I0138064

CALAMITY JANE

Also by Richard W. Etulain *(a selective listing)*

AUTHOR

Owen Wister

Ernest Haycox

Re-imagining the Modern American West: A Century of Fiction, History, and Art

Telling Western Stories: From Buffalo Bill to Larry McMurtry

Beyond the Missouri: The Story of the American West

Seeking First the Kingdom: Northwest Nazarene University, A Centennial History

Abraham Lincoln and Oregon Country Politics in the Civil War Era

The Life and Legends of Calamity Jane

COAUTHOR

Conversations with Wallace Stegner on Western History and Literature

The American West: A Twentieth-Century History

EDITOR

Jack London on the Road: The Tramp Diary and Other Hobo Writings

Writing Western History: Essays on Major Western Historians

Basques of the Pacific Northwest: A Collection of Essays

Contemporary New Mexico, 1940–1990

Does the Frontier Experience Make America Exceptional?

César Chávez: A Brief Biography with Documents

New Mexican Lives: Profiles and Historical Stories

Western Lives: A Biographical History of the American West

Lincoln Looks West: From the Mississippi to the Pacific

COEDITOR

The Popular Western: Essays toward a Definition

The Idaho Heritage

The Frontier and American West

Basque Americans

Fifty Western Writers: A Bio-bibliographical Guide

A Bibliographical Guide to the Study of Western American Literature

Faith and Imagination: Essays on Evangelicals and Literature

The Twentieth-Century West: Historical Interpretations

Religion and Culture

The American West in the Twentieth Century: A Bibliography

Researching Western History: Topics in the Twentieth Century

Religion in Modern New Mexico

By Grit and Grace: Eleven Women Who Shaped the American West

Portraits of Basques in the New World

With Badges and Bullets: Lawmen and Outlaws in the Old West

The Hollywood West

The American West in 2000: Essays in Honor of Gerald D. Nash

Wild Women of the Old West

Chiefs and Generals

CALAMITY JANE

A Reader's Guide

Richard W. Etulain

UNIVERSITY OF OKLAHOMA PRESS : NORMAN

LIBRARY OF CONGRESS CATALOGING-IN-PUBLICATION DATA

Etulain, Richard W.
    Calamity Jane : a reader's guide / Richard W. Etulain.
        pages cm
    Includes bibliographical references and index.
    ISBN 978-0-8061-4871-7 (hardcover : alk. paper)
1. Calamity Jane, 1856-1903.   2. Calamity Jane, 1856-1903—Sources.   3. Women
pioneers—West (U.S.)—Biography.   4. West (U.S.)—Biography.   I. Title.
    F594.C2E879 2015
    978'.02092—dc23
    [B]

                                                                    2015006403

Th e paper in this book meets the guidelines for permanence and durability of the
Committee on Production Guidelines for Book Longevity of the Council on Library
Resources, Inc. ∞

Copyright © 2015 by the University of Oklahoma Press, Norman, Publishing Division
of the University. Manufactured in the U.S.A.

All rights reserved. No part of this publication may be reproduced, stored in a
retrieval system, or transmitted, in any form or by any means, electronic, mechanical,
photocopying, recording, or otherwise—except as permitted under Section 107 or
108 of the United States Copyright Act—without the prior written permission of the
University of Oklahoma Press. To request permission to reproduce selections from
this book, write to Permissions, University of Oklahoma Press, 2800 Venture Drive,
Norman OK 73069, or email rights.oupress@ou.edu.

For
Professor James D. McLaird
superb researcher-scholar
good friend
the *source on Calamity Jane*

Contents

PREFACE

FOR WELL MORE THAN a century, biographers and historians have touted Calamity Jane as the most-written-about woman of the Old West. They point to the hundreds—even thousands—of newspaper stories, biographies, novels, and movies made about this western demigod. In the earliest years of her public career in the 1870s, when her name changed from Martha Canary to Calamity Jane, she was depicted as a Wild Woman of the frontier. But another legend began to emerge alongside that of the red devil in britches, Calamity as an Angel of Mercy, nursing the sick and aiding the poor and disfranchised. A third legend, although less widespread, surfaced before Calamity died in 1903. In a few scattered interviews, works of fiction, and probing journalistic writings, she was described as a young woman yearning to marry, bear children, and gain and maintain a stable home. Calamity herself added to this legend by speaking about her two children and her "husbands." She was even legally married in 1888, a fact not revealed until more than eighty years after her death.

Unfortunately, the earliest accounts to appear both while Calamity was still alive and shortly after her death were incestuous. When archives and libraries had little information about Calamity, and certainly in pre-digital days, writers (especially male journalists), gathering their information from newspaper morgues, repeated earlier stories about Calamity, even though many contained inaccuracies and were missing critical information. The first semi-dependable biography did not appear until the late 1920s, and no one revealed that Martha and her family had been recorded in the U.S. census of 1860, and Martha again in an 1869 census, until toward the end of the twentieth century, nearly one hundred years after her death.

This borrowing from previous distorted accounts often led to dead-end conclusions. Frequently, from-the-hip newspaper reports, Calamity's own exaggerations in her interviews and her autobiography *Life and Adventures of Calamity Jane, By Herself* (1896), and the dime novels of Edward L. Wheeler published in the 1870s and 1880s became *the* misleading sources for other stories before and after her death. False stories about a Calamity Jane–Wild Bill Hickok romance, trips to California and the Southwest, and her being childless, once enshrined in print and in the reservoir of accepted memory, continued endlessly during the twentieth century.

The purpose of this guide is to counter these distortions and oversights by providing solid, dependable information on Martha Canary/Calamity Jane. The guide opens with a brief introduction to Calamity's life and a summary overview of the legends about her that have surfaced in roughly the past 140 years. Keeping in mind the necessity of revealing the mountains of false information on Calamity for readers and pointing them toward correct reports, I have included two kinds of comments in most bibliographical annotations: (1) a brief summary of the item's content and emphases; and (2) a terse evaluation of the source's information. If these annotations work as intended, readers will be saved from misleading or valueless sources and informed of the most trustworthy newspaper stories, books and essays, novels, and movies about Calamity Jane.

A few words to explain the volume's format. All sections, save for three, are organized alphabetically. The exceptions are the section on legal documents and the two parts dealing with newspaper articles, before and after 1903 (the year of her death). I have arranged these three sections chronologically because the documents should be viewed in the order they were created. Structuring the newspaper sections chronologically allows readers to see how journalists, over time, built on previous stories. Moreover, an alphabetical listing for the newspaper stories is virtually impossible because some carry bylines, titles, and newspaper names; but many are missing one or another of these identifiers.

I hope that these thorough listings will become the first stop for scholars and general readers wanting to see what has been written about Calamity Jane. Even though this book provides the most extensive guide thus far to writings and movies about the western heroine, it is by no means exhaustive. Although I have tried to deal with the most important items within each category, I have not been able to discuss everything. For example, a summary and evaluation of the hundreds—even thousands—of newspaper stories about Calamity would more than fill a volume. I have had to be frustratingly selective in the newspaper stories I have included. I have provided particularly extensive comments on Edward L. Wheeler's Deadwood Dick dime novel series and J. T. Edson's Westerns because these fifty or so items have not received extensive commentary. I have also furnished expansive comments on the books and essays of James D. McLaird, the leading interpreter of Calamity Jane. Even if not exhaustive, this guide will introduce readers and writers to the most important sources on Calamity Jane.

My primary approach in this volume is that of the diligent biographer or historian attempting to turn up the most thorough and dependable information on the life of Martha Canary/Calamity Jane. Although the summaries and evaluations make some allowance for artistic experimentation and achievement, my chief purpose here is to point readers toward the most helpful and trustworthy sources on Calamity. Other investigators may focus on the literary qualities of innovative novels and movies. That is certainly an acceptable approach that would help readers to know and understand fictional and cinematic treatments of Calamity Jane over time. But emphasis on aesthetic achievement is not the central approach of this volume.

This volume draws heavily on several sources. It is, first of all, a partner to my earlier book, *The Life and Legends of Calamity Jane* (2014), published by the University of Oklahoma Press, and borrows sentences, and a few paragraphs, from that full-scale biography. It is also based on my other previous writings about Calamity Jane, particularly "Calamity Jane: A Life and Legends," *Montana: The Magazine of Western History* (Summer 2014). The brief biographical and interpretive overviews in this volume are taken nearly verbatim from this recent essay. I am also much indebted to the books and essays of Professor McLaird. His pioneering and diligent research and valuable publications are bedrock sources for this volume.

I wish also to thank several persons who have helped me along the way in my Calamity research and writing—stretching all the way back to the early 1990s. The University of New Mexico provided small research grants that allowed visits to archives and libraries by day and travel by night to the next Calamity Jane collection. I worked my way through dozens of libraries and wrote a handful of essays (listed later). Along the way, librarians and archivists in Montana, South Dakota, Oregon, Washington, New Mexico, Wyoming, Idaho, Colorado, and Utah were particularly helpful. Editors David Holtby and Chuck Rankin helped to bring my Calamity research into print. I am also very grateful to William R. Whiteside, expert genealogist and diligent researcher; see his invaluable research lists in the "Manuscript Collections and Manuscripts" section. My western pard, Glenda Riley, in reading the manuscript caught and corrected many writing errors and infelicities. Recently, my good buddy David Gowan helped with South Dakota backgrounds and with the photographs. More than to any other person, I owe a huge debt to James D. McLaird. For more than twenty years, Jim, now professor emeritus at Dakota Wesleyan University, has provided regular assistance in my work on Calamity Jane. His readings and evaluations of my writings dealing with Calamity, including this book, have been invaluable.

At the University of Oklahoma Press, I am most indebted to Chuck Rankin, who encouraged the project from its first mention. Also supportive at the Press were Steven Baker and Rowan Steineker. In addition, copy editor Kirsteen Anderson saved me from a bundle of errors and smoothed over more than a few stylistic problems.

Along the way, others helped with photographs. Laurie Langland of Dakota Wesleyan University was particularly helpful. So were Lory Morrow of the Montana Historical Society; Judy Cox of the Mercer County Library in Princeton, Missouri; and Bob McCubbin and Coi Drummond-Gehrig of the Denver Public Library. They pointed me toward needed photographs and other useful sources.

Finally, I am indebted to two wonderful library ladies for their support and help—my wife, Joyce Oldenkamp Etulain, and my daughter Jackie Etulain Partch.

CALAMITY JANE

A LIFE IN BRIEF

THE *NEW YORK TIMES* reporter was puzzled. How was he to write the obituary of that mysterious Wild Woman of the West, Calamity Jane, when he knew so little about her? Even though Calamity may have been the most written-about woman of the pioneer West, the facts of her life seemed but a molehill beside the mountainous legends already stacked around her. Facing this dilemma, the journalist chose to play on the legends rather than investigate the facts. Like so many stories about Calamity, the narrative he produced was as distant from the truth as he was from faraway Montana, South Dakota, and Wyoming.

In writing his obituary of Calamity the New York journalist was whistling in the dark. Appearing one day after her death on 1 August 1903 in Terry, South Dakota, the brief story relied heavily on hearsay and Calamity's own suspect, undependable autobiography of 1896. The subhead of the obituary foreshadowed its truckload of errors. The writer declared that Calamity was a "Woman Who Became Famous as an Indian Fighter" and that "thousands of tourists went miles out of their way to see her." Generally, the obituary was off to the races in repeating Calamity's falsehoods about scouting, serving with General Custer, and capturing Jack McCall (Wild Bill Hickok's assassin) with a threatening cleaver. He also repeated exaggerations from frontier magazines and newspapers that had labeled Calamity as "The Beautiful White Devil of the Yellowstone" and as a young woman who laid "around with a lot of road agents on the prairies."

The *Times* obituary, a harbinger of the future, exuded tall tales and did little to illuminate Calamity's actual life. At its center, the New York story reiterated the most popular legend about Calamity: she was a Wild Woman of the Old West who spent her life prancing around the frontier fighting Indians, marching with the military, taking on the bad guys, and helping a roaring frontier pass through its final stages.

But the newspaper obituary overlooked two other legends that congealed around Calamity in the last twenty-five years of her life, from roughly 1876 to 1903. The better-known of these two stories portrayed Calamity as a veritable Angel of Mercy, courageously helping smallpox victims no one else would aid and giving freely to down-and-outers. Less widely touted but nonetheless in circulation by the end of Calamity's life was her desire to be a Pioneer Woman who married, bore children, and had a steady, safe home.

In the days and weeks immediately after Calamity's demise, numerous newspapers across the country cobbled together obituaries and retrospectives of her life no more dependable than that in the *New York Times*. Building on wild journalistic stories and sensational dime novels, the obituary writers continued the legends that had grown up about her since the 1870s. It would be several decades before careful, diligent biographers and historians dug out the obscure details of Martha Canary and her deification as Calamity Jane. Indeed, a full century transpired after Calamity's death before the definitive biography of her appeared.

Two especially useful approaches to Calamity's life and legends lie before a writer. One could illuminate her story through gender analysis, clarifying how her roles as an unusual woman in the West illuminate and expand meanings of frontier history. Or, one could deal with Calamity's biography and career in light of shifting climates of opinion during her lifetime and in the following century. The following pages primarily rely on the second approach, without overlooking insights gained from gender analysis.

❦

Martha Canary's rather traditional early life carried no hints of what she would become after her teenage years. She was born in 1856, perhaps on 1 May, near the town of Princeton, in north-central Missouri. Her parents, Robert and Charlotte, were a farm family, as Robert's parents had been. As U.S. census records revealed, Martha's paternal grandparents, James and Sarah Wilson (or Willson) Canary, began life in Virginia, moved to Ohio early in their marriage, parenting a large family of five boys and four girls, and continued to farm in eastern Ohio until 1852. (Robert was the youngest of the children, born in 1825.) On their way west, the Canary family stopped briefly in Iowa, before James (without Sarah, who may have died) arrived in Mercer County, Missouri, in the mid- to late 1850s. Perhaps James was looking for more-available, less-expensive land for each of his sons and sons-in-law, about half of whom followed him west. On 14 June 1855, in Polk County, Iowa, son Robert married fifteen-year-old Charlotte Burge. Robert and Charlotte arrived in Mercer County within the next year with father James; brother James Thornton Canary and his wife, Delilah; two sisters, Lana and husband James Kilgore, and Mary and her husband, Robert Southers. They all congregated not far from one another in northern Missouri.

The census of 1860, too often overlooked, provides the most revealing evidence about the Canarys before dramatic changes invaded the family. Robert and Charlotte were by then the parents of three children, all born in Missouri: Martha (the future Calamity Jane), in 1856; Cilas (Silas?), in 1857; and Lana (or Lena), one year old. Robert was literate, Charlotte was not; their land was worth $1,500, and their personal estate $400.

More than sixty years later, biographer/journalist Duncan Aikman traveled to Princeton, hoping to mine the memories of Mercer County residents who recalled the Canary family. Robert, they remembered, was at best a phlegmatic, unenthusiastic farmer, preschool Martha a lively tomboyish girl. But it was mother Charlotte who remained fresh and controversial in the neighbors' minds. Repeatedly Charlotte bruised the social expectations of neighborhood wives. Her brightly colored and eye-catching clothing, her cigar smoking, her public flirtatiousness and swearing, and her drinking (sometimes to drunkenness) branded her in contrast to the upstanding mothers who were innocent of all these untoward actions.

Soon after Grandpa James died in 1862, Robert and Charlotte fell out with other members of the Canary family and left Mercer County. When an administrator for the James Canary estate attempted to regain money, livestock, and farm implements from Robert and Charlotte and return them to the rightful heirs in James's estate, they refused to deliver the goods. Vague rumors of Charlotte's pro-Southern sympathies (she was called a "Secesh," or secessionist) and of Robert's antipathy for farming may have been reasons for the Canarys' exiting Missouri, but the most likely explanation lies buried in the Mercer County Court records. When Robert and Charlotte refused to return the requested goods to James's estate, other members of the family sued them. The probate and county courts hailed Robert into court several times between 1862 and 1864, but the proceedings indicated that Robert "comes not." In late 1862 Robert and Charlotte sold their farm and hustled off to a less threatening place. Perhaps they were drawn to a West rumored to be mineral rich. Whether they headed directly west or went north, stopping off for a few months in Iowa before striking out for the Montana goldfields, is not clear.

The next decade of Martha Canary's life is a virtual tabula rasa of dependable documentation. In her ghostwritten autobiography, Calamity Jane played up the adventure and dangers of the long trip west. She also claimed she became "a remarkable good shot and fearless rider for a girl of my age."

The Canary family disappears from the scene in these years save for one important newspaper document in Montana. The Canarys were evidently drawn to the new strike in Alder Gulch in the early 1860s. Robert, Charlotte, and their children most likely arrived in 1864, and by the end of the year, they were in deep trouble. Jammed in among the five thousand or more who crowded into the Virginia City, Montana, area, the Canarys lost their way in the chaos and costs of the boomtown. A brief story in the 31 December 1864 issue of the *Montana Post*, headlined "Provision for the Destitute Poor," highlighted the difficulties of "three little girls, who state their names to be Canary." Then the angry reporter turned on the parents: "The father, it seems, is a gambler in Nevada [City]. The mother is a woman of the lowest grade." The writer concluded this was "a most flagrant and wanton instance of unnatural conduct on the part of parents to their children."

Things quickly got worse. Charlotte died in Blackfoot City, Montana, probably in 1866. Robert, hoping to get help in raising his brood, headed south to be among the Mormons, or perhaps he may have been heading back home to Missouri. A year later he too was gone, rumored to have died in the Salt Lake City area.

Now, Martha, not yet a teenager, was an orphan and responsible for her siblings. What could she do? She had no family in the far-off West, no community of support, or any other kind of help on which to rely. She would make do. Rumors suggest that Martha's younger sister Lena and brother Elijah (Lige) were farmed out to Mormon families in Utah. Martha was on her own, very young but a survivor.

The period from 1868 to early 1875 is a challenge for biographers because scarcely more than a handful of sources disclose Martha Canary's whereabouts and activities. Much later, Calamity said that after the death of her parents, she "went to Fort Bridger during 1868, then to Piedmont, Wyoming, with the U. P. Railroad." In 1869 the census taker caught up with Martha in Piedmont, where she claimed to be fifteen (but was actually thirteen) and evidently was helping in a boardinghouse and babysitting. Martha's controversial actions got her in trouble. The woman with whom she was staying, Emma Andrews Alton, "blew up and fired" Martha. In the next few years, strong rumors place her in the Wyoming mining boomtowns of Miner's Delight and South Pass City, where again her antisocial activities impelled her out the door and back to the "hell-on-wheels" railroad towns stretching across Wyoming. Martha was reported in Cheyenne in the early 1870s, and about this time reconnected with her sister, Lena, who relocated to western Wyoming, married German immigrant John Borner, and gave birth to a large family before her early death in 1888, at age twenty-nine. Martha's brother Lige also came to western Wyoming, but his footloose, roughneck activities kept him running from place to place. Later, Calamity claimed to have been with General Custer and other military commanders during the early 1870s, but there is no proof of such activities, save on expeditions with General George Crook in 1876.

The best evidence places Martha in Cheyenne and other sites to the north, such as Fort Laramie, in 1874–75. One trader along the Cheyenne-to-Deadwood stagecoach route claimed Martha was in a "hog ranch" (house of prostitution) selling sex by the mid-1870s. In 1875 she clandestinely joined the Newton-Jenney Expedition sent north by the U.S. government to check out the rumors of gold in the Black Hills. Younger brother Lige may have been with her. It was Martha's first trip to the Hills, perhaps as a surreptitious teamster after she was tossed out trying to dress up as a soldier and march with the troops. During this trip north Martha became Calamity Jane. "Mac," a reporter for the Chicago *Inter-Ocean*; Dr. Valentine McGillycuddy, the expedition's topographer and engineer; and Harry "Sam" Young, a teamster and later Deadwood bartender; all spoke of her traveling with the expedition. Dr. McGillycuddy described her as "crazy for adventure," and Mac reported her to be a more "unctuous coiner of English, and not the Queen's pure either, than any (other) man in the command." In other words, Martha, now being called Calamity Jane, was already a prolific, unrepentant swearer of world-class caliber.

The year 1876 proved the turning point in Calamity's career. It began with two quick trips to the Black Hills with General George Crook and his army in the winter and spring of that year. Calamity may have served informally as a scout (so a good source claims), but primarily she was a camp-follower, hitching rides with soldiers and sneaking in among the teamsters and bullwhackers until she was discovered, chased out, and sent back south. Several travelers on these trips and other observers reported her with Crook—and not always traditionally dressed or sober. One teamster described her as "dressed in buckskin suit with two Colts six shooters on a belt." To him, she was one of the roughest persons he had ever seen. In the town of Custer, Calamity headed for the nearest saloon and "was soon made blind as a bat from looking through the bottom of a glass." In the 1880s and 1890s when Calamity began to make a name for herself as a Wild West performer, she made much of these experiences, claiming that she had been an active scout for General Crook.

Calamity's travel itinerary in the late spring and early summer of 1876 was chockablock, and more. In March she was with Crook to the north, in May back in Cheyenne, where she was arrested for stealing clothes, but was declared "Not. Guilty" [*sic*]. In early June she zipped back north for a second jaunt with Crook. Heading out of Cheyenne, "greatly" rejoicing "over her release from durance vile" (jail), she "borrowed" a horse and buggy. After overindulging in "frequent and liberal potations" of "bug juice," she headed for Fort Laramie, ninety miles up from Cheyenne. By mid-June, Calamity was celebrating with soldiers from Fort Laramie. The rhythm of her life, already in uncertain high gear, whirled into overdrive in the coming months.

At the end of June, an encounter took place that would forever change Calamity's story. In spring 1876, Wild Bill Hickok, newly married to circus owner Agnes Lake, and his partner Charlie (also Charley) Utter were in Cheyenne, making plans to ride north. Hickok would try his hand at mining, he promised his new wife, who stayed in Cincinnati. Charlie hoped to establish a stage line into the Black Hills. Soon after mid-June they were on their way. When the Hickok-Utter train stopped just north of Fort Laramie, the officer of the day at the fort asked them to take along several prostitutes, to keep them away from the soldiers. Calamity may have been among these prostitutes. One creditable source describes her as drunk and "near naked." Here in late June, in northeast Wyoming, Calamity met Wild Bill for the first time. They would know one another as acquaintances, and no more, for about the next five weeks. Members of the train gave Calamity a suit of buckskins for their trip into the Hills.

Contemporaries made much of the dramatic entrance of Wild Bill, Calamity, and other members of the train into Deadwood in early July, picturing them as prancing along the entire main street, greeting friends. But in the weeks to come Wild Bill and Calamity were rarely together. Then tragedy struck on 2 August, when Jack McCall, a drifting ne'er-do-well, sneaked up behind Hickok while he was playing poker and shot him in the back of the head. Those who have tried to conjure up a love affair between Hickok and Calamity, in Deadwood or in previous years, have no facts on which to base those stretchers. But the rumors have become a major, shaky legend surrounding Calamity.

From 1876 to 1881 Calamity was in and out of Deadwood. In man-deluged, female-starved Deadwood, Calamity became an in-demand worker, hostess, and dancer in the boomtown saloons and lively theaters. But a transformation was necessary. "Boys," she told the men camped with Wild Bill and Charlie Utter, "I wish you would loan me twenty dollars. . . . I can't do business in these old buckskins." The men dished out the money, and the redressing worked. A few days later, Calamity returned to the men's camp dressed attractively as a woman. "She pulled up her dress," one eyewitness recalled, "rolled down her stocking and took out a roll of greenbacks and gave us the twenty she had borrowed." Saloons and all-night dance halls, theaters, and the ubiquitous, undefinable "hurdy-gurdies" offered positions to the very small group of women as hostesses, entertainers, and "dance hall girls." Calamity worked in several of these establishments but mostly in the Gem, ruled over by the unsavory manager Al Swearingen, who turned the theater into a "notorious den of iniquity."

One observer claims that it was "generally well-established . . . that Jane was a prostitute." Perhaps, but unproven. No irrefutable evidence exists that Calamity sold sex in Deadwood. That she worked in houses of prostitution and hog ranches, where the main occupation was selling sex, and that she had several "husbands" without benefit of clergy is established. Still, no patron of the "joy palaces" nor any madam or worker therein ever testified to Calamity's being an out-and-out prostitute. Despite this lack of substantiating evidence, one part of the Wild Woman legend that began to gather around Calamity in Deadwood, and soon thereafter, indicated she was a prostitute.

During the Deadwood years, strong evidence suggests Calamity often served as a nursemaid for the sick or a helper for the needy. Granted, sometimes these stories of Calamity as Ministering Angel seemed attempts to balance harsh criticism of her unwomanly and socially aberrant acts. Illustrating this ambivalence are the stories of Jesse Brown and A. M. Willard, two early arrivals in Deadwood. At first they labeled Calamity as "nothing more than a common prostitute, drunken, [and] disorderly." They quickly countered that negativity by praising her efforts as a nurse, particularly during a devastating invasion of smallpox. Other sources were more certain of Calamity's positive actions. One memoirist remembered her as "the heroine of the Deadwood smallpox epidemic"; another recalled her as "a perfect angel sent from heaven when any of the boys was sick." Several others agreed, with another acquaintance stating that "Calamity was a great friend in a time of trouble. If anyone got sick or hurt, she nursed them until they got well."

A mishmash of rumors and solid information about Calamity exploded onto the national scene from 1876 to 1878. She first appeared in regional news-papers in 1875–76, then her notoriety spread in 1876–77 through much of the northern West but particularly in the northern Rockies and upper Great Plains. In 1877–78 her name and stories about her fanned out from the West and into the national media. Journalist Horatio N. Maguire profiled Calamity in his two books *The Black Hills and American Wonderland* (1877) and *The Coming Empire: A Complete and Reliable Treatise on the Black Hills, Yellowstone and Big Horn Regions* (1878). The second of these books also featured a lively illustra-tion entitled "Miss Martha Canary ('Calamity Jane'), The Female Scout," which pictured Calamity as a young, electric heroine galloping through a Wild West landscape. Information from the books was picked up and printed in New York newspapers. Journalist T. M. Newson furnished even more extensive treatment of Calamity in his play, *Drama of Life in the Black Hills* (1878). Newson's drama also carried rather amateurish illustrations of Calamity as both a masculine and feminine frontier woman, as well as a revealing photo of her, the original of which is now lost.

The most important of Calamity's sudden appearances, the most significant venue for turning her in a nationwide heroine, was in dozens of dime novels, beginning with *Deadwood Dick, the Prince of the Road; or, The Black Rider of the Black Hills* (15 October 1877). The first of thirty-three novels in the Deadwood Dick series by veteran dime novelist Edward L. Wheeler, it presented Calam-ity as a rambunctious, devil-may-care heroine who could outride and outshoot many of her male companions. Calamity appeared in nearly all these dime nov-els, sometimes as Deadwood Dick's companion in thwarting evildoers, less fre-quently as his wife, but nearly always as a frenetic female helping to tame an uncivilized frontier. She appeared in the titles of two of the series: *Deadwood Dick on Deck: Or, Calamity Jane, The Heroine of Whoop-Up* (1878) and *Dead-wood Dick's Doom; or, Calamity Jane's Last Adventure* (1881) and on the cover of two novels, *Deadwood Dick on Deck* and *Deadwood Dick in Leadville; or, A Strange Stroke for Liberty* (1879). Nearly all the content about Calamity in these novels was imagined nonsense, and even some pretending to be authentic biog-raphy was wide of the mark. Wheeler knew very little about Calamity and illus-trated one cynic's comments about dime novelists: they wrote without fear—or research. But the series caught on and became one of—if not the most—popular dime novel series of all time. The Deadwood Dick series made Calamity an over-night sensation. In less than three years, Martha Canary had been transformed into a national heroine. Her life would never again be the same.

In less than a decade, Martha Canary had become Calamity Jane, notorious woman of a legendary Wild West. Never again would she be known as the farmer's daughter from Princeton, Missouri. Over the next two decades, Calamity was increasingly identified as a lively female protagonist of the "yellowback" novels. These continuing moments of recognition were not always pleasant for her. When journalists or other writers quoted lurid lines about her from dime novels, Calamity usually blew up in anger, labeling the stories and descriptions as packs of lies.

Underneath the layers of sensation was a needy woman who seemed, for some of the time, to find a stable and happy existence. That searching heroine took to the road in the early 1880s, hoping to find a husband, family, and home (as she had begun to do in the 1870s) and to discover how to make a living. Calamity wandered incessantly for most of the last twenty years of her life—first in Montana and then in Wyoming in the 1880s. She also returned to South Dakota for brief stops after the mid-1890s. In the first half of these years she seemed like a modern Energizer Calamity, never stopping; but in the latter part of the second decade, her batteries lost their power, leading to a sharp decline and death.

Through these years Calamity often displayed her desire to be like other pioneer women. She sought a husband and a home. As early as 1877, she told an inquiring reporter in the Black Hills, "I want you to understand my name ain't Calamity Jane, it's Maggie Cosgrove." Two years later she elaborated, "Boys, . . . I am married to George [Cosgrove] now and am living straight and don't do any business on the outside." As is true of most of Calamity's "husbands," no record exists that she and Cosgrove were ever legally married. In fact, in 1881 in Montana, Calamity was said to be living with another man, possibly ranch worker Frank King. Late in 1882, Calamity became the mother of a baby boy, whom she called "Little Calamity." Sadly, the baby died soon after birth.

By the mid-1880s, Calamity, now living in south-central Wyoming, in Rawlins, had a new "husband," William S. (Bill) Steers. She became a new mother—and wife—in that order. That relationship proved to be her stormiest. In regional newspapers she and Steers were often reported as fighting. In 1885, Steers would have been twenty, nine years younger than Calamity. One Rawlins journalist harpooned Steers as "one of the most worthless curs unhung." Another reporter indicted Steers for beating up Calamity and stealing her "watch and chain." In October 1887, Calamity gave birth to a second child, a baby girl she named Jessie Elizabeth. To gain respectability, Calamity and Steers traveled to Pocatello, Idaho, where they were legally married on 30 May 1888. Calamity now had a husband, but more importantly, a father for her seven-month-old daughter. Inexplicably, Steers disappeared, and Calamity never mentioned him again.

Instead, Calamity asserted later that Clinton Burke, her next "husband," whom she claimed to have married in Texas, was Jessie's father. There is no evidence for the claim. Indeed, Calamity and Burke probably did not meet until the early 1890s, perhaps in eastern Montana. They were together off and on until about 1896, with Jessie sometimes accompanying them. In the early 1890s, Burke, the son of a Missouri minister, worked at odd jobs on ranches and farms. He, Calamity, and Jessie traveled through Montana and parts of Wyoming and South Dakota, then Calamity and Burke began a trip with the Kohl and Middleton dime museum group in 1896 before the relationship ended.

After the breakup with Burke, Calamity tried again to establish a home with a new companion. She and Robert Dorsett, a laborer in eastern Montana, were together by 1898, if not sooner. They were spotted in Billings, then in Lewistown, and next in the small towns of Utica and Gilt Edge. The "marriage" did not last long, although a recent discovery in the census of 1900 reveals that Calamity and Dorsett were living in northwestern North Dakota and were at least together in 1900. Perhaps a rumor explains their breakup. One source states— and daughter Jessie said much the same many years later in the 1930s—Dorsett stole Jessie away and took her to live with his mother in Livingston. If so, he may have believed that Calamity could never be the mother Jessie needed.

On occasion, Calamity half-humorously referred to her abilities to entice a new companion, but in doing so covered up a more significant point. When observers teased her about the young, handsome men she attracted (Steers, Burke, and Dorsett were all about ten years younger than Calamity), she retorted, "I never had a fellow with a h— of a lot of money; [but] I always did pick a good-looker." The problem and achievements went much deeper. In a male-dominated society Calamity could not find work that would pay sufficiently to support Jessie and herself. Even when she was with a "husband," Calamity was pinched for financial resources. Part of the problem, of course, was Calamity's excessive drinking, rambling, and unwise use of money.

During the 1880s, Calamity tried several ways to make a living in a society that expected women to be stay-at-home wives and mothers. She was a domestic worker in hotels, did men's work in hauling wood to nearby towns, and served variously in saloons. In addition, when the Northern Pacific Railroad laid new rails across Montana in the early 1880s, she rode west as far as Spokane, Washington, where she dealt faro and other card games. Then, backtracking and attracted by the new mineral strike in the Coeur d'Alenes in northern Idaho, she tried something new. In February 1884, Calamity and a small corps of female dancers hiked over snow-covered mountains from the Northern Pacific railroad junction to the boomtown of Eagle City, where they entertained miners crowded into a tent saloon. Calamity, telling exaggerated yarns about her life, became the "star of the evening," and after her monologue the women danced with the female-hungry miners until morning. One month later Calamity returned to "mine the miners" with further entertainment, but a pretty Irish lass, Molly b'Damn, outsparkled Calamity, pushing her out of the Coeur d'Alenes. Later in 1884, trying to capitalize on her brief experience as an entertainer, Calamity evidently joined Tom Hardwick's Great Rocky Mountain Show, but it collapsed financially before she could become one of its featured attractions.

For several years, Calamity kept the entertainment possibilities in mind. And a decade later she had her largest success when, after tiring of ranch work, she returned to Deadwood in 1895, with Burke and Jessie in tow. Early the next year she signed on with Kohl and Middleton, the dime museum entertainers, and barnstormed across the northern United States from Minneapolis to the East Coast. Calamity was sold as "The Famous Woman Scout of the Wild West," the "Heroine of a Thousand Thrilling Adventures," the "Terror of Evildoers in the Black Hills!" and "The Comrade of Buffalo Bill and Wild Bill!" All of this was hype, but it worked. One newspaper revealed that Calamity was earning $50 a week for presentations, and an acquaintance who heard one of her performances said that the Wild West heroine was drawing crowds with her interesting, sensational monologues. Just before the tour left, Calamity, with the aid of a ghostwriter, turned out a nine-page autobiography, *Life and Adventures of Calamity Jane: By Herself* (1896), which, with a few nods toward authenticity, overflowed with exaggerations and inaccuracies. Over the years, too many unsuspecting biographers and historians uncritically embraced what Calamity said in the little pamphlet. Although the tour went smoothly, when Jessie, whom Calamity left with a friendly family in South Dakota, was reported sick, Calamity came home to help her daughter.

After Calamity returned, probably in May or June 1896, she was unable to capitalize on her recent experiences, and her off-track pattern resumed. Picking up Jessie in Sturgis, Calamity began traipsing from town to town, in Wyoming and then in Montana. After her brief time with Dorsett, she began a downward tumble during the next two or three years. Trying to eke out a living selling her autobiography for fifteen cents and her photographs for a dime or more, Calamity rarely found other work that lasted more than a few days or weeks. She wandered into and around the Yellowstone Park area, where she lived off generous acquaintances and resided briefly in a "pest house" set aside for those suffering from communicable diseases.

A new challenge with new employment possibilities suddenly came on scene in early 1901. Calamity, experiencing health difficulties and unable to pay for her care, was taken to a poorhouse in Bozeman. She soon bounced back and went on her way. Still, the story of Calamity Jane being in a poorhouse burst into national newspapers and caught the attention of an East Coast writer.

Josephine Winifred Brake, a New York journalist and author, read a story about the down-and-nearly-out Calamity and dreamed up an idea. She would come west, rescue Calamity, take her east, introduce her to the public at the Pan-American Exposition then in Buffalo, New York, and provide a home and stability for the western heroine. When Brake arrived, she located Calamity in the "hut of a negress" near Livingston. Critics of Brake—especially the most cynical of the commentators—accused her of ulterior motives, of planning to use Calamity and her Wild West reputation to reap some unnamed reward for herself. Recently discovered documents suggest that Brake was working with the Pan-American Exposition in Buffalo to bring Calamity east as an attention-attracting feature, but she also exhibited genuine concern for Calamity then and later.

Not surprisingly, Brake's dream did not go well. On the trip east it was difficult to keep Calamity on the wagon, and once in Buffalo she was not easy to handle. In a few days Calamity tired of working for Brake and signed on with Colonel Fred Cummins and his Indian Congress. Less than a month after she went east, Calamity wanted to return home to Montana and the West. Binge drinking got her into trouble, and in despair she went to Buffalo Bill Cody, recently arrived in Buffalo with his Wild West arena show, and begged for money to pay her fare back west. Cody anted up, and despite a few hiccups of delay, Calamity was back west in the late fall of 1901.

The next two years witnessed a steady decline. Calamity's drink-fueled wandering recommenced—and continued. For nearly a month in early 1903, Calamity (Jessie was with her) worked for madam Dora Du Fran's "house of joy" in South Dakota, cooking and doing the laundry for Dora's sex workers. Then she fell off the wagon. "For five days she whooped it up," Du Fran wrote later. In her noisy celebrating Calamity went howling up the street, competing with the coyotes who were sounding their own barbaric yawp across the Black Hills.

The next months were depressingly similar—and worse. A few weeks in Sundance, Wyoming, more trips around to Black Hills towns, and back to Deadwood in midsummer. Photos taken in July show Calamity a wrinkled wreck. In late July she boarded an ore train for the mining town of Terry, a few miles out of Deadwood. Soon after her arrival in Terry, an incapacitating illness overtook her. Doctors said there was nothing further they could do, and Calamity seemed to accept that she was dying. In her final hours, she may have told acquaintances that she was already a grandmother, with Jessie having given birth, but she would not give information about her daughter's whereabouts. Calamity may also have told these listeners she wanted to be buried next to Wild Bill Hickok in Deadwood.

Death came on the afternoon of 1 August 1903. Probably the main cause of Calamity's demise at age forty-seven was chronic alcoholism. The funeral service at Deadwood's Methodist church drew a huge crowd of friends, acquaintances, and curious bystanders. Charles B. Clark, the father of later well-known writer Badger Clark, officiated at the service. Drawing from Psalms 90, Dr. Clark emphasized Calamity's humanitarian actions, praising her "deeds of kindness and charity . . . [she was a] heroine." After the service, a hearse took Calamity's remains to the Mount Moriah Cemetery, where she was buried near Wild Bill's grave. The companionship Calamity may have wished for in life seemed possible only in death. Ironically, the headstone prepared for Calamity's grave misspelled her name and gave a wrong age and birth date (as age 53, and thus born in 1850). A similar combination of facts and misinformation had marked her life and legends while she was living—and continued after her death. The marriage of truth, distortion, and legend, as we shall see, has continued to define Calamity Jane in the more than a century since her death.

Legends in the Making

Journalists, biographers, and historians were not sure what to say about Calamity Jane at the end of her life. Their indecision continued what had been true over the twenty-five years or so before her death when images of her had been neither monolithic or static. During her lifetime, journalists often tried to counterbalance the less palatable facets of her controversial character—the cross-dressing, drinking, and promiscuity—with images of an Angel of Mercy. These positive treatments included her care for smallpox victims, her aid for the poor, her attentions to mothers and children, and her bailing out of the penniless. Missing in nearly all accounts of Calamity during her lifetime, however, was her desire to be a rather traditional pioneer woman, with a family. A handful of hints reveal this desire. As we have seen, Calamity wanted to be married, to be with a "husband," to be near children. In 1895–96, in an extraordinary interview, she told a female interviewer that her daughter, Jessie, was her reason for living, that she wanted to make sure Jessie got the education she herself had missed. Almost a decade earlier, novelist (Mrs.) William Loring Spencer had portrayed Calamity as an energetic, go-ahead frontier figure, on the one hand, but also as a warm, supportive friend for the novel's heroine. In the novel, Calamity bonds with Meg Stevens, even though other, snooty Deadwood females dismiss her as below their social station. A few writers and moviemakers would pick up on this feminist interpretation of Calamity in the following century.

Although interest in the pioneer West boomed in the period from roughly 1905 to 1930, less than a handful of important works were written about Calamity. Several barriers faced those who wanted to write about her. Information about Calamity remained nearly nonexistent, with many of the reliable facts buried in newspapers, census reports, and other legal records not easily accessible to researchers. In addition, many of the stories about Calamity, including her own, were unreliable, often more fanciful—even downright false—than truthful. Third, myths about Calamity were already hardening into assertions: (1) that she had served as a scout, (2) that she was an Indian killer, and (3) that she had been romantically attached to Wild Bill Hickok. Fourth, novelists and moviemakers were telling masculine stories; women were the companions of these heroes, not the central characters in novels and films made in the 1900 to 1930 period. Biographers who wished to provide veracious and soundly researched accounts of Calamity had to find their way through or around these almost impassable or insurmountable barriers. The patterns that emerged revealed that moviemakers and biographers were frequently more interested in embracing the legendary stories than in turning up newer or more truthful accounts

The first two films featuring cinematic Calamities illustrated how much myths about her had already solidified in the teens and early twenties, and how often she would be the supporting female character, not the star. The silent film *In the Days of '75 and '76* (1915) issued not out of Hollywood but from the outback of northwestern Nebraska. Like such later movies as *The Plainsman* (1936) and *Calamity Jane* (1953), this film is the romance story of Calamity and Wild Bill. Played by Freeda Hartzell Romine, Calamity is a perky, pretty tomboy who learns to shoot well and carries a sidearm along with her rifle. But she is also portrayed as domestic and in a very positive light, before she marries Wild Bill halfway through the film and later helps him with scouting and mining. The plot carries through Wild Bill's violent death. At times Calamity seems like one of the guys, but not the slightest bit of immorality or alcoholism is suggested. As in most of the early Calamity movies, the gray side of the historical Calamity—the possible prostitution, aberrant behavior, and alcoholism—is entirely elided.

The second silent film with a role for Calamity, William S. Hart's *Wild Bill Hickok* (1923), is somewhat shrouded in mystery since all copies of the movie have disappeared. And, because of Hart's reputation as the leading Western star of the time, neither he nor Paramount could allow Calamity's character, played by Ethel Grey Terry, to steal the limelight in her supporting role. Hart flatly declared the movie to be historically accurate (he himself had written the screenplay), but it put forth a false story that Calamity and Hickok had been acquaintances in Dodge City before they reconnected in Deadwood. At the end of the movie, Hickok, the famous pistoleer, suggests he and Calamity might forge a life together, but before that can happen, Jack McCall dashes on camera and guns down Wild Bill. Here again the romantic attraction of Wild Bill and Calamity dominates the plot. These sentimental stories, not substantiated in history and biography (a fact not yet clear in the 1920s), were the plotline necessary to bring together *the* story of an Old West hero and heroine. In addition, with but a few exceptions, it would be several years before Calamity could stand as the center pivot, by herself, in cinematic works and novels.

The first nonfiction book on Calamity, Duncan Aikman's *Calamity Jane and the Lady Wildcats* (1927), excessively traveled the legendary Wild West image of Calamity. Aikman, a journalist possessing the sardonic wit of his friend and cultural critic H. L. Mencken, devoted a bit more than a third of his 350-page book to Calamity, along with other provocative sections on Cattle Kate Watson, Belle Starr, Lola Montez, Madame Moustache, and other Wild West women. Supposedly a work of nonfiction, most of its pages about Calamity reeked of imagined scenes and what-ifs—even though Aikman interviewed a few persons who knew Calamity, read dozens of newspaper clippings, and perused other published information about her. If the author had utilized only the hard facts of his research—and avoided artistic verbiage—his account of Calamity could have been condensed into a twenty-five-page essay.

Instead, addicted to a frenetic Old West, Aikman distorted the lives of Calamity and the other "Lady Wildcats." When he wrote to Wyoming historian Grace Raymond Hebard, he asked for stories about their gambling and shooting; never does he request information about them as wives, sisters, daughters, or mothers. Aikman's Calamity is rarely a pioneer woman, almost entirely a frontier hellcat. He spilled no ink about her giving birth to two children or about the lives of her children, and he debunks almost entirely her rumored actions as an Angel of Mercy. Given his intentions, Aikman found what he wanted: Martha Canary, the wild "lynx's kitten" who becomes the Wild Woman of the West. Unfortunately, his unreliable account remained the most widely circulated historical source on Calamity for more than two decades, with subsequent biographers capitalizing on his disclosures but also victimized by his slanted evidence, misstatements, and blatant fabrications.

In the next three decades, from 1930 to 1960, biographers, novelists, and filmmakers followed the legend of Calamity as a Wild Woman of the Old West, but they also traveled other avenues of explanation. These interpretations sprang up during a time of growing interest in the Old West, one that spiraled upward and hit a peak in the 1930s. Most remarkable of all, two women came forward to claim they were, respectively, a granddaughter and daughter of Calamity.

The accounts of Jessie Elizabeth (Oakes) Murray and Jean Hickok McCormick, appearing suddenly on the scene in the 1930s and 1940s, reveal much about Americans' hunger for mother-daughter stories. In the late 1920s but especially in the early 1930s Murray emerged to claim she was Calamity's granddaughter or niece. Jessie appeared a few times from her birth on 28 October 1887 until her mother's death. Then, except for the records of two marriages in Montana in 1904 and 1908, she disappeared for more than three decades, only to reappear suddenly, telling many to whom she wrote that she was Calamity's granddaughter or niece, not her daughter. Throughout the 1930s and sporadically in the next few years Jessie queried librarians, archivists, and historians for information about her grandmother or her aunt and sometimes about the man she considered her father, William Hickok, a relative of Wild Bill. When her informants failed to turn up the information she requested, she upbraided them for not getting "the scum off your brain." Along the way, Jessie frequently changed her story, especially after another woman's claim to be Calamity's daughter surfaced.

Adding new ingredients to the mother-daughter theme, Jean Hickok McCormick dashed onstage on Mother's Day, 6 May 1941, announcing to a nationwide radio audience on *We the People* that she was the genuine daughter of Calamity Jane and Wild Bill Hickok. She claimed Calamity and Bill had fallen in love in Kansas, had married, and Calamity had given birth to Jane (or Janey). Bill abandoned Calamity and Janey. Thinking she would be unable to raise her daughter, Calamity gave her up for adoption to James O'Neil and his wife to raise in England. To answer skeptics, Hickok McCormick produced an unpublished diary that Calamity reportedly kept and also letters unsent to Janey. More than a few aficionados of the Old West and others who wanted so much to see a mother-daughter strain in Calamity's life embraced Hickok McCormick's story and sources without asking the needed questions. Unfortunately, many writers and moviemakers used Jean's story for nearly a half century before biographer James McLaird showed it to be a shabby fraud.

The McCormick followers included historians and biographers in the 1940s. Clarence S. Paine, a librarian who amassed an unusually large collection of Calamity documents for his planned biography of Calamity, could never free himself from the McCormick story, even though he was a thoughtful, diligent researcher. Another local historian, who was a medical doctor by occupation, Noley Mumey, was so smitten by the Hickok-McCormick story that he published, for the first time, the diary and letters, without questioning their authenticity. More annalist than analyst, Mumey provided a valuable summary of key newspaper articles about Calamity but failed to use much of the Hickok McCormick story in his own narrative.

The Hickok McCormick virus also infected another biographer, Glenn Clairmonte, in her book *Calamity Was the Name for Jane* (1959). Touted as

"The Only Complete Life of Calamity Jane," and a "distinguished biography," the volume fell far short of these salutes. Instead, the author, taken in by the Hickok McCormick tale and adding false facts to prove Calamity's warmheartedness toward her putative daughter, Jean, produced a deeply flawed book. Clairmonte also refused to deal with Calamity's "husbands," and Calamity's profanity and early drinking are muted. And nearly everything about the Wild Bill–Calamity relationship is imagined, sometimes being even more far-fetched than the McCormick story. Clairmonte's biography illustrated how difficult it had become to produce a defensible biography of Calamity if one relied heavily on the McCormick materials and tried to make the Calamity–Wild Bill relationship the central plot of the story.

Two films did exactly that, however, dramatizing Calamity's story as a love affair with Hickok. These two movies, *The Plainsman* (1936) and *Calamity Jane* (1953), probably did more than anything else to shape the dominant romantic image of Calamity from 1930 to 1960.

When famed movie director Cecil B. DeMille announced in early 1936 his plans for a film on Wild Bill Hickok, with a major role for Calamity Jane, he set tongues to wagging. Would he place an emotional romance at the center of the film, how would he treat the darker side of Calamity, and would he remain true to history and end the film tragically? Even though Hickok family members tried to warn DeMille away from the falsity of a Calamity–Wild Bill romance, DeMille stayed on track, with appealing roles for Gary Cooper as Hickok and Jean Arthur as a hybrid Calamity trying to sort out her competing masculine and feminine impulses. Calamity drives a wild stagecoach and swings a wicked bullwhip, but she is also appealingly feminine in her form-fitting buckskins, her hair nicely arranged. She acts like a man but also wants to be an attractive woman, wife, and mother. One memorable scene reverberates with symbolic meaning and encapsulates DeMille's interpretation. Preparing to secure help for soldiers pinned down by Indians, Calamity steps out of the nearly ruined skirt of a stylish dress she had donned earlier in hopes of proving her femininity, and rides for reinforcements in the buckskins she was wearing beneath her dress. Moving back and forth from dress to leather pants, Jean Arthur's Calamity personifies the oxymoronic Calamity that had appeared by the 1930s. Spunky, perky, and pretty but also assertive and courageous (but not boozy or loose), Calamity plays a romantic, vernacular woman of the frontier who wishes to marry.

The second film, the musical *Calamity Jane* (1953), starring Doris Day, revealed how far moviemakers were willing to go in featuring a romantic Calamity in full flower. Like most musicals, this film—with huge doses of glitz,

uplift, and nonstop action—shoved history aside in its dash toward entertainment. Day was ideally suited for her role in this musical Western. Her singing
talents, physical attractiveness, agility, and vivaciousness matched the need for
a romantic rather than gritty Wild West Calamity. There would be no alcohol,
only "sarsaparilla"; and her swearing was limited to her denunciation of recalci-
trant miners as a "mangy pack of dirt-scratching beetles" or "slab-sided coyotes."
The plotline of *Calamity Jane* follows the heroine's transition from a careless and
seemingly carefree tomboy to a woman aching for a man's love and marriage.
When Calamity discovers her love for Wild Bill (who is definitely not a leading character in the film), she transitions toward love and marriage, emotional
transformations that come front and center in Sammy Fain's Oscar-winning
song "Secret Love," whose lyrics reveal that Calamity's "heart is now an open
door" and "her love is secret no more." Nothing of Calamity's alcoholism and
sexual experience is evident here, nor is the historical fact that Wild Bill died in
Deadwood somewhat less than a month after he arrived in midsummer 1876. In
its excessively romantic depiction of Calamity, Doris Day's role sacrificed nearly
all historical veracity on the altar of cinematic popularity.

At the same time that the false story of Jean Hickok McCormick and the
romantic depictions of Calamity in *The Plainsman* and *Calamity Jane* greatly
distorted history, two biographers were trying to bring historically accurate
portraits of Calamity in front of readers. J. Leonard Jennewein, a journalist and
professor, set out to write a full-scale biography, but concluded he "had neither
the time, money, nor talent" to complete the project and reduced his 50,000-
word (150–200-manuscript-page) document to a pamphlet-length book.
Jennewein was a truth-teller who combed hard-to-find newspaper sources and
interviewed oldsters who knew Calamity before issuing his *Calamity Jane of
the Western Trails* in 1953. In his brief work, Jennewein addressed most of the
controversial topics: Calamity's birthplace, her death, her drinking and prostitution, her claims of scouting, her physical appearance, and the McCormick
story. Consider his one-line summary of Calamity's drinking: "Alcohol pushed
and pulled and pounded on Calamity Jane." Or his comment on the Hickok
McCormick and Wild Bill narrative: "We buy no stock in the Calamity Jane–
Wild Bill corporation." Word-for-word Jennewein's abbreviated work remains
eminently valuable.

The same hard-headed realism exudes from Roberta Beed Sollid's *Calamity
Jane: A Study in Historical Criticism* (1958). This work quickly became accepted
as the best-researched biographical study of Calamity. Via Greyhound buses, Sollid visited nearly all the major collections of Calamity material and interviewed

aged men who had known Calamity personally. She was no romantic sycophant; she may even have disliked Calamity. As she said bluntly at the beginning of her valuable book, "No career is so elusive to the historian as that of a loose woman." Her diligent research turned up new information on such topics as Calamity's nickname, her so-called husbands, nursing, jailings, gun handling, and death. Sollid's work was not so much a biography as a critical study of the stories told about Calamity and their validity. Nor was it a thesis-driven book; rather, it debunked misconceptions, lies, and folklore. Sollid achieved much of her corrective goal, and her book became the most reliable study of Calamity for most of the next half century.

By the end of the 1950s, no coherent, long-lasting, single image of Calamity Jane had come into focus. Instead, divergent and changing images dominated the scene. Historians and biographers wrestled with the chaotic, differing stories of Calamity's life. Moviemakers—though accepting some of Calamity's rough, uncouth side—were more interested in peddling romantic stories about her. And for nearly twenty years the variant story of Jean Hickok McCormick being the daughter of Calamity and Wild Bill troubled and diverted many Calamity storytellers. If these diverse, often shifting images dominated the period from 1930 to 1960, an even sharper shift transformed Calamity images after 1960. A New Gray Calamity bounded onto the scene, influencing—indeed transforming—much of what was written and filmed about her up to 1990.

The new images of Calamity Jane in the years between 1960 and 1990 paralleled the tipping points of change occurring in American culture and were also consonant with the interpretive shifts of the American West. The sociocultural upset following the assassination of President John F. Kennedy in 1963, and of his brother Robert and civil rights leader Martin Luther King, Jr., in 1968, as well as the Vietnam War and the dissent that boiled up vis-à-vis that war, transformed the tone of many novels, histories, and movies during the sixties. These dramatic incidents and events also reshaped interpretations of the American West. Western novels such as Thomas Berger's *Little Big Man* (1964), Robert Flynn's *North to Yesterday* (1967), and John Seelye's *The Kid* (1972) illustrated the expanding emphases on violence, ethnic and racial topics, and new roles for women. Similar topics received major attention in Western films such as *A Fistful of Dollars* (1964), *The Wild Bunch* (1969), and *Little Big Man* (1970). Western historians likewise participated in the transformation, gradually moving away from earlier narrative and romantic storytelling toward more analytical/evaluative studies of Native Americans, Chicanos, women and families, and environmental history. By the end of the 1980s a historical work like Patricia Nelson

Limerick's *Legacy of Conquest: The Unbroken Past of the American West* (1987) illustrated the marked changes going on in western historical writing.

These sociocultural shifts clearly molded images of Calamity Jane that surfaced between 1960 and 1990. None was published more widely than the nearly twenty novels of English author J. T. Edson featuring a nonromantic—if not an antiromantic—Calamity as a central or supporting character. In his Calamity novels, Edson introduced bits of biography, but had key facts wrong, stating, for example, that Calamity's mother Charlotte, now widowed, took her daughter "Mary Jane Canary"[*sic*] to a convent. At sixteen "Mary Jane" escapes and quickly begins her new life as a cook and then a skilled rider, wielder of a long whip, and fearsome gun-woman. His Calamity heroine is an attractive (but not beautiful) woman, sexually voracious, a moderate drinker and smoker, a stout but well-built female, and romantically intertwined with more than two or three equally handsome and virile heroes. No drunkenness or prostitution here; instead youth, robustness, competitiveness, and success.

The imagined Calamities in Edson's novels juxtapose her Wild Women legend with the incipient New Gray Calamity image. In Edson's first Calamity novel, *Trouble Trail* (1965), Calamity and three other women get into a vicious brawl, tearing off one another's clothes and ending in a sweaty heap. In another novel, *The Cow Thieves* (1965), Calamity rides nonstop, gallops through a series of threatening violent scenes, and beds down with the hero Danny Fog two or three times. In one of the last books of the series, *Calamity, Mark and Belle* (1980), Edson exhausts his list of adjectives in describing Calamity: she is pretty, red-haired, sexy, well endowed, raunchy, promiscuous, foul-mouthed, adventuresome, courageous, and forever young. Again, her conflicts are with equally alluring and daring—and physically strong—women. Even though Edson's fictions were mostly innocent of factual history, they kept Calamity's name continuously before a huge reading public.

Edson's emphases on sexuality and violence (hallmarks of the Gray Calamity images) became steady fare in the so-called Adult Westerns that several publishing houses printed in multivolume series. Most of the series, although carrying just one author's name, were written by a stable of house-hired, anonymous writers. The most voluminous of these was the Jake Logan series, launched in the mid-1970s and containing more than four hundred volumes by 2010. In one of the Logan series novels, *Dead Man's Hand* (1979), Calamity rides and sleeps with superhero John Slocum. She comes on scene as a sexual toy of the macho men, eventually simultaneously taking on Slocum and also Wild Bill Hickok as lovers, on the same night, in the same blankets. *Longarm in Deadwood* (1982), an installment in another sex-and-violence series, features Calamity as a drunken nymphomaniac, trying to seduce the hero Longarm and other men who come to her attention. The novel presents an excessively negative and distorted picture of Calamity as a filthy, ugly, clap-ridden, and hopeless liar.

Pete Dexter's novel *Deadwood* (1986) also featured the New Gray Calamity who appeared after the 1960s. In his novel, Calamity smells like the ripe mules and horses she rides. Nor is she much cleaner than the filthy tents and lean-tos where she flops. Calamity is so rancid that a fresh crop of mold grows unnoticed on her neck. No man pays much attention to her even though fornication and sexual violence are rife in Dexter's Deadwood. Unwashed, unloved, and underappreciated, she seems less a woman in Dexter's novel than a two-legged screaming eagle bent on shooting off toes, bragging of her "husband" Wild Bill, and out-drinking all others, men and vile drunkards included. Unfortunately, Dexter's Calamity is unbelievable—a flat, one-sided figure of parody instead of a full-bodied, round character of memorable fiction.

Larry McMurtry's novel *Buffalo Girls* (1990) also featuring a New Gray Calamity, contains redeeming qualities. McMurtry's Calamity symbolizes a closing frontier, a once-heroic past disappearing into nostalgic haze. The author also depicts Calamity as a failure in nearly all her endeavors. She falls off the stagecoach in Buffalo Bill's Wild West, cannot use a gun, and fails to *do* anything except live off others. Although McMurtry's novel and heroine suffer from excessive grayness, the work raises significant cultural questions about the impact of a closing frontier.

The most important film released in this period was the TV movie *Calamity Jane* (1984), starring a feminist Jane Alexander. The movie used the Hickok McCormick story as its plotline and also illustrated the increasing tendency of Calamitists to create an ambivalent character, rambunctiously masculine and less assertively feminine. Here the thematic emphasis, less successfully, is Calamity as Hickok's wife and mother of his daughter, but her role as a strong, independent woman is on much stronger ground. Her desire for independence clashes with her lust for a partner. Alexander superbly portrays these clashes of desire and actuality. And she revealingly tells her daughter Janey (who does not know that Calamity is her biological mother), "What I know about wifeing you could stuff in a saddlebag." Or, even more sensationally, "Well, I guess it's the same for us ladies here and there. You either get paid for washing a man's drawers or for pulling them down." In her unvarnished, gritty actions, Alexander's Calamity, foreshadowing even more realistic images in coming movies, illustrates the large distances Calamity portrayals had traveled since Doris Day's Calamity of the 1950s.

Revealingly, during the 1960–90 period, historians and biographers seemed uninterested in Calamity. A few local historians wrote essays or pamphlet-length studies of Calamity, but no full-length biography of her appeared in these decades. Historian Watson Parker produced two important studies of Deadwood and the Black Hills boomtowns, although he did not much care for Calamity. Calling her "the notorious harlot" and that "notorious bawd," and describing her as "built like a busted bale of hay," Parker even suggested "that if indeed she cured any smallpox victims, she probably gave them the great pox in return." Biographers of Wild Bill Hickok were kinder. Englishman Joseph Rosa, who turned out the most important life story of Hickok, *They Called Him Wild Bill* (1964), denied any Wild Bill–Calamity romance and denounced Jean Hickok McCormick's story as a fraud.

The most important essays on Calamity were by historian-biographer James D. McLaird. Beginning his long, fruitful career as the leading authority on Calamity, McLaird published a path-breaking essay on the developing legends surrounding her. He also filled in information on Calamity's role in the Newton-Jenney Expedition of 1875 and furnished background for Mrs. William Loring Spencer's novel about Calamity Jane.

By the end of the 1980s the mushrooming images of a New Gray Calamity in some ways gained more headway than the declared truth-tellers in the race to reveal Calamity's story. But many segments of Calamity's life had not been uncovered. Much of this missing information would be discovered and pieced together in the next quarter century.

A variety of Calamity Janes marched across the stages of U.S. and global cultures following 1990. Some image-makers advanced new feminist interpretations, others preferred the New Gray Calamity, still others followed the outdated Jean Hickok McCormick story, and more than a few preferred Calamity as a bona fide Wild Woman of the Old West. Most important of all, James McLaird provided a full, historically sound life story of a complex woman of the pioneer frontier.

In 1995, two major motion pictures furnished even more pronounced feminist interpretations of Calamity. The *Buffalo Girls* film, based on McMurtry's novel of the same name, followed the discredited Jean Hickok McCormick story. Despite its unauthentic source, *Buffalo Girls* furnishes intriguing depictions of gender relations, sexuality, maternal desire, and a disappearing Old West. Calamity is a very intimate girlfriend of madam Dora Du Fran, who is equally intimate with cowboy/rancher Teddy Blue. Calamity, played by Anjelica Huston, wants to stay emotionally connected with her daughter Janey, now in Europe. This mother-daughter relationship played well with American audiences. But viewers seemed less interested in an equally important theme: Calamity's role as a symbol of a vanishing Old West. When Buffalo Bill Cody invites her to be a part of his Wild West arena show, which will make her "famous," she retorts "I *am* famous."

Similar gender themes appear in *Wild Bill* (1995), with Jeff Bridges as Hickok and Ellen Barkin as Calamity. The movie accepts much of the Jean Hickok McCormick plot yet promotes a strongly feminist rendition of Calamity. Barkin's Calamity has much to say about male-female relationships, about sexuality, and about the significance of these relationships. She wants Wild Bill to love her, but is willing to accept much less than that, including having sex on a saloon table. By and large, Calamity is depicted as a female nurturer in a heathenish male world. Serving as something of a saloon housewife, she cleans up and serves up necessities. Although based in part on Pete Dexter's novel *Deadwood*, this cinematic Calamity is not the dirty and foul heroine of Dexter's fiction who seems to have bundled with a skunk. In all, Barkin epitomizes a New Gray Calamity reflecting on subjects of love, sex, class, and gender.

The HBO made-for-TV series *Deadwood* (2004–2006) probably attracted more viewers than any other vehicle portraying Calamity in the years following 1960. Lasting three seasons with thirty-six episodes, the series proved unusually fascinating for television audiences. *Deadwood* illustrated how much a New Gray Calamity Jane had come on scene, and it showcased the talents of gifted writer and producer David Milch, bringing to life a new kind of Western for movie and television viewers.

Even though Milch and several of his actors claimed the series episodes were "historically accurate," they rarely were. Milch skewed the lives of lead characters to fit his dramatic purposes, imagined many characters and events that never happened, and greatly overplayed the theme of violence. For example, he depicts the Gem Theater/Saloon as a den of death, with about a dozen murders occurring at that site alone over the series' three years. In one interview, Milch also asserts, rather arrogantly, "that's not the way they talked in the West" (in criticizing the critics of his characters' profane language), when almost no scholar of the West would make that claim because evidence is lacking on how frontier men and women spoke.

Robin Weigert performed superbly as Calamity but within a narrow focus. Described ambivalently as a profane drunkard but also as a nurse of the sick and a lover of children, Weigert's Calamity appears in major or minor roles in about three-fourths of the thirty-six episodes. But Calamity is so often inebriated and isolated from the community she cannot function as a dancer and entertainer. Producer Milch exhibits outright silliness too. Contemporary sources did not refer to Calamity as "Hickok's woman," as occurs several times in *Deadwood*. Then Milch rushes into a morass of unbelievability when he ventures: "I don't think he ever banged her . . . [but] she told everyone he did." No writer at the time, or since, has Calamity saying she and Hickok were bedmates. When Robin Weigert was interviewed about her role in the series, she showed no knowledge—in fact, little interest—about the historical Calamity. The inadequate depiction of Calamity in *Deadwood* is all the more disappointing since the program had such an amazing following.

In 1995, Montana museum owner Stella Foote published her biography, *A History of Calamity Jane*, which proved to be the last hurrah for full-length books adhering to the Jean Hickok McCormick line. Foote and her husband, Don, had known McCormick, hired her at their museum, and supported her in her declining years before her death in February 1951. The Footes bought the so-called Calamity diary and letters and published portions of them in small pamphlets. In her biography, Foote's reach far exceeded her grasp when she tried to force contradictory information into the McCormick mold. Overall, the obvious limitations of Foote's vanity-published biography further undermined the already weakened McCormick story.

Finally, in the 1990s and beyond, the solid, exhaustively researched essays and books of James D. McLaird provided the dependable historical accounts Calamity Jane aficionados had lacked for nearly a century. The most important of McLaird's several essays was "Calamity Jane's Diary and Letters: Story of a Fraud." Published in *Montana: The Magazine of Western History* in 1995, the invaluable essay, point by point, dismantled the Jean Hickok McCormick story, showing where the documents were wrong, falsified, and hedged about with misleading assertions. McLaird proved that no one should place any reliance on the diary and letters for further research on Calamity. He also speculated that McCormick had trotted out the fraudulent documents because she hungered and thirsted after notoriety. Replacing her own nondescript background with a life linked to two western legends would give her the headlines she desired. Hickok McCormick did get newspaper and radio attention, but the notice quickly melted away. Even if the documents were undoubtedly forgeries, Hickok McCormick gained, in some measure, what she presumably wanted to achieve in claiming to be the daughter of Calamity and Wild Bill.

McLaird's notable research in this and other essays prepared the way for his extensive biography, *Calamity Jane: The Woman and the Legend* (2005). Thorough, measured, and thoughtful, McLaird's biography is by far the most important publication on Calamity. His exhaustive research jumps out from every page, including his near-definitive coverage of frontier newspapers, manuscript collections, and published books and essays. McLaird chops out the cluttered underbrush of misconceptions: Hickok McCormick's fable, the exaggerations of Calamity herself, and the misleading conclusions about the Calamity–Wild Bill relationship. Readers who examined closely McLaird's text and notes could avoid the noxious weeds of unsubstantiated rumors, falsehood, and downright lies that clutter the Calamity landscape.

The major contributions of McLaird's turning-point biography are two. For the first time we have a full-scale, veracious account of Martha Canary/Calamity Jane's life. We are also given a valuable overview of the legends that grew up around her, both during her lifetime and in the following decades. Three years later McLaird dealt with the most widely trafficked legend surrounding Calamity in *Wild Bill Hickok and Calamity Jane: Deadwood Legends* (2008). Showing how exaggerated tales in sensational magazine and newspaper accounts and in dime novels helped spawn the flood of legends about Hickok and Calamity, McLaird moves on to show the wrongheadedness of those views that turned them into a much-touted couple. McLaird presents a complex Calamity, noting the jostling images of her as a young woman dressed as a dancer, waitress, and entertainer in Deadwood saloons and the conflicting depictions of her as a buckskin-clad rider and teamster among workers and soldiers, usually dressed as a man. Equally rewarding is McLaird's tracing of Calamity's evolving notoriety from a young waif to a local celebrity to a nationally recognized dime novel heroine, and on to a notorious wanderer and distressed, aging woman. Unfortunately, in the decade since the publication of McLaird's biography in 2005, other authors have not moved notably beyond his contributions. Nor have they made good use of his prodigious research in their own essays and books.

By the end of the twentieth century, readers, viewers, and a variety of other participants in popular culture had a veritable smorgasbord of Calamity Jane representations spread before them. These representations often reflected the increasing interest of many Americans in feminist themes. TV shows, dramas, and one-person impersonators presented some of these womanly images of Calamity. Several communities also began celebrating Calamity. Princeton, Missouri, finally stopped overlooking that Martha Canary/Calamity Jane was born there and initiated and continued its Calamity Jane Days. Livingston,

Montana, commenced sponsoring a Calamity Jane Rodeo. And probably most widely known, Deadwood launched its Days of '76 in the 1920s, a celebration that continues to draw large groups of spectators and tourists into the twenty-first century.

In two other areas—clothing stores and restaurants—entrepreneurs also played on diversifying Calamity Jane themes. One clothing line carries a shout-out line: "I figure if a girl hankers to be a legend, she ought to go ahead and be one." Calamity Jane clothing stores opened across the United States and also in Calgary, Canada, where offerings included canvas trench coats, dresses, boots, lingerie, and wedding dresses, all sold under the slogan "Be What You Want to Be."

Calamity Jane restaurants also spread from coast to coast. A Calamity Jane restaurant in Seattle urges customers to "celebrate the spirit of our namesake." The café promises to serve up "great grub," with no dishes proving to be calamities. Another Calamity Jane restaurant in faraway northern New Mexico provides a spicy menu of green chile stew, burritos, and enchiladas. The most unusual of these restaurants is the Calamity Jane Saloon in the Basque area of southern France. This establishment, its publicity indicates, will "cultivate the meaning of the heroes of the American West."

Racehorses, show dogs, household pets, artworks, and footwear also carry the Calamity Jane sobriquet. Athletes adopted her name, too, with famed golfer Bobby Jones naming his erratic putter Calamity Jane. The web page for Indiana University's Ultimate Frisbee team is exceptionally direct, catching the varied implications of Calamity's divergent identities: "Give 'em Hell, Give 'em Fear!"

By the early twenty-first century, Calamity Jane's name had taken on a hodgepodge of diverse meanings, well beyond the mere identification of a nineteenth-century woman of the frontier West. Journalists, biographers, historians, and some filmmakers and novelists may have made her the most written-about woman of the American West; they focused primarily on the well-known and notorious western female. But other entrepreneurs, cultists, and purveyors of popular culture found a catchy brand that captured buyers, attendees, and hangers-on. Much as dime novelist Edward L. Wheeler had in the nineteenth century, people in the late twentieth and early twenty-first centuries discovered or rediscovered that the name of Calamity Jane snapped up attention. Like the names of leading athletes, political leaders, other historical figures, and the newest sensations on morning TV or evening news shows, Calamity's name grabbed buyers, curiosity-seekers, and tourists. She had become a powerful magnet of popular culture. That was not likely to change soon.

Bibliographies and
Reference Volumes

Entries in this section are arranged alphabetically by first author. Numbers in parentheses cross-reference other numbered entries.

1. Adams, Ramon F. *Six-Guns and Saddle Leather: A Bibliography of Books and Pamphlets on Western Outlaws and Gunmen*. 1954, 1969. New ed., Cleveland, Ohio: John T. Zubal, 1982.

The leading bibliographer of western outlaws and gunmen, Adams, a candy maker by trade, chose to include such characters as Calamity Jane, Poker Alice, and Madame Moustache in his listings. Although the women were not outlaws or gunmen, Adams reasoned that "these unique characters deserve a place here as part of the gunman's West" (p. xviii). This hefty volume is essentially an annotated bibliography of 2,500 books and pamphlets that Adams considered the most important on Old West subjects.

Adams cites more than 180 items on Calamity, most of which are annotated. Although Adams refrains from giving high marks to any of the early accounts of Calamity, he notes that Mumey (302), Jennewein (278), and Sollis [*sic*, Sollid] (326) provide new, dependable information. Duncan Aikman (230), Adams avers, "is unreliable" (p. 8). He likes the general findings of John S. McClintock (288) on the Black Hills, but does not point out the significant shortcomings of Horan (275) and Clairmonte (243). Interestingly, even though Adams rarely deals with fiction, he does mention the novels by Mrs. William Loring Spencer (481) and Ethel Hueston (469). Because Adams is primarily a fact man, he says little about the literary artistry of historians and biographers. Revealingly, Adams doubts the spurious tale of a Wild Bill–Calamity marriage, but he does not weigh in on Jean Hickok McCormick's claim (198–99, 376) of being the daughter of these Old West notables.

Overall, a very useful listing, especially when understood in light of Adams's fascination with facts. Always the energetic bibliographer, Adams added to his listings, which include Calamity, in *Burs Under the Saddle: A Second Look at Books and Histories of the West* (Norman: University of Oklahoma Press, 1964), and *More Burs Under the Saddle: Books and Histories of the West* (Norman: University of Oklahoma Press, 1979, 1989).

2. Browning, James A. *The Western Reader's Guide: A Selected Bibliography of Nonfiction Magazines, 1953–91*. Stillwater, Okla.: Barbed Wire Press, 1992.

   This helpful guide lists hundreds of essays dealing with the frontier West that appeared in popular historical magazines. Its listings include several essays about Calamity Jane.

3. Chamberlain, Kathleen, comp. *Wild Westerners: A Bibliography*. Albuquerque: Center for the American West, University of New Mexico, 1998.

   A handy guide to nearly all the leading notorious figures of the Old West, this bibliography also includes sections on other bibliographies and general reference books and essays on the frontier West. The volume lists more than eight hundred unannotated items.

4. Etulain, Richard W. "Calamity Jane Bibliography," manuscript, 1994, 1997.

   This unpublished bibliography of 150 items, which circulated widely in the mid to late 1990s, includes sections on novels; books; essays, chapters, and introductions; films; and photographs dealing with Calamity. The items are arranged in chronological order, from the beginnings to the late 1990s, and are unannotated. This bibliography is superseded by the list in the Etulain biography of Calamity (5, 257).

5. Etulain, Richard W. *The Life and Legends of Calamity Jane*. Norman: University of Oklahoma Press, 2014.

   The fifteen-page bibliography in this recent biography of Calamity lists more than three hundred items. Separate sections are devoted to manuscripts, bibliographies and histories, novels, dime novels, essays, newspapers, films, and television programs. In addition, the author provides a ten-page "Essay on Sources" discussing the major sources of information on Calamity.

6. Etulain, Richard W., and N. Jill Howard, eds. *A Bibliographical Guide to the Study of Western American Literature*. 2nd ed. Albuquerque: University of New Mexico Press, 1995.

This 477-page guide to interpretations of western American literature lists nearly 6,500 items. In addition to citing general reference volumes and essays and several subject categories —such as regionalism, dime novels, popular Westerns, environmental and ethnic literature—the guide includes references to the books and essays of more than five hundred western authors. The most useful listings on Calamity Jane are those in the topical sections on dime novels, Western films, and women and family. The citations carry no annotations.

7. Jennewein, J. Leonard. Bibliography in *Calamity Jane of the Western Trails*. 1953; 4th ed. Rapid City, S.Dak.: Dakota West Books, 1991, 40–47.

This listing of eighty-two entries includes biographies, histories, novels, and a few other items. No newspaper stories are cited, and the South Dakota entries are the most numerous. Most items are annotated, providing both summary and evaluative comments. Jennewein sometimes steers readers away from a less-than-satisfactory source but finds useful information in most sources. He also notes the photographs that enhance the value of some items. Overall, the first edition of this pamphlet, published a few years before Roberta Beed Sollid's path-breaking study (326), provided the first extensive bibliography of publications about Calamity Jane.

8. Lamar, Howard R., ed. *The New Encyclopedia of the American West*. 1977; New Haven, Conn: Yale University Press, 1998.

A revised and expanded version of a nonpareil reference volume on the American West, this huge, oversized volume belongs on the shelves of every aficionado of the topic. Thousands of entries in this 1,300-page guide to the West cover the major (and many of the minor) characters, events, and ideas associated with eastern and western frontiers and the pioneer and modern American West. The entry on Calamity Jane (pp. 150–51), by volume editor Lamar, is a model of balanced, judicious comment.

9. McLaird, James D. Bibliography in *Calamity Jane: The Woman and the Legend*. Norman: University of Oklahoma Press, 2005, 337–63.

This exhaustive bibliography is the starting place for anyone interested in researching the life and legends of Calamity Jane. McLaird divides his more than twenty-five-page listing into several parts: manuscript collections, documents, books, Deadwood Dick dime novels, articles, newspapers, and popular culture. Although the bibliography does not cite the specific newspaper stories the author has consulted, his very detailed endnotes (pp. 291–335) do. The entries here are not annotated, but many of the major books, essays, novels, and films are discussed in the text and footnotes of McLaird's superb biography (290).

10. McLaird, James D. Bibliography in *Wild Bill Hickok and Calamity Jane: Deadwood Legends*. Pierre: South Dakota State Historical Society Press, 2008, 157–66.

The bibliographical listing in this dual biography is particularly valuable because it provides readers with all the major sources dealing with the much-touted relationship between Wild Bill and Calamity. McLaird furnishes sources on documents/manuscripts, books, articles, newspapers, and videotapes. Explanatory footnotes comment on many of the sources.

11. McLaird, James D. "Dakota Resources: A Reader's Guide to the Historical Literature of South Dakota." *South Dakota History* 22 (Summer 1992): 173–99.

This very helpful annotated bibliography of one hundred South Dakota historical sources "is targeted for the general reader" (p. 173). After a section on general and reference sources, McLaird moves chronologically from Indians to twentieth-century South Dakota. One section on the Black Hills (pp. 188–92) contains thirteen items. Nearly all the books in this section contain information on Calamity Jane. There is a brief but very useful bibliography.

MANUSCRIPT COLLECTIONS
AND MANUSCRIPTS

Entries in this section are arranged alphabetically by repository or collection name, or in the case of individual manuscripts, by the author's surname.

12. American Heritage Center, University of Wyoming, Laramie.

    This well-organized center contains an unusually full vertical file of Calamity Jane materials. It also houses the papers of early Wyoming historian Grace Raymond Hebard, which contain a good deal of information on the frontier Rocky Mountain West, including interviews with persons claiming to have known Calamity.

13. Buffalo Bill Center of the West, Cody, Wyo.

    The vertical files and the Mercado Collection at the Buffalo Bill Center of the West contain information on Calamity Jane.

14. Cerney, Jan. "Elijah Canary, Calamity Jane's Brother," [ca. 2012]; copy in Etulain's files.

    A fifty-nine-page, closely spaced manuscript, this story of Calamity's younger brother Elijah (Lige or Lije) is well researched and full of valuable information. The author has made good use of newspapers, legal documents, other unpublished sources, and the most significant essays and books on Calamity. After further revision to heighten the narrative power of its unusual story, the manuscript clearly deserves publication.

15. Robert Beebe David Collection, Casper College, Casper, Wyo.

    The "Earnest, Boney, Reminiscences" in the David Collection state that Boney met the Canary family on their way to the Montana goldfields. This is an important reference, but Boney dates the meeting as occurring in 1872, whereas the Canarys were traveling in 1863 or 1864.

16. Foppes, Ellen K., "Calamity Jane Chronology," [1990s]; in Etulain's files.

    This forty-seven-page chronology traces the story of the Canary family and Calamity Jane from 1788 through the published obituaries for Calamity. The listing cites census and other manuscript sources and many newspaper citations. This chronology was prepared by a doctoral student for a never-completed dissertation at the University of New Mexico.

17. Fort Collins Pioneer Museum, Fort Collins, Colo.

    This collection includes considerable information about Jean Hickok McCormick and her fraudulent claim to be the daughter of Calamity Jane and Wild Bill Hickok. It also contains copies of some of Hickok McCormick's writings. See also the revealing letter from Joseph F. "White Eye" Anderson to C. M. Lawrence, 28 January 1943, concerning his meeting with Calamity on her way north to Deadwood in June–July 1876.

18. Homestake Adams Research and Cultural Center, Deadwood, S.Dak.

    This center contains all the information formerly housed at the Adams Museum in Deadwood. It also contains rich materials on Deadwood and the Black Hills areas in general.

19. McGovern Library, Dakota Wesleyan University, Mitchell, S.Dak.

    This collection houses the papers of J. Leonard Jennewein, longtime Calamity Jane scholar. In addition, it contains one of the most extensive holdings of Calamity Jane photographs.

20. Mercer County Courthouse, Princeton, Mo.

    This site contains the important land records of the Canary families in the 1850s and 1860s. In addition, the courthouse retains the legal and probate records dealing with the Canary family squabbles in the early 1860s.

21. Montana Historical Society, Helena.

    The Montana Historical Society's (MHS) collections include an extensive vertical file on Calamity Jane. The MHS also holds many photographs of Calamity and the locations in the Rocky Mountain West where she visited.

22. Clarence S. Paine Research Files, Center for Western Studies, Augustana College, Sioux Falls, S.Dak.

This valuable collection gathers research materials from librarian Clarence Paine's projected full-scale biography of Calamity Jane. It includes important bibliographies of pertinent books, essays, and manuscript sources. Also available is Paine's correspondence with Jean Hickok McCormick, who claimed to be Calamity's daughter.

23. South Dakota State Historical Society, Pierre.

The most important Calamity collection at the South Dakota State Historical Society is the Lloyd McFarling Papers. A writer who focused on topics of the northern West, McFarling gathered abundant materials, especially from newspapers, for a book-length biography of Calamity. A copy of several chapters of a drafted book, to be entitled "The Legend of Calamity Jane," drawing heavily on newspaper research, is included in the McFarling Papers. Other collections contain scattered items on Calamity Jane and her daughter, Jessie Elizabeth Oakes Murray.

24. William R. Whiteside Working Papers; copies in Etulain's files.

"Family of James Canary of Virginia," 14 July 1997 (18 pp.); "Calamity Jane Novels," 3 August 1998 (3 pp.); "Calamity Jane in Periodicals," 3, 8 August 1998 (8 pp.); "The Trip West," 4 August 1998 (3 pp.), revised 5 September 1998 (2 pp.); "Canary Family: Iowa Chronology," 7 August 1998 (3 pp.); "Chronology: Canary Families in Iowa," 15 August 1998 (4 pp.); "Chronology: Canary Families in Idaho," 15 August 1998 (6 pp.); "Public Appearances: Calamity Jane," 3 September 1998, revised 9 August 2000 (22 pp.); "Family of Elijah Canary," 5 September 1998 (17 pp.); "Hardwick's Great Rocky Mountain Show: Chicago," 2 October 1998 (5 pp.); "Calamity Jane and General Crook," 17 December 1998 (6 pp.); "Calamity Jane in Film and TV," 4 July 1999, revised 16 August 2000 (5 pp.); "Canary Marriages: Idaho," November 1999–January 2000 (2 pp.); "George Cosgrove," 13 November 1999–January 2000 (5 pp.); "Could Calamity Jane Read and/or Write?" 1 January 2000 (2 pp.); "Thomas McLean Newson Newspaper Articles: Deadwood, SD, 1877," 26 June 2000 (9 pp.); "Madam Bull Dog," 24, 26 June 2000 (29 pp.); "The Unknown (Smith) Bloxsom," 30 June 2000 (9 pp.); "Calamity Jane in the Coeur d'Alenes," 12 July 2000 (11 pp.); [James Thornton Canary family], 12 July 2000 (32 pp.); "Calamity Jane and Tobacco Spitting Incident: Two Versions," revised 16 August 2000 (13 pp.); "Robert Dorsett," 2001, revised 16 May 2013 (12 pp.).

These invaluable research guides include information from census, marriage, probate, and other genealogical records. They also draw on published books and essays. The guides are especially worthy tools for serious researchers.

25. Wyoming State Archives and Research Division, Cheyenne.

    Available here are valuable legal, photographic, and newspaper materials on Calamity Jane. The archives also contain useful information on the many Wyoming sites Calamity visited or stayed in.

26. **Public Libraries**

    Important information about Calamity Jane is available in the following public libraries.

27. Deadwood Public Library, Deadwood, S.Dak.

28. Denver Public Library, Denver, Colo.

29. Lander Public Library, Lander, Wyo.

30. Parmalee Public Library, Billings, Mont.

31. Princeton Public Library, Princeton, Mo.

LEGAL DOCUMENTS

Entries in this section are arranged chronologically within subdivisions pertaining to the Canary Family, Martha Canary/Calamity Jane, Calamity's siblings, and her husbands and partners. Parenthetical numbers in the text cross-reference other entries in the bibliography.

32. Canary Family (Grandparents and Parents)

33. U.S. Censuses, 1820–1850, Malaga Township, Monroe County, Ohio.

These decadal reports hold biographical information on Martha Canary's grandparents, aunts and uncles, and father, as well as limited information on their backgrounds, wealth, and literacy.

34. U.S. Census, 1850, Appanoose County, Iowa.

This census report includes information on Charlotte Burge, Martha's mother-to-be, who was then ten years old.

35. Polk County, Iowa, Marriage Records, 1855, Book 1, p. 174.

This listing records the marriage of Robert W. Canary and Charlotte Burge, Martha's parents-to-be, on 14 June 1855, in Iowa.

36. Land Records, Mercer County, Mo., 1850s–1860s.

These records reveal when Grandpa James Canary came to Missouri in the late 1850s, bought land, and quickly sold it to his children, well before his death in 1862. Some of these documents are reprinted in Foote, *A History of Calamity Jane*, pp. 231–36 (265).

37. U.S. Census, 1860, Ravanna Township, Mercer County, Mo.

This listing of the R. W. Canary family includes information on Martha's parents, Robert and Charlotte, Martha herself (born in 1856), and her siblings, Cilus (Silas?, 1857), and Lana (or Lena, 1858 or 1859). Information on Grandfather James Canary follows the R. W. Canary entry, no. 411. Information on Aunt Lana and her husband, James Kilgore, is in the next entry, no. 412, that on Aunt Mary and her husband, Robert Sowders (or Southers), follows, no. 413. Uncle James T. Canary lived about five miles south of Ravanna in Medicine Township and is listed as no. 568.

38. Probate Records, Circuit Court of Mercer County, Mo., 1862–1865.

These files contain an extensive account of the squabbles among the Canary descendants after the death of James in 1862. These conflicts were probably the main reason Robert and Charlotte and their family left Missouri soon after 1862, although the possible attraction of "getting rich quick" in western mineral rushes may have been another "pull" factor to the frontier.

39. Martha Canary/Calamity Jane

Many legal records important for tracing Calamity's complex career are seemingly nonexistent. For example, although she was jailed multiple times, those records have not been located. Nor have the birth records of her two children. Thus far, she has not been located in the censuses of 1870, 1880, or 1890. Even her death certificate, once said to be in Deadwood, has disappeared. More diligent research may turn up some of these important legal documents.

40. U.S. Census, 1860, Ravanna Township, Mercer County, Mo.

This listing of the R. W. Canary family (Martha and her parents and siblings) is the strongest evidence for dating Martha's birth in 1856, not in 1852 as she stated in her autobiography (241). Surprisingly, this census report did not appear in publications about Martha/Calamity until the mid-twentieth century.

41. Census of Wyoming[,] Unorganized Territory, Carter County, 1869.

Person no. 144 in this little-known enumeration is Martha Canary. She is listed as a female of fifteen years [*sic*, actually thirteen years], a resident of the railroad town of Piedmont, Wyoming, for five months, and born in Missouri. The census taker indicates Martha intends to become a citizen of Wyoming, but her occupation is not revealed. Other contemporary sources reveal she was helping in the boardinghouse of Mrs. Emma Alton, listed as no, 145, tending children. Martha probably added two years to her age to make her actions seem less controversial than they would be for a thirteen-year-old.

42. *Territory of Wyoming vs. Maggie Smith, Indictment for Grand Larceny,*
    Doc. 2, No. 269, 22, 24 May 1876; Territory of Wyoming vs. Maggie Smith,
    verdict, No. 269, filed 8 June 1876. Wyoming State Archives, Cheyenne; copy
    in Paine Papers, Augustana College, Sioux Falls, S.Dak.

    The court indictment for grand larceny against Maggie Smith (alias Calamity Jane, as local newspapers revealed) ended in a "Not. Guilty" [*sic*] verdict. Maggie/Calamity was accused of stealing a bundle of clothes. This is one of the few legal documents substantiating Calamity's times in jail. After the not guilty decision, Calamity celebrated joyously and dashed north to rejoin General George Crook.

43. Certificate of Marriage, Bingham County, Idaho Territory, 30 May 1888.

    Calamity and William Steers traveled to Pocatello, Idaho, to marry. Steers, probably the father of Calamity's daughter, Jessie, born in October 1887, disappeared after the marriage. Perhaps Calamity married to give her baby girl a legal father, but later, after she and Steers had broken up, she claimed that Clinton Burke, her next "husband," was the father of Jessie.

44. U.S. Census, 1900, Billings County, N.Dak.

    Calamity is listed in this census as residing in Billings, North Dakota, as Mattie Dorsett, the wife of R. H. Dorsett, a stock herder. Her birth date is given as August 1867, and her age as thirty-two. The census report says she was born in Missouri, as were her mother and father, and that she had been married to Dorsett since 1896. She reported having no children. A "yes" appears in columns asking if Mattie Dorsett could read and write. Interestingly, the date of her birth, her childlessness, the site of her parents' births, her marriage to Dorsett, and her literacy are all at odds with other legal and personal records. But this document, recently uncovered, places her where no other previous source had.

45. **Canary Siblings and Calamity's Daughter**

46. *Lena Canary Borner (Younger Sister)*

    Other than her appearance in the census of 1860 and mentions in local histories of western Wyoming, not much is known about Calamity's younger sister Lena. She married German immigrant John G. Borner, and his application for a pension and his obituary indicate the couple was married 20 August 1898. John G. Borner, Bureau of Pensions, Department of the Interior, 14 June 1898, no. 824,030. There is no legal documentation on the birth, marriage, or death of Lena, although a newspaper obituary was published (125).

47. Elijah Canary (Lige or Lije, Younger Brother)

48. *Docket No. 93, District Court, Unita County, State of Wyoming vs. Elijah Canary, 3 December 1895; Report of Convicts Discharged, No. 253, 12 August 1900.* Elijah was arrested for "Obstructing a Railway" and sentenced to five years in prison. He and a confederate had stolen horses, placed them on a train track, then sued the railroad for damages after the destruction of the animals. He entered prison in 1895 and was released on 12 August 1900.

49. U.S. Census, 1900, Albany County, Wyoming.

    Lige's age is given as thirty-two.

50. *Report of Convicts Discharged or Removed,* Idaho State Penitentiary, AR 42/200063158/1007.115/1176.

    Elijah was arrested in Fremont County for horse stealing and sentenced to one year in prison for grand larceny. He entered the Idaho prison on 30 November 1905 and was released on 30 October 1906.

51. Death Certificate, 20 November 1922, Town of Roosevelt, Duchesne County, Utah.

    Lige's birth date is given as 20 November 1862, and his age at death as sixty. Burial was in a potter's field in Roosevelt Cemetery.

52. Jessie Elizabeth Oakes Murray (Daughter)

53. Marriage License No. 3883, County of Lewis and Clark, State of Montana, 8 April 1904.

    Marriage license of Jessie Oakes of Helena, Montana, age eighteen and single, to Fred S. Schwabe, age twenty-one; Jessie's parents were listed as William Oakes and Mattie Oakes, and she was born in Denver in 1886 ("estimated").

54. Marriage License no. 4969, County of Lewis and Clark, State of Montana, 20 July 1908.

Marriage license of Jessie Oakes, age twenty-two, divorced, to Ralph Kennedy, age twenty-seven. Jessie's parents are John Oakes and Martha Canary, and she was born in Denver in 1886 ("estimated").

55. Affidavit of Robert H. Dorsett, 23 June 1934.

See entry 66 under "Robert H. Dorsett."

56. Application for Social Security Number, SSN 546-28-2649, 11 April 1939.

Birth, Denver, 28 October 1887; parents William Hickok and Belle Jane Somors; residence San Diego, unemployed; name listed as Jessie Oakes (by adoption—stepfather) Murray; signed Jessie Murray.

57. Death Certificate 0190-013225, State of California, Department of Health Services, 14 March 1980.

Death in Whittier, California; usual residence in Industry, California. Widowed, unknown parents, no name of surviving spouse. Jessie may have been institutionalized in later years, with "severe organic brain syndrome"; cause of death, "acute pneumonia" and colitis.

58. Husbands (Legal and Companions)

Legal records for at least two other supposed husbands, George Cosgrove (with Calamity Jane ca. 1877–79), and Frank[?] King (with Calamity Jane ca. 1881–83) are missing.

59. William P. Steers

Steers was with Calamity Jane ca. 1885–88; life dates, 1865–1933.

60. U.S. Census, 15 June 1880, Rawlins, Carbon County, Wyoming Territory, p. 173.

Steers was born 11 March 1865 in Iowa; in 1880, at age fifteen, he is listed as a boarder with nearly thirty other men in the Smith family boardinghouse. He is described as a laborer.

61. Certificate of Marriage, Bingham County, Idaho Territory, 30 May 1888.

See entry 43 under "Martha Canary/Calamity Jane."

62. Death Certificate 33-008846, State of California, Department of Health Services.

Date of death 15 February 1933, age sixty-seven; name of wife (divorced) Mamie Steers; profession, solicitor, door to door; length of residence in California, forty-five years.

63. *Clinton E. Burke*

Burke was with Calamity Jane, ca. early 1890s to 1896 or 1897; life dates 1867–1929.

64. Death Certificate 2501, Texas State Department of Health, Bureau of Vital Statistics.

Date of death 6 November 1929, age sixty-two; name of wife Mrs. C. E. (Mary Belle) Burke; profession, watchman; birth, 5 October 1867, Missouri; son of Rev. William E. Burke and Mary Lilla Mack. Place of death, Houston, Texas.

65. *Robert H. Dorsett*

Dorsett was with Calamity Jane, ca. 1898–1900; life dates, 1874–1954.

66. Affidavit, Hotchkiss, County of Delta, State of Colorado, 23 June 1934.

This affidavit asserts that Dorsett has known Jessie E. Hickok (Oakes) as the granddaughter of Calamity Jane and the daughter of William Hickok of South Dakota "since she was seven years old." He "was a confidential friend of Calamity Jane's." Copy in Meade County Records, South Dakota State Historical Society, Pierre.

67. Application for Social Security Number, SSN 523-20-3014, 3 March 1942.

Robert Harrison Dorsett, Denver, Colorado; born 28 July 1874, Union Villa, Putnam County, Missouri; unemployed.

68. California Death Index, 1940–1997.

Death date 13 May 1954, Santa Cruz, California.

Newspaper Articles during Calamity's Lifetime

Entries in this section are arranged chronologically. Parenthetical numbers in the text cross-reference other entries in this guide.

69. "Provision for the Destitute Poor." (Virginia City) *Montana Post*, 31 December 1864.

    Of major importance, this rarely cited newspaper article about the Canary family places them in the Virginia City–Nevada City, Montana, area in the last days of 1864. The writer speaks of Robert as a gambler and Charlotte as "a woman of the lowest grade" (prostitute?). The children are described as scantily dressed in very cold weather. They are begging for food. "The oldest girl," probably Martha, is said to be twelve (but she was only eight in 1864), and "carried in her arms her infant sister, a baby of 12 months of age." The reporter calls this scene a "most flagrant and wanton instance of unnatural conduct on the part of parents to their children."

70. Lane, J. R. "The Gold-Hunters." *Chicago Tribune*, 19 June 1875.

    Datelined 4 June 1875 in the Black Hills, this long story is the first to identify Martha Canary as Calamity Jane. Calling Calamity one of the "Lesser Notables," Lane, detailing the Newton-Jenney Expedition into the Black Hills in 1875, describes "Calam" dressed as a man, riding astride, and taking care of her sixteen-year-old brother (Elijah or Lige). The writer incorrectly places Calamity in Omaha, Nebraska, running a millinery shop before a fit of itchy feet brought her to this expedition. A year before, in an episode on the Powder River, when she got lost, a comrade said it would be a "calamity" if Indians captured her. Hence her nickname. This is a pioneering piece on Calamity's emerging national reputation.

71. Mac [Thomas C. McMillan]. "Gold Galore." *Chicago Daily Inter Ocean*, 3 July 1875.

Written by a journalist traveling with the Newton-Jenney Expedition, this piece provides extensive descriptions of the wild, unsettled Black Hills area. The final section of the piece, titled "A Strange Creature," asserts that Calamity could have served as the model for Bret Harte's Local Color fictional character "Cherokee Sal" in his acclaimed short story "The Luck of Roaring Camp." But Harte's "Luck" story was first published in 1868, well before Martha was on the scene and known as Calamity Jane. Nonetheless, Mac writes that Calamity lives out the eccentric life of Cherokee Sal. She wears a "costume" similar to that of soldiers. Then comes the widely quoted description of Calamity: she "has the reputation of being a better horseback rider, mule and bull whacker (driver), and a more unctuous coiner of English, and not the Queen's pure, either, than any (other) man in the command." This and the Lane article (70) were the first newspaper stories about Calamity, and they were published outside the Black Hills area.

72. "Latest News from the Black Hills." *Cheyenne* (Wyo.) *Daily Leader*, 24 February 1876.

In this story, a letter by Captain Jack Crawford from Custer City, he speaks of the recently named Calamity Bar, a mining claim three miles from Custer. It got its name, Crawford notes, "from a woman who accompanied the soldiers last summer. They called her Calamity Jane."

73. *Cheyenne* (Wyo.) *Daily Leader*, 9 June 1876.

A jury in Cheyenne declares Calamity not guilty of grand larceny charges. The case is titled *Territory vs. Maggie Smith, alias Calamity Jane.*

74. "Jane's Jamboree." *Cheyenne* (Wyo.) *Daily Leader*, 20 June 1876.

After being found not guilty on grand larceny charges, Calamity celebrated on 10 June by "borrowing" a horse and buggy from a stable and, fortified by "liberal potations . . . [of] bug juice," dashed north to Chug. Not yet entirely sober she traveled on the next day to Fort Laramie rather than her intended destination, Fort Russell. About two weeks later the Hickok-Utter train accepted her into their group traveling to Deadwood. This story clarifies some of the full schedule Calamity was following in the winter, spring, and early summer months of 1876.

75. *Cheyenne* (Wyo.) *Daily Leader*, 30 July 1876.

An important announcement appears here: "'Calamity Jane' has arrived." These words were reprinted from an account in the *Deadwood Black Hills Pioneer* of 11 July 1876.

76. *Cheyenne* (Wyo.) *Daily Leader*, 23 November 1876.

"Calamity Jane, a lady not unknown to fame, both eschewed the wine-cup and her other minor imperfections, and now slingeth hash as a waiter in a Custer City Hotel." Here is another substantiation of Calamity's wandering through other parts of the Black Hills outside Deadwood in 1876.

77. *Cheyenne* (Wyo.) *Daily Leader*, 26 January 1877.

"Calamity Jane is reported to have married and settled down at Custer City." Was this George Cosgrove, reportedly Calamity's first "husband," who had come to Deadwood in June–July 1876 with the Hickok-Utter party?

78. *Jackson* (Mich.) *Daily Citizen*, 28 April 1877.

This brief piece quotes, word for word, some of H. N. Maguire's description of Calamity in his book *The Black Hills and American Wonderland* (1877) (286). Over the next few months, articles using much the same wording appeared in Massachusetts, Ohio, New Jersey, Idaho, Illinois, Utah, and West Virginia. This fanning out of Maguire's story about Calamity indicates that it most certainly must have come to the attention of dime novelist Edward L. Wheeler about this time, and that the information from Maguire became central to Wheeler's description of Calamity as the heroine in the Deadwood Dick series, 1877–85 (404–37).

79. (Denver, Colo.) *Rocky Mountain News*, 10 June 1877.

The biographical information in this brief piece closely resembles that in Edward L. Wheeler's first dime novel, *Deadwood Dick, The Prince of the Road* (1877) (405). Probably the information for this newspaper story and the first dime novel in the Deadwood Dick series came from H. N. Maguire's book, *The Black Hills and American Wonderland*, also published in 1877 (286). This journalist's descriptions and words closely follow those in Maguire's early profile of Calamity. Much the same story appears in the

Cheyenne (Wyo.) *Daily Leader*, 14 June 1877; the *Salt Lake* (Utah) *Tribune*, 7 July 1877; and other regional newspapers.

80. *Cheyenne* (Wyo.) *Daily Leader*, 7 July 1877.

Calamity tried to rent a horse and buggy from a Cheyenne livery stable, but the owner, recalling that Calamity had taken a rig from another stable a year earlier and not returned it, refused.

81. *Cheyenne* (Wyo.) *Daily Leader*, 7 July 1877.

This account of Calamity's run-in with a newspaper editor seems embellished and perhaps the product more of an imaginative reporter than a fact-finding journalist. At the story's end is a brief, explicit challenge said to be from Calamity to the editor. "Print in the *Leader* that Calamity Jane, the child of the regiment and pioneer white woman of the Black Hills is in Cheyenne, or I'll scalp you, skin you alive and hang you to a telephone pole. You hear me and don't you forget it. Calamity Jane." Perhaps journalistic hyperbole since Calamity was illiterate and could not write? An attempt to grab readers with sensation? Possibly. The letter is without substantiation.

82. *Laramie* (Wyo.) *Daily Sentinel*, 11–12 July 1877.

Herein are reports of the capture of outlaw Bill Bevins (Bevans) and some of his road gang. But another gang member and a woman dressed as a man, said to be Calamity Jane, got away with the "swag." Bevans was trying to locate them and take back the loot when he was captured. Probably Calamity was not with the Bevans gang, even though she claimed to have been.

83. "Calamity Jane." (Deadwood, Dak. Terr.) *Black Hills Daily Champion*, 16 July 1877.

This piece, quoting Dr. A. R. Hendricks of Des Moines, Iowa, says Calamity's real name is Jane Coombs, and she is from Burlington, Iowa, the daughter of a Baptist minister. The story goes far astray in stating that Jane married as a teenager, but when her husband died in the Civil War, she dressed as a man, went off to war, and afterwards drifted into Texas. Wandering over the West she became known in many parts of the region and now had returned to Cheyenne. Far-fetched; no other sources support this information.

84. *Cheyenne* (Wyo.) *Daily Leader*, 7 August 1877

"Calamity Jane is 'tripping the light fantastic' in a Deadwood dance house." This and a few similar contemporary newspaper reports identified Calamity as a dance hall entertainer.

85. Adrienne. "A Lady Among the Miners: The Experience of a New York Belle in the Black Hills." *Wheeling* (W.Va.) *Register*, 3 September 1877.

Originally dated 11 August 1877 and taken from the *New York Graphic*, this story by a woman tourist from New York in the Black Hills extols all the intriguing novelties of life in the Deadwood area. Among the sights are "fast women," and they "are very plentiful" in the Hills. Calamity Jane "stands at their head." The author advances the probably false story about Calamity having been with the Bevans gang after a stagecoach holdup, getting them drunk, and running off with the stolen loot. Calamity, writes Adrienne, "rides on horseback without a side saddle, is a good shot, and as a frontiers-woman, is better than a good many men." Although the story illustrates the booming reputation of Calamity as a Wild Woman of the West, it seems mostly secondhand.

86. *Laramie* (Wyo.) *Daily Sentinel*, 1 October 1877.

This account briefly summarizes the activities of road agents along the Black Hills stage line since the then-recent arrest of the leading robber, "Bill Bevins" (Bevans). The reporter says one of the highwaymen and his mistress, said to be Calamity Jane, have run off with "the heist" of the group. Later, Calamity liked to tell others she was among the robbers.

87. (Deadwood, Dak. Terr.) *Black Hills Daily Times*, 17 December 1877.

When a reporter calls Martha "Calamity Jane," she retorts, out of sorts, "I want you to understand my name isn't Calamity Jane; its [*sic*] Maggie Cosgrove." Calamity is speaking of having married George Cosgrove, who had come to Deadwood with the Hickok-Utter party. No record of such a marriage has surfaced.

88. *New York Daily Tribune*, 3 January 1878.

Among the characters available to the "poet-novelists" of the Black Hills are several lively women and men. There are Petite Kittie, Monte Verde, Aunt Sally, and Captain Jack, as well as the late Wild Bill. "Another nice girl is Calamity Jane." About twenty-two, she reportedly has worked in hurdy-

gurdies, traveled through the Hills, and scouted for the army. Her movements "have an unstudied grace," but when upset her "eyes emit a greenish
glare." These words are lifted from Thomas Newson's *Drama of Life in the
Black Hills* (304). An intriguing if abbreviated depiction. Reprinted in the
(Denver, Colo.) *Rocky Mountain News*, 11 January 1878.

89. (Deadwood, Dak. Terr.) *Black Hills Daily Times*, 3 January 1878.

"Calamity Jane, disgusted with Deadwood, has taken up her residence at
Rapid." Still another illustration that Calamity Jane was ever on the move.

90. *Yankton* (S.Dak.) *Daily Press and Dakotaian*, 10 January 1878.

Datelined Central City, Black Hills, 18 December 1877, this brief sketch
provides a strong, balanced portrait of Calamity. It speaks of her "wild
whirlwind" beginnings "with a mother incapacitated to love her" and a
deceased father. She is about twenty-two, "her movements are free and
unstudied," and "her heart warm and generous." She has wandered much
but is now in the Hills, "dancing in a hurdy-gurdy house in Deadwood for a
living." Despite a few errors, this is a valuable early newspaper portrait, fair
and quite thorough.

91. (Deadwood, Dak. Terr.) *Black Hills Daily Times*, 22 January 1878.

"Calamity Jane had her photograph taken to-day for the first time in her life."
Perhaps Calamity went to a photographer's studio for the first time; previous
photos of her date back to 1875 (see 516–17).

92. "City and Vicinity." (Deadwood, Dak. Terr.) *Black Hills Daily Times*, 18 February 1878.

"'Calamity' and her 'darling Jim' and one or two other attendants at a Saturday night dance, succumbed to the green-eyed monster, and made things
live until Officer Clark put a quietus to the difficulty." "Darling Jim" is not
identified.

93. (Deadwood, Dak. Terr.) *Black Hills Daily Times*, 22 June 1878.

When Deadwood resident Frank Warren was viciously stabbed, Calamity
"kindly" undertook his care. The writer salutes Calamity's humanitarian
efforts: "There's lots of humanity in Calamity, and she is deserving of much
praise for the part she has taken in the particular case." A typical incident on
which the Angel of Mercy legend was built.

94. *Cheyenne* (Wyo.) *Daily Leader,* 28, 30 August 1878.

The death of a second "Calamity Jane" (Mattie Young) in Denver in a buggy accident complicated stories about the real Calamity Jane (Martha Canary). The Denver Calamity similarly combined negative qualities (drunkenness and sexual promiscuity) with positive characteristics (love of her mother and a good education). In the late 1870s newspapers frequently mixed up the stories of the two nontraditional young women.

95. (Deadwood, Dak. Terr.) *Black Hills Daily Times,* 5 September 1878.

Reporting on the death of Mattie Young in Denver, the other "Calamity Jane," this story makes clear she is not "our Calamity." The Calamity of the Black Hills "is alive and well." She is a western product, no "tenderfoot from Iowa," as was Young. The reporter considers Iowa in the East, Missouri in the West.

96. (Deadwood, Dak. Terr.) *Black Hills Daily Times,* 24 September 1878.

Calamity has headed out on the stagecoach for Bismarck. She is probably traveling "down [up?] to see the boys in blue." Calamity appeared frequently in the Black Hills newspapers in the late 1870s, with her attraction to soldiers often mentioned.

97. (Deadwood, Dak. Terr.) *Black Hills Daily Times,* 8 February 1879.

Calamity "walloped two women" in Sturgis yesterday, the journalist reports. She "can get away with a dozen ordinary pugilistic women when she turns loose," the reporter adds, "but she never fights unless she is in the right, and then she is not backward to tackle even a masculine shoulder hitter." Mostly exaggeration.

98. *Cheyenne* (Wyo.) *Daily Leader,* 6 June 1879.

"Calamity Jane has started a ranche at Fort Pierre with the $16,000 she received for her quartz claim in the Hills." No other source supports the veracity of this very doubtful story.

99. "Calamity Jane's Virtues." (Deadwood, Dak. Terr.) *Black Hills Daily Times,* 20 July 1879.

Reporters often criticized Calamity Jane for her offending behavior, but this story takes a different path. Calamity, the author states, "possesses so many good and tender qualities of heart" that when she is sick more than a few Black Hills residents rally to her aid. They do so largely because they realize that "this rough diamond of the border" has helped so many needy and sick men. Her watchful care is among her "solid virtues" and "make Calamity solid with the good people of the West." A convincing case for Calamity as an Angel of Mercy.

100. (Deadwood, Dak. Terr.) *Black Hills Daily Times*, 7 November 1879.

Quoting the *Yankton* (Dak. Terr.) *Press* of the previous 31 October, this column speaks of Calamity's "tripping the light fantastic at Fort Pierre." The reporter adds that "Calamity Jane is the most elegant waltzer in the Fort Pierre dance house."

101. "Ft. Meade." (Deadwood, Dak. Terr.) *Black Hills Daily Times*, 3 December 1879.

On the day after payday, the "girls and gang are down from Deadwood . . . and have everything their own way." And Calamity, "queen of the demi monde," is in from Pierre. Reporters, in very general stories like this one, stated that Calamity worked in—or even was in charge of—a house of joy.

102. "Personal News." (Deadwood, Dak. Terr.) *Black Hills Daily Times*, 10 December 1879.

"Calamity Jane has gone to Rapid City to spend the winter. Deadwood is too puritanical for her." Calamity's incessant wanderings caught the attention of newspapermen, but they rarely provided reflection/interpretation about why she was so often on the move.

103. *Cheyenne* (Wyo.) *Daily Leader*, 10 December 1879.

On the same day as the previous story reporting Calamity to be in Rapid City, the Cheyenne newspaper states "Calamity Jane is the queen of the dance house in Scooptown" [Sturgis, Dak. Terr.].

104. (Deadwood, Dak. Terr.) *Black Hills Times*, 27 August 1880.

Over time, more than a few journalists wrote about Calamity's owning or operating a ranch, a hotel, or some other kind of business. This story states that Calamity, a partner George Baker, and others were establishing "a bagnio" (brothel) along a South Dakota railroad. Whether that happened is not clear because while they were trying to set up the business, a fight broke out, and Baker was seriously injured. Later, Baker turned outlaw and was chased out of the area. Other information on the Calamity-Baker connection appears in the *Yankton* (Dak. Terr.) *Daily Press and Dakotaian*, 21 August 1880.

105. (Deadwood, Dak. Terr.) *Black Hills Journal*, 2 August 1882.

"The famous nymph du pave" (Calamity Jane) "has made things lively about Pierre, the past two months." The reporter states that Calamity tried to "start a fancy house near the Missouri [River]," and a fight broke out between Calamity and one of "her paramours," bringing about "hair and blood in wild confusion." This very typical brief newspaper report supports the Wild Woman of the West stereotype of Calamity, repeating information in the immediately previous entry.

106. *Miles City* (Mont.) *Daily Yellowstone Journal*, 19 November 1882.

Quoting "the Deadwood newspapers," this Miles City reporter refers to the "eulogizing [by] Calamity Jane [of] the recently born little Calamity." Not many reports are available on the "little Calamity" boy. Sadly, he died soon after birth. A man named Frank[?] King was Calamity's companion in Montana in 1882 and may have been the father of her son "Little Calamity."

107. "Calamity Jane's Simplicity." (Deadwood, Dak. Terr.) *Black Hills Daily Pioneer*, 12 December 1882.

Citing the *Miles City* (Mont.) *Journal*, the Deadwood newspaper speaks of the "jewel garter craze" capturing eastern jewelers and customers. Some are willing to pay up to "$250 for a single pair of stocking supports." But Calamity, displaying her simplicity, is satisfied to use an old pair of her husband's suspenders to hold up her stockings. Calamity might embrace simplicity, but she could also rage and attack, as editor Charley Collins of the *Deadwood* (Dak. Terr.) *Daily Champion* discovered when he "denounced her as a fraud and mopsqueezer." She tore after him, and he retreated to a nearby gulch for safety, until she cooled off. This anecdote illustrates the humor and hyperbole often evident in news stories about Calamity, particularly before her decline and fall.

108. *Livingston* (Mont.) *Daily Enterprise*, 14 March 1884.

Calamity is currently in Livingston, "taking in the sights." But she "has pulled up stakes and joined the stampede for the Coeur d'Alenes." In fact, she is already "on her way thither."

109. "Calamity Jane." *Eagle City* (Idaho) *Coeur d'Alene Nugget*, 9 April 1884.

Calamity Jane, "the most noted woman of the Western frontier and the heroine of many a thrilling nickel novel," has moved again and "joined the stampede for Coeur d'Alene." Also, quoting the *Belknap* (Mont.) *Enterprise*, the reporter says Calamity has just returned to Eagle, Idaho, "penniless, not even able to pay for her lodging." But the very next morning she was cooking at a restaurant. It was a draw for the café since "many had a desire to see the charming old lady." (Calamity was twenty eight!) Here is one of the few sources to indicate that Calamity made two trips to the Coeur d'Alenes in early 1884.

110. *Livingston* (Mont.) *Daily Enterprise*, 16 April 1884.

Calamity is back in Livingston after escaping "various trials and tribulations" on a trip to the Coeur d'Alenes. "She has had enough of the mines."

111. (Rawlins, Wyo.) *Carbon County Journal*, 20 December 1884.

During 1884, Calamity moved to Livingston, Montana, to the Coeur d'Alenes in Idaho, back to Livingston, down to Buffalo, Wyoming, in the summer, and completed a full year of roaming by arriving in Rawlins, Wyoming, by the end of 1884. The reporter ventured that Calamity had "probably crowded a little more experience and frontier life into her career of some forty odd years [she was twenty-eight in 1884] than any other woman in the country." For most of the next three to four years, Calamity was in and out of Rawlins as her home base.

112. *Cheyenne* (Wyo.) *Daily Leader*, 21 March 1885.

"'Calamity Jane' that once noted heroine of the Black Hills has concluded to make Lander her permanent place of abode." Calamity made many such pronouncements to reporters, but she never found a "permanent place"— then, or ever.

113. (Rawlins, Wyo.) *Carbon County Journal*, 25 July 1885.

"Miss Mattie King, the great and only 'Calamity Jane' . . . loaded up with a more than average 'Elbow croaker'" and took on "any and all comers." She is now in "durance vile until Monday morning." A man named Frank[?] King was Calamity's companion in Montana in 1882.

114. "Calamity Jane: The Heroine of Yellow-Back Literature Appears Again." *Cheyenne* (Wyo.) *Daily Leader*, 3 November 1885.

This story, dispatched from Lander, Wyoming (30 October), says Calamity has chosen that site as her new hometown. The reporter then speaks of Martha's early years in Wyoming, providing details of her having lived with the Gallagher family in Miner's Delight in 1868, "at the age of 11 years." Trying to discipline the unruly preteen caused such an uproar that Martha was sent out of town, down to the railroad camps to the south. Next, the reporter turns controversial, labeling Calamity a "female bandit" who holds up stages and plunders others. Although no proof is available for such assertions, the information on Martha staying with the Gallaghers in Miner's Delight *before* her stay in Piedmont (1869) merits further consideration.

115. *Cheyenne* (Wyo.) *Daily Leader*, 25 November 1885.

Calamity Jane "is leading a quiet life at Fort Washakie." Calamity was rumored to be, on at least a couple of occasions, at Fort Washakie, Wyoming. One shaky rumor states she found a short-term "husband" in that area.

116. (Rawlins, Wyo.) *Carbon County Journal*, 18 September 1886.

Appearing on the same day as the next item, this story draws on the *Meeker* (Colo.) *Herald* in reporting that Calamity, "the she-son-of-a-gun, swore out a warrant for the arrest" of Bill Steers, her consort. He had tried to injure her with the handle of a knife and hit her on the lip with a rock. She accused Steers of not being a real husband; he countered that Calamity was a "damn liar." Following a trial, Steers was jailed and Calamity got plastered. Yet soon after Steers was released, the couple left Meeker, Calamity "carrying the pack." The reporter concluded: "They are a tough pair."

117. (Rawlins, Wyo.) *Carbon County Journal*, 18 September 1886.

On the same day the local editor of the *Journal* was more sympathetic to Calamity than the reporter for the Meeker newspaper (116). Both were extremely negative about Bill Steers. Noting that Calamity's "post office name" was Mrs. Martha King, the Rawlins reporter concluded that Calamity was "not half as bad as the human ghouls that abuse her." She was "the victim of passion, with generous impulses, . . . a poor pilgrim . . . made the scapegoat of the outlaw, the assassin, the tin horn, and at last the outcast of man." Warmly, the journalist asks in closing, "Kind Christians, what will you do with her?" But for Steers he had only opprobrium: the young man deserved "a hangman's knot."

118. (Rawlins, Wyo.) *Carbon County Journal*, 30 October 1886.

Calamity is "an inmate of Hotel Rankin," the county jail. She and husband-to-be William "Bill" Steers have gotten into another row. Steers, whom the reporter labels "one of the most worthless curs unhung," hit Calamity over the head with a wrench, leaving a large gash. When patrons at the nearby saloon seemed less sympathetic to Calamity than she wished them to be, she threw rocks through a large glass window. Steers fled south toward Colorado, and Calamity is resting in the clink.

119. (Rawlins, Wyo.) *Carbon County Journal*, 6 November 1886.

Bill Steers has been captured and jailed for thirty days for walloping Calamity with a wrench. The reporter then vents his wrath on Steers: "It is time that this individual received the punishment he so richly deserves. He is a miserable stick and deserves a more severe punishment than a month's free board, but the law will not allow it."

120. (Laramie, Wyo.) *Boomerang*, 28 February 1887.

Calamity, back in Laramie, is "the wreck of what might once have been a woman." She was earlier in Douglas, Wyoming, but "the whiskey of that village was not flavored to her taste and . . . society was below her standard." Calamity got drunk the previous night, "and if she didn't make Rome howl she did Laramie." Another piece that contains insight as well as journalistic license. The reporter cannot stick to a straightforward story, instead loving too much his own rhetorical sleights of hand, as did many, many journalists who wrote about Calamity.

121. "After Many Years." (Cheyenne, Wyo.) *Democratic Leader*, 12 March 1887.

After having been absent from Cheyenne for eleven years, Calamity has reappeared. That "notorious" woman, "who used to figure so prominently in police courts and circles in this city," has come back in "a very dilapidated condition." She is reportedly widely known here and in the Black Hills area. "Only a few months ago . . . her picture appeared in one of the New York illustrated police papers." This last reference is unclear; perhaps it points to (Mrs.) William Spencer's novel *Calamity Jane: A Story of the Black Hills* (1887) (481), parts of which appeared in a New York magazine.

122. "Calamity Jane: The Heroine of Dime Novel Takes in Town." *Cheyenne* (Wyo.) *Daily Leader*, 21 June 1887.

Purporting to be an interview with Calamity when she returned from visiting the family of her husband-to-be, Bill Steers, in Wisconsin, the story wobbles between facts and exaggerations. The reporter speaks of Calamity as formerly a "beautiful and dangerous courtesan," who is now a "wreck." He also quotes Calamity as saying she was "born over forty years ago" (she was thirty-one) and that two or three men have lost their lives in competing for her attentions. She denounces a recent "history of . . . her life published in an Eastern paper" as a pack of lies. Were the reporter and Calamity referring to the novel *Calamity Jane: A Story of the Black Hills* (1887) by (Mrs.) William Loring Spencer (481), or might they have been speaking of the earlier *Street and Smith* serial by Reckless Ralph, "Calamity Jane: Queen of the Plains" (January–March 1882) (401), or even pointing to one of the Edward L. Wheeler dime novels in the Deadwood Dick series (404–37)? All were works of fiction in publication at this time and were far from dependable biographical sources.

The most important revelation in this skip-and-run story is that the night before its publication Calamity had been released from jail on a charge of drunkenness. She had been "released upon the presentation of a physician's certificate that she was in a rather delicate condition." Calamity had gotten drunk even though pregnant. Her daughter, Jessie Elizabeth, was born four months later, and she married Bill Steers, likely the biological father of Jessie, the next year in Idaho (43). But here Calamity evidently told the reporter that she had married Steers two years earlier, in 1885, thus disguising her pregnancy outside legal marriage.

123. "About Calamity." *Sundance* (Wyo.) *Gazette*, 2 September 1887.

Bill Steers and Calamity are now residing in Lander, Wyoming. In a recent letter to a friend, Steers bragged about "getting away with the old woman's [Calamity's] watch and chain." The journalist rightly concluded that "Steers and Calamity separate about four times every year, and as often reunite." Steers is described as a "slightly built, sickly looking and unassuming genius, about 25 years old."

124. *Livingston* (Mont.) *Enterprise*, 17 September 1887.

Calamity appears in a new venue as the heroine of a novel written by Mrs. William Loring Spencer (Mrs. George Spencer) (481). The reporter is mistaken in stating that Calamity first appeared in "a story of this kind, we believe" a few years earlier, written by Montanan "Harry Horr of Cinnabar," Montana, and published in the *New York Ledger*. He is probably referring to the dime novel serial "Calamity Jane, Queen of the Plains," said to be authored by Reckless Ralph and appearing in Street and Smith's *New York Weekly* (January–March 1882) (401). The writer goes on to state that a biography of Calamity "would make a large book, more interesting and blood-curdling" than the fiction written about her, "but it would never find its way into a Sunday school library." The most recent stories about Calamity have her "on a ranch down in Wyoming trying to sober up after a thirty years' drunk." A typical news story of the time, trying to peddle a few facts (often mistaken) alongside the Wild Woman of the West legend concerning Calamity.

125. "At Rest." *Wind River* (Wyo.) *Mountaineer*, 17 October 1888.

An obituary for Lena Canary Borner, this piece salutes her as "one of the most industrious women in the valley." She was the mother of seven (some say eight or nine) children, the oldest only ten years of age. Lena died from the aftereffects of a debilitating farm accident. These details of Lena's adult life and family are at dramatic odds with the corresponding years in her older sister Martha/Calamity Jane's life.

126. *Cheyenne* (Wyo.) *Daily Sun*, 3 January 1890.

At the end of 1889, Calamity was in Wendover, Wyoming, which she described as like Deadwood with its "wood sawed off." A Cheyenne reporter described Calamity in Wild West terms: "as a female holy terror she has no living superior." She could be at times "one of the most amiable of women," but on other occasions ornery and far too often drunk. Even "her worst enemies will not deny that she is an able drinker."

127. *Omaha* (Neb.) *Morning World-Herald*, 3 February 1892.

In the late 1880s and early 1890s, Calamity was usually on the road—even traveling to Nebraska in 1892. She told this reporter that she was on her way to visit her relatives in Iowa. The story then dropped into a swamp of misinformation, stating that Calamity had been in dozens of frontier battles, killing more than fifty Indians and whites in these murderous conflicts. "She has had dozens of narrow escapes from assassination and lynching." Where these journalistic fictions came from—Calamity's or the reporter's imagination—is not clear.

128. (Rawlins, Wyo.) *Carbon County Journal*, 9 December 1893.

At the end of 1893, Calamity was back in Rawlins, not with William Steers, whom she had legally married in 1888, but with a man named King. Perhaps she had returned to the rancher/cowboy Frank[?] King, who may have been the father of her "little Calamity" son born in 1882. The writer states that Calamity had with her "a little girl she had stolen" and introduced her companion as King, her husband. Probably the little girl is daughter Jessie Elizabeth, born in 1887.

129. (Deadwood, S.Dak.) *Black Hills Daily Times*, 26 May 1894.

By 1893–94, Calamity (and daughter, Jessie, with her) had returned to Billings. She was older, the journalist reported, retaining "few traces of that beauty which had at once been her pride and fatal gift." Nor was she "a society woman."

130. *Billings* (Mont.) *Weekly Times*, 16 August and 25 October 1894.

Calamity stayed perhaps a year in Billings. The local newspaper reported that she was gone by August 1894. She had "been running a restaurant on the South side," but had "packed her saratoga" and left. In October, the same newspaper noted that "Hotel Calamity" was for sale. Whether that was the café Calamity had operated is not clear.

131. "'Calamity Jane'! This Fearless Indian Fighter and Roamer of the Western Plains, in Deadwood." (Deadwood, S.Dak.), *Black Hills Daily Times*, 5 October 1895.

Calamity is back in Deadwood after a many-year absence. A little girl "who has seen probably nine summers" is with her. Word of mouth that "Calamity Jane's in town" has attracted a good deal of attention. Old friends greeted her, and she sat in the sheriff's office and "talked over the olden days for fully an hour." She has arrived from Ekalaka, Montana, where she lived [with Clinton Burke], but, detesting that life, she has come to Deadwood to find work and "give her child the benefit of the schools." She dislikes what reporters and other authors have written about her and does not want to play on her notoriety; "she does not like the idea." Three months later she was on the road with a traveling group, touted as the wildest woman of the Old West.

132. Deadwood (S.Dak.), *Black Hills Daily Times*, 6 October 1895.

Calamity arrived on 4 October, spent time in Deadwood, and the next day traveled to Lead, where her appearance "created considerable excitement." Her actions were at odds with "the flowery account of her in yesterday's paper." She "had to be assisted into a hack," and "she used vile language" to the officer assisting her.

133. "An Attraction." *Lead* (S.Dak.) *Evening Call,* 7 October 1895.

Hearing that Calamity was in Lead, old-timers and curiosity seekers flocked to a "street resort" to see her. Many danced with her. Calamity "had a fair sized jag on board, and this, together with a vile cigar, which she smoked, made her look anything but the beautiful woman which novelists and story writers have said so much about."

134. (Deadwood, S.Dak.), *Evening Independent,* 24 October 1895.

Journalists rarely said much about Calamity or photographs taken of her. This account states, however, that Locke and Peterson, Deadwood photographers, have taken "a lot of pictures of . . . [Calamity] in frontier costume" to sell "them about town." These photographs probably were used on her trip with the Kohl and Middleton dime museum tour early the next year. Calamity traded the photographs for drinks in more than a few saloons.

135. "The Bloomer Ball for Calamity Jane." *Lead* (S.Dak.) *Evening Call,* 11 November 1895.

Not to be outdone by a benefit gathering for Calamity in Deadwood to raise funds for her daughter's schooling (Calamity squandered much of the contributed money on drinks for herself and those gathered), neighboring Lead decided to sponsor their own Bloomer Ball benefit. But Calamity, that "grand old ruin . . . in temporary retirement at Hot Springs [S.Dak.]," failed to show as the guest of honor. The outcome was "a regular calamity."

136. *Belle Fourche* (S.Dak.) *Times,* 28 January 1896.

Last night Calamity left on the train for Minneapolis and her first presentations with the Kohl and Middleton touring group. She will be in Minneapolis for a week, followed by presentations in Chicago and elsewhere. "Mr. Burke, her husband, will accompany her."

137. *Chicago Daily Inter Ocean,* 26, 27, 28 January; 1, 2, 3, 9 February 1896.

This series of commentaries about Calamity and advertisements for the Kohl and Middleton museum touring group kept her name before the Chicago public for about two weeks. Sensationalism abounded. Calamity was headlined as the "woman who has won distinction on the western plains" (28 January) and "the most remarkable woman of the century" (3 February). The come-ons were equally hyperbolic and often downright lies. For example, General Crook never said Calamity was the "Bravest and Noblest Scout I Ever Knew, Regardless of Sex," and General Custer, unacquainted with Calamity, did not state she was "Worth a Regiment of Soldiers in Fighting Indians." Statements from Buffalo Bill and General Miles were also whole-cloth lies. The marketing machines were running overtime to portray Calamity as *the* Wild West Woman of her time.

138. (Deadwood, S.Dak.) *Black Hills Daily Times*, 30 May 1896.

This news story reports that Calamity has cut short her tour with Kohl and Middleton because she has received news that her daughter, Jessie, has become ill. Some see this decision as a sign of Calamity's strong mothering instincts. Jessie had been staying with the Ash family in Sturgis, South Dakota, while her mother was on tour. The story also touts Calamity as a "drawing card" performer who is planning to return to touring in the fall. Whether she did so is not substantiated.

139. "Calamity Jane as Agent." *Anaconda* (Mont.) *Standard*, 30 October 1896.

Datelined from the *Baltimore American*, this story is as distant from the truth as its East Coast origins were from Montana. The opening sentence should have slammed the door shut on any Montana publication: "A woman who has killed more than five score of Indians [there is no record that Calamity killed any Native Americans], who has met and conquered a dozen bad men and has been in more deadly rows than falls to the lot of a hundred average men is now earning a living as a book agent." True, Calamity peddled her published autobiography from 1896 onward, but there is not a shred of evidence for the other claims. A litany of misinformation follows: Bret Harte did not make Calamity famous in his short story "The Luck of Roaring Camp"; Calamity did not write her autobiography (she was illiterate); her mother did not die when Martha was a baby; the family did not move to Virginia City, Nevada; her father was not killed by Indians; and she did not lead a contingent of female scouts in the Indian wars. No matter. Other howlers abound. One bit of helpful information, however, is that Calamity was selling her autobiography, hoping to earn sufficient income to educate her daughter.

140. *Anaconda* (Mont.) *Standard*, 29 April 1897.

Calamity is in Billings, selling her autobiography. Several residents of the Black Hills, who knew Calamity in earlier years, think her pamphlet life history "a very tame presentation of some remarkably stirring facts." Intriguingly, many later readers thought, to the contrary, Calamity's autobiography was unrealistic in its sensationalist treatment of her life and actions.

141. (Lewistown, Mont.) *Fergus County Argus*, 16 June 1897.

Calamity has been in town for about two months selling her brief autobiography. She plans, about the first of August, to travel again with the Kohl and Middleton troupe through several eastern cities. Calamity will appear as a female scout dressed in buckskins; her male counterpart will "represent the wild and wooly puncher of the much-abused West." Calamity will be paid $100 per month. Did the tour take place? The absence of confirming evidence suggests it did not.

142. *Klondike* (Yukon Territory) *Nugget*, 23 June 1898.

The *Nugget* reports that Calamity is "in Dawson." The journalist adds, with an absence of confirming facts, that Calamity has "on more than one occasion . . . been forced to take a human life in defense of her own." Still, after recounting ambivalent legends about Calamity already in place, the reporter states "a kinder, truer character would be hard to find." Although naysayers dismiss this and other stories about Calamity's traveling to the Yukon, this report at the place and at the time suggests that she was indeed there in the summer of 1898. How she got to the Yukon and how long she stayed are not clear. This newspaper story is quoted in Bankson (233).

143. Vaughan, John D. "Hearts Are Pretty Much Alike the World Around." *Denver* (Colo.) *Times*, 30 November 1899.

Here is what seems to be an authentic story about Calamity's helping a miner who fractured a leg in a mining accident. The helping hand is Calamity's, without fanfare or notoriety. Although a bit sentimental and dated (it deals with happenings in the 1870s), the account fits smoothly within the legend of her as an Angel of Mercy.

144. *Livingston* (Mont.) *Enterprise*, 2 February 1901.

Calamity Jane, or Mrs. R. S. [*sic*, H.] Dorsett, is in court, suing Yee Sam Lee of the L and L Restaurant. Calamity "claims that Lee is withholding from her a trunk containing dresses and bedding valued at $500." One of the few references to Calamity as Mrs. Robert Dorsett, her last named "husband."

145. Bozeman (Mont.) *Avant Courier,* 16 February 1901

While on a train from Livingston to White Sulphur Springs, Montana, Calamity became ill and was taken to the Gallatin County Poor House. Staying for only a short time under a physician's care, Calamity was released "and went on her way rejoicing." She was trying to eke out a living selling her photograph "and the little pamphlet purporting to be a history of her life."

146. "It Is Calamity Jane." *Anaconda* (Mont.) *Standard,* 23 February 1901.

Calamity came to Bozeman, Montana, fell ill, and spent a few days in the Gallatin County Poor House. Without money or friends, she, for the first time, "was obliged to accept aid from the county," but is now headed to eastern Montana. She evidently told the reporter that some of her family members in Missouri found "little enjoyment in the fame" she had gained. The writer then pointed out that Calamity "has always been touchy concerning her matrimonial experience." Recently she was "married" to [Robert] Dorsett, but "they parted soon afterward." She carries several pieces of lead in her body from fighting in dangerous battles with Indians." Typically, the story carries important information (the poorhouse stay and separation from Dorsett), but there is no evidence Calamity was ever in a battle with Indians or was shot. Reprinted in the *Montana Standard,* 12 April 1953.

147. "Calamity Jane in Poor House." (Denver, Colo.) *Daily Rocky Mountain News,* 25 February 1901.

Ill and penniless, Calamity Jane has been forced into the poorhouse of Gallatin County, Montana. "Calamity Jane is about 70 years of age now," the reporter mistakenly wrote (she was forty). In early years she "was a member of Montana's famous vigilantes . . . and was on the staff of General Miles." Her "body bears the scars of a dozen bullets" received in fights with Indians. She has also scouted with Buffalo Bill. Once dressed as a man, she "has never returned to the dress of her sex." Married many times, she shot and killed her first husband. A litany of errors and false assertions, save for the momentary stop in the poorhouse.

148. "Calamity Jane." *Billings* (Mont.) *Gazette,* 19 March 1901.

Dr. D. Frank Powell wants to help with the financial support of Calamity Jane. He has written from St. Paul, Minnesota, to the Commissioners of the Poor in Butte to provide funding for Calamity. Will they send him the needed details? He knows that Calamity's "foster brother and lifelong companion Colonel Cody" will "join in adding his contribution." Then, the journalist, contradicting Powell's letter, states that Calamity will not need help as long as "she is able to perambulate." The Livingston journalist who launched the story about her being at the poorhouse "narrowly missed annihilation" from Calamity, making "him feel smaller than 30 cents." Calamity is off on a new jaunt visiting friends in Big Timber and probably headed next to Billings.

149. "Calamity Jane." *Livingston* (Mont.) *Enterprise*, 13 April 1901.

Reprinted from the *Anaconda* (Mont.) *Standard*, this extensive story speaks of Easterners who, hearing of Calamity's financial reverses and brief stay in the poorhouse, have sent monies to help her. The writer reports that she is now doing well financially and "able to look the world in the face." But the journalist falls into a slough of misinformation: that Calamity helped settle Kansas; that she led a group of vigilantes who captured and strung up Wild Bill's assassin, Jack McCall; and that several years earlier Calamity divorced her second husband in California. Another example of a useful report that veers off-track with misinformation and exaggerated legend.

150. "Local News." *Livingston* (Mont.) *Post*, 13 June 1901.

Calamity, recently at Mammoth Hot Springs, has come to Livingston to pick up a new batch of her autobiographies to sell. She tells the reporter that she has had "great success in 'hot airing' the tourists." The money is flooding in but, says Calamity, she has not been able to keep it. If she had, "she would be a bloomin' millionaire."

151. "Local News." *Livingston* (Mont.) *Post*, 11 July 1901.

Calamity is going east "to spend the rest of her days eating spring chicken and living like a prince." J. W. Brake, a woman writer, hearing of Calamity's financial problems, came west to offer Calamity a life free from poverty if she went east to live with Mrs. Brake. This morning, Brake and Calamity headed for New York. Brake, a philanthropist, will serve as "chaperone of the famous old scout and champion rifle and pistol shot of the Untamed Yellowstone Valley." A few facts married to tongue-in-cheek descriptions.

152. "'Calamity' in St. Paul." *Helena* (Mont.) *Evening Herald*, 16 July 1901.

A Minnesota reporter captures Calamity Jane and her ways for Montanans. He speaks particularly of Josephine Brake's difficulties in trying to keep Calamity in line as they travel to the East Coast. Although Calamity asks

Mrs. Brake's permission to drink whiskey, taking a nip four times a day, it's obvious that Calamity's companion is feeling the challenges of getting her from Montana to New York. As the reporter notes, Brake's handwriting, when she registered at the St. Paul hotel, "shows plainly that she was more or less agitated and nervous." Not surprisingly, Calamity has "a faculty . . . of producing a ruction at any time and place and on short notice." Calamity has been dressed in buckskins, but innocently tried out the face powder Brake gave her. As a result, Calamity was a "sight to behold," powdered from face to toes. Before the interview ended, Calamity pulled the journalist's leg, telling him she had fought alongside General Custer, Buffalo Bill, and other noted Indian fighters. Reprinted in *Billings* (Mont.) *Gazette*, 19 July 1901.

153. "Calamity Jane at a Social Function," *Buffalo* (N.Y.) *Enquirer*, 30 July 1901.

The Buffalo newspaper targets Calamity's personality. It is of note, especially "for a woman who, over thirty years ago, was the heroine of popular dime novels." She is bright, attentive, and with a "striking personality." Yesterday, she wore her "battle-field attire": her buckskins, chamois blouse, and sombrero. She also visited Niagara Falls and attended a reception hosted by Josephine Winfield [*sic*] Brake. "At a formal dinner, [she] seems out of atmosphere."

154. "Calamity Jane Sees the Falls," *Buffalo* (N.Y.) *Evening Times*, 31 July 1901.

Calamity enjoyed a trip to Niagara Falls and its environs. Later, she was part of a reception, where, as guest of honor, she impressed attendees as youthful despite being "something over 60 years." Her reputation goes before her: "her word is as good as her bond and she was loved and respected by everyone in the West." Then, the journalist lists the soldiers with whom Calamity served while with General Crook. Obviously, Calamity was puffing her story with misinformation, and the writer's conclusions were not uniformly accepted in the West. Calamity has sealed a deal to participate in Fred Cummins's Indian Congress.

155. *Buffalo* (N.Y.) *Enquirer*, 1 August 1901.

Calamity will take part in a gigantic parade in Buffalo as part of the Pan-American Exposition. She will be sandwiched among Geronimo and an Apache band, other Indian groups, and Winona, a famed Sioux girl sharpshooter.

156. *Buffalo* (N.Y.) *Evening News*, 9 August 1901.

Drunk and wandering the streets, Calamity was arrested in Buffalo. When a policeman found her, she was "reeling from side to side and did not appear to know where she was." She was held in jail for the night, taken before a judge, and "released on a suspended sentence." "Mrs. Dorsett said it was the first time she had been arrested."

157. (Lewistown, Mont.) *Fergus County Argus*, 2 October 1901.

Calamity is heading back to Montana after her upsetting experiences at the Pan-American Exposition in Buffalo, New York. Now temporarily in Chicago, she hopes soon to return to the Treasure State. Calamity tells the reporter that she had been sold a bill of goods by Josephine Brake. "She had been lured into a net and that New York woman had secured her for exhibition purposes." But if promised funding arrives, she will soon be home. If the money fails to come, she will "adopt the role of a hobo" to get back.

158. "Jane Was Hostile." *Minneapolis* (Minn.) *Journal*, 19 October 1901.

A Minneapolis reporter told a lie to get an interview with Calamity Jane when she traveled through Minneapolis with Josephine Brake on their way to the Pan-American Exposition in Buffalo, New York. Calamity was unhappy with reporters because of incidents back in the West. But the reporter in Minnesota lied, claiming to be the cousin of Mrs. Brake (with her blessing). When Calamity refused an interview with a second reporter, he pointed to the first and uncovered that reporter's falsehood. Realizing what had happened, Calamity tore up the first journalist's notes. Passing back through Minneapolis on her return from her traumatic weeks in Buffalo, she ran into the mendacious reporter. She went after the liar. He escaped, but not without trembling knees after Calamity's blast at him.

159. *Anaconda* (Mont.) *Standard*, 4 April 1902.

Quoting the *Jamestown* (North Dakota) *Alert*, this story reports that Calamity Jane has just visited Jamestown and is on her way to Livingston, Montana. She startled men in a saloon when, after they had joshed "the old lady," she pulled her guns and warned them "now it's my turn." She yelled at the cowboys, while making them dance, you "don't know as much as the calves on my Montana ranch." Calamity with a ranch? Probably not.

160. *Livingston* (Mont.) *Enterprise,* 24, 31 May and 6 June 1902.

One Richard Lee has been arrested for "rolling" Calamity Jane and stealing a ring from her. Lee was charged with larceny, but when Calamity failed to show up to testify against him, Lee was released.

161. "'Cherokee Sal,' Bret Harte's Heroine." *Denver* (Colo.) *Times,* 1 June 1902.

This reporter's facts are not to be trusted. He has Calamity as a famous Indian fighter, "a regular scout" for the U.S. Army, and "the most remarkable woman the frontier has ever developed." Most of the piece, however, consists of quotations from Buffalo Bill about Calamity (quoted elsewhere as well). He too sees her as a unique woman of the West. "A more daringly eccentric woman I have never known," Cody states. She is a sensational pioneer female, "one of the old frontier types, and she . . . [has] all their merits and most of their faults." She drinks far too much (Cody himself was a notorious tippler) and has often been jailed. Cody goes off the deep end in stating that Calamity served on vigilante committees in early Deadwood "and took part in every lynching bee."

Conversely, Cody continues, Calamity was "a big-hearted woman, generous to a fault." Cody's story goes on to tell of his financial support for Calamity in the late summer of 1901 when she was adrift in Buffalo, New York, at the Pan-American Exposition and homesick for Montana. Buffalo Bill paid her way back.

The reporter then returns to his own off-the-wall assertions in stating that short story writer Bret Harte used Calamity as a model for his Local Color heroine "Cherokee Sal" in his famous short story "The Luck of Roaring Camp." The story was published in 1868, when Calamity was still the twelve-year-old Martha Canary.

162. (Helena) *Montana Weekly Record,* 3 June 1902.

Calamity is to be taken to the Poor Farm in Park County. She has been sick for the past week in her shack in Gardiner, Montana. (Once at the Poor Farm, however, Calamity borrowed money for a railroad ticket and whiskey and departed westward from Livingston.)

163. "They Want Calamity Pensioned." *Anaconda* (Mont.) *Standard,* 19 June 1902.

Several friends of Calamity's, including her benefactor Josephine Brake of Buffalo, New York, are gathering support to establish a government pension for her. Supporters contend that Calamity "rendered efficient service to her country as a scout and Indian fighter, and many an old pioneer owes his life to her careful nursing." One old stage driver supports the pension movement, telling the journalist, "I tell you she [Calamity] is an angel when a fellow is in trouble." The pension is necessary because "Calamity will not accept charity."

164. "To Pension Calamity Jane." *Lewistown* (Mont.) *Democrat*, 11 July 1902.

The move to raise a pension for Calamity receives no support from this reporter. He is certain that Calamity has had the freedom and opportunities to work, travel, and display herself before paying audiences. "She has had about all that was coming to her." To pension her would establish a bad precedent. If Calamity has had her opportunities and she "is not content with all these honors[,] she must indeed be hard to satisfy."

165. *Livingston* (Mont.) *Enterprise*, 13 September 1902.

A movement is under way to gather funds to support Calamity in her "poverty and old age" (she was forty-six). A guardian will administer the funds to see that she does not spend the money on whiskey "for every sheepherder she meets at cross roads saloons."

166. "'Calamity Jane' Gets Sixty Days." *Anaconda* (Mont.) *Standard*, 22 November 1902.

Liquored up, Calamity entered the Yegen Bros. store in Billings, Montana. Spying a scalp she coveted, she tried to yank it away. When the clerk screamed, Calamity was apprehended, "disarmed and landed in jail." She was "tried on a charge of disturbance" and sent to the clink for two months. "She registered as Mattie Burke."

167. "Calamity Jane, Last of the Old Indian Fighters." *Denver* (Colo.) *Post*, 11 January 1903.

Seven months before Calamity's death, this reporter for the *Post* provided a lengthy overview of her controversial life—loaded with spurious information. She had married twelve times, and all of the husbands "had met a violent death," including the first, whom she had killed. Her real name is not known, nor the names of her husbands. They were usually known as "Calamity Jane's man." Calamity was also a brave Indian fighter, ready to do in "redskins" at any time.

The latter part of the piece, containing information on Calamity's recent trip to the East Coast, is more true to facts because it closely follows other, more veracious newspaper accounts. The author also salutes daring and kindly nursing. In conclusion, the journalist notes, "everybody knows more or less of Calamity, . . . the last of the old Indian fighters and army scouts." Almost all the story is nonsense or imagined puffery.

168. "Talk of the Town." *Belle Fourche* (S.Dak.) *Bee*, 15 January 1903.

Calamity is in town with her daughter. Then a familiar refrain follows: "she is tired of traveling and desires to locate somewhere, where she can lead a quiet life, earn her living in an honorable manner and spend the balance of her days in peace and quiet." Now, "she seeks only the opportunity to work, that she may support herself and her daughter in a proper manner." (Sadly, a persisting, disruptive alcoholism kept Calamity from ever finding that peace and quiet.)

169. "Calamity Jane as She Was and as She Is." *Great Falls* (Mont.) *Daily Tribune*, 18 January 1903.

Readers must remember the Calamity of the past, the reporter claims. The present-day Calamity is "old and poverty stricken and wretched." The reporter understands what has happened. "The country has outgrown her and her occupation is gone." When she tries to shoot up the town, as she had two decades earlier, she is now thrown in jail to cool her heels.

Her experiences in Buffalo at the Pan-American Exposition did not turn out well. Calamity was earning only about forty cents a week and did not enjoy being treated like a sideshow freak. Her host, Josephine Blake [*sic*], according to Calamity, was "coining money at her expense." So she came back west as soon as she could.

Calamity Jane was a wild woman in earlier years, but "she was [also] a good nurse and took care of every such person she could reach." In addition, "behind all the rough exterior there is a good deal of woman to Calamity Jane."

An insightful piece touching on all the major Calamity Jane legends: Wild Woman, Nursemaid, and Pioneer Woman.

Newspaper Articles after Calamity's Death

Entries in this section are arranged chronologically. Parenthetical numbers in the text cross-reference other entries in this guide.

170. "'Calamity Jane' Is Dead." *New York Times*, 2 August 1903.

Published one day after Calamity's death, this obituary egregiously peddles dozens of erroneous facts. Following closely many of Calamity's off-track contentions in her autobiography and information from other false rumors, the New York journalist has Calamity as a scout for Custer, helping to capture Wild Bill Hickok's assassin, carrying government mail, and marrying Clinton Burke in Texas—all falsehoods. Moreover, the obituary covers all of Calamity's life after 1876 in one paragraph and concludes that "in her dotage speculators fenced in her house and charged an admission fee to tourists." Misinformation compounding misinformation in one of the country's leading newspapers.

171. (Deadwood, S.Dak.) *Daily Pioneer-Times*, 2 August 1903.

The obituary in the Deadwood newspaper proved that close-at-hand outlets could be as distorted in their coverage as those on the East Coast. The reporter says Calamity's real name was "Mary E. Canary"; Wild Bill was her "consort"; her mother, Charlotte, had lived in Montana "for a long time" (though it was two years at most); and Calamity had married "several times"—all falsehoods. But the journalist balances this incorrect information with praise for Calamity's "kindly heart and . . . generous disposition." He also states that Calamity's daughter [Jessie] was newly married and living in North Dakota, but evidently an "estrangement" kept Calamity from speaking further on the matter.

172. "Death of Calamity Jane." *Lead* (S.Dak.) *Evening Call*, 3 August 1903.

The obituary from the nearby Lead newspaper encapsulates nearly all of its information from the day-earlier obituary in the Deadwood *Daily Pioneer-Times* (preceding), including many of its miscues. Calamity's real name was "Mary E. Canary," but she was known more recently as "Mrs. Mary E. Burke."

173. "Noted Woman Calamity Jane Dies Saturday." *Rawlins* (Wyo.) *Republican*, 5 August 1903.

The newspaper in Rawlins, where Calamity and Bill Steers (her only legal husband) lived for several years in the 1880s, mixes untruths and facts in this combined obituary and retrospective story. Calamity "was nearly 73 years of age," the piece begins (she was forty-seven at death). She "would fight the most notorious tough in the country," but she was also "a very pretty woman" and on the staff of General Miles in his Nez Perce campaign. Not so. But the writer provides helpful information on Calamity's years in Rawlins, her life there with Steers, and her return some years later with another "husband" King and her daughter.

174. "Talk of the Town" column, *Belle Fourche* (S.Dak.) *Bee*, 6 August 1903.

This obituary states that Calamity died at age fifty-two and "has a married daughter residing in North Dakota somewhere, the address of whom she will not divulge." Mary E. Canary was her maiden name, and her mother, a washerwoman, died in Blackfoot, Montana. She received her nickname from writer Bill Nye, editor of the *Laramie* (Wyo.) *Boomerang* and was married often. She was buried in Deadwood, next to Wild Bill Hickok, one of her consorts. "Now Deadwood will have a double attraction to exhibit to visitors from the east." The prediction proved to be prescient—with one addition: visitors from all directions and countries. A montage of useful facts, mis-statements, and a provocative final observation.

175. "Calamity Jane Dies," *Livingston* (Mont.) *Post*, 6 August 1903.

This obituary calls Calamity "the most unique character the great west has produced." The writer attempts to balance his description of Calamity's character because it was "many sided." She drank excessively, married often,

and had difficulty making a living. Overall, she was "almost entirely lacking in that high moral sense possessed in a great measure by the majority of
woman-kind." There was a good side of Calamity too: she did help the needy
and sick. The reporter is wrong in stating that Calamity and Wild Bill were
longtime friends and companions on many scouting and military expeditions. The chronology of Calamity's life is also jumbled. Most useful here
are the tidbits of information about Calamity's life in Livingston and Horr,
Montana, and other nearby areas.

176. "Calamity Jane Finally Does the Right Thing," *Gardiner* (Mont.) *Wonderland,*
6 August 1903.

The blaring headline of this story reveals the hostility of some journalists to
positive reports about Calamity. The writer accepts almost nothing positive
about Calamity and highlights several negative comments. In the last years
of her life, Calamity had spent several months, off and on, in the Gardiner
area, on her way to Yellowstone Park.

177. "'Calamity Jane,' the Wild West's Wildest Product, Dead." (Bozeman, Mont.)
Avant Courier, 7 August 1903.

This obituary asserts that "Calamity Jane was the most remarkable woman
the frontier has developed." But, surprisingly, the reporter misfires on so
many facts that he presents an undependable retrospective on Calamity's
life. For example, she cornered Jack McCaul [*sic*] with a cleaver after Wild
Bill's assassination, she participated in the lynching of McCall, and she was
a "celebrated . . . Indian fighter"—all dead wrong. Nor did she scout and
prospect "in every state of the West." The second half of the story is primarily
material quoted from Buffalo Bill Cody describing Calamity Jane.

178. "'Calamity Jane': 'Buffalo Bill' Recollections." *London Star,* 7 August 1903.

Interviewed in England, Buffalo Bill Cody recalled Calamity as a lively
frontier woman he had met on two or three occasions, although he also
said that he "knew her very well." Curiously, Cody's chronology is all out
of whack: he says he met her first in 1874 (when he thinks she was already
known as Calamity Jane), but at that first meeting she tells him of Deadwood happenings of 1876–78. Similarly, the journalist speaks of Buffalo Bill's
seeing Calamity at the Pan-American Exposition in 1891, when that event
took place a decade later. Perhaps the English writer misunderstood what
Cody said. Buffalo Bill admitted Calamity's drunkenness, her tendency to get

involved in upsets and disruptions, and her unwomanly actions; but he also praised her skills as a shooter and hunter. Cody also stated that "everyone knew and liked her."

179. "'Calamity Jane' Feared No Man." *Princeton* (Mo.) *Press*, 12 August 1903.

This combined obituary–retrospective mini-biography occupies the first column of the newspaper's front page. The writer asserts that Princeton residents will be interested in the account of Calamity's death because some elderly residents would remember her parents, and some even the little girl Martha. Sadly, the piece contains more miscues than facts, probably because it follows too closely wrong information in Calamity's autobiography (241) and repeats other stories for which there is no evidence. The author clearly did not examine the information available in the Mercer County Courthouse.

180. *White Sulphur Springs* (Mont.) *Meagher Republican*, 14 August 1903.

This reporter found nothing positive and much negative to say about Calamity. She was a "notorious prostitute" who hung out with "roughs, rogues, robbers," and other unsavory characters. She was often a soused drunk, frequently "obscene" and "indecent." Journalists must, argues the writer, tell the truth and avoid touting Calamity, or they would be "embark[ing] in the cultivation of rattlesnakes."

181. "Calamity Jane Was Never an Indian Scout Nor a Killer." (Great Falls, Mont.) *Daily Leader*, 16 July 1906.

George Hoshier, an old-time Westerner, first met Calamity in 1875 in Cheyenne and was one of her pallbearers nearly forty years later in Deadwood in 1903. Now, says this reporter, Hoshier "has just told the true story of Calamity's life." Her real name was "Mary E. Canary," and she "was never a scout." She got her nickname because "she was always getting into trouble." But she helped the sick, despite all her wandering. "The reason she got so much notoriety was because she was always doing some crazy thing, and partly because she wanted to be notorious." This story is a combination of fact and fiction.

182. Ward, Josiah M. "A Wild West Heroine the Movies Overlook." *New York Tribune*, 16 October 1921.

Ward argues that Calamity, a western woman of lively and individualistic ways, deserved to be featured in Western movies, but hadn't been. Problem

is, much of what Ward relates about her life is absolute nonsense. He bun-
gles the facts and introduces absurd new and unsupportable yarns, thereby
vitiating the strength of his contention. Disappointing.

183. *Casper* (Wyo.) *Tribune Herald*, 26 November 1921.

The reporter wrongly states Calamity "came from Pennsylvania as a young
woman." Nor is the writer correct in asserting she worked for two years as a
"cowboy" in Nebraska, served as a scout of General Crook at Fort Kearney
and as an Indian scout beside Buffalo Bill and Red Wing, or sent her one
daughter to a convent in Nebraska to be educated. He may be right, though,
in stating that Calamity married "one Tom King." Where the writer gathered
most of this incorrect information is a mystery, although he does mention
old-timer Tom Fales and his interest in Calamity.

184. McGillycuddy, Valentine. Letter to the Editor, *Rapid City* (S.Dak.) *Journal*,
   1 October 1924.

McGillycuddy's published letter became a central source for historians' and
other writers' off-track story of Calamity actually being a young woman
named Jane Dalton. Like Harry (Sam) Young's *Hard Knocks* (342), which
McGillycuddy may have been following too closely, this letter asserts that
Calamity's origins were in Wyoming, near Fort Laramie. McGillycuddy,
Young, and several others then spun a tale about Jane Dalton's becoming an
orphan after Indians killed her parents, and being raised by soldiers. A later
letter by a believer in this story to the military archives in Washington, D.C.,
revealed that none of the soldiers named in the story had been at Fort Laramie when the Dalton story said they had. Because of McGillycuddy's solid
reputation as a sound source, many Wyoming and South Dakota historians
and popular writers fell for the Jane Dalton story. The original letter is on file
in the McGillycuddy Papers (H74–87) in the South Dakota State Historical
Society in Pierre (23).

185. Pond, Seymour G. "Frontier Still Recalls 'Calamity Jane.'" *New York Times
   Magazine*, 18 October 1925, 9.

One of the few newspaper stories about Calamity in the national media
during the 1920s, this article overflows with errors. The author repeats
several of Calamity's offbeat stretchers in her autobiography, as well as
several other faulty assertions from other sources. Pond has Calamity killing
Indians, capturing Jack McCall after his shooting of Wild Bill Hickok, saving

a stagecoach attacked by Indians, and marrying three times—all wrong
Overall, the writer portrays a wild Calamity, but also a woman of courage
and daring and an agent of charity. "In time of need, Calamity was never
known to fail." Some conclusions click, but this is primarily an inferior piece
afflicted with errors and vague generalizations.

186. Conway, Dan E. "Calamity Jane: Unique Character of Old Frontier—Her
Deadwood Romance; 'Wild Bill' Hickok Was Her Ideal of Man." *Montana
News Association* (*Cascade Courier*), 8 October 1926.

A long newspaper account filling several paragraphs, this retrospective
story opens with the false Jane Dalton origins story (289). It then shifts
to the Martha Canary origins story in Missouri, without explaining the
story-line conflicts. Additional mistakes occur when the author follows
too closely Calamity's error-ridden autobiography (241). Conway trots
out most of the Wild West Calamities: scout, Indian fighter, soldier with
Custer, crack shot, balanced against ministering angel episodes: helping
the poor and caring for the smallpox-afflicted. The author accepts a Wild
Bill–Calamity romance in Deadwood and gives her death date as 2 August
1903, exactly twenty-seven years after Wild Bill's demise. Almost all these
statements are incorrect, and no mention is made of Calamity's traveling
with tour groups, performing in Buffalo, New York, in 1901, or working in
dance halls. Disappointing. Virtually the same story, almost word for word,
appears in John K. Standish, "Calamity Jane Often Traveled over Cheyenne
& Deadwood Stage Line; Notorious Character." *Lusk* (Wyo.) *Herald*, 28
May 1936.

187. "Calamity Jane, Famous Wild Woman of Frontier, Spent Much of Latter Part
of Her Life in Billings." *Billings* (Mont.) *Gazette*, 30 January 1927. Reprinted
in *Anaconda Montana Standard*, 12 April 1953.

This curious piece is almost entirely a reprint of Seymour G. Pond's essay in
the *New York Times* (185). It does not deal specifically with Calamity's later
years in the Billings area.

188. "Calamity Jane Was Real Wild West Heroine to Those Who Knew Her."
Bozeman (Mont.) *Courier*, 17 May 1929.

A sympathetic portrait of Calamity, this piece accepts her unorthodox
actions but also touts her warmhearted help for the sick and needy. Most
of the article deals with her early life, although the piece is short on details

and long on anecdotes. The writer says men accepted Calamity, but women "failed to understand her." Calamity had her flaws, the author contends; however, "there are none of us in a position to condemn her."

189. Standish, John K. "Calamity Jane, a Real Robin Hood among Needy on Frontier." *Great Falls* (Mont.) *Tribune,* 22 March 1931.

This informative and rather lengthy piece is based largely on the memories of Mrs. L. N. Walker who was a schoolgirl in Pierre when Calamity lived there in 1901–1902. Walker (and author Standish), while admitting Calamity drank and swore, chose to emphasize her kindly deeds, her separation from well-to-do townspeople, and her silence about her personal affairs. Neither the informant nor the author knows the real name of Calamity. One incident Walker relates concerned Calamity's helping a sick woman with several children. When the kids became disruptive in their small, intimate home, Calamity sat them down and told them, "D— you little devils, now you stay there." The remembered details, if recalled correctly, reveal a good deal about Calamity, but the reporter misdates Calamity's death, says she drank only at home, and denies that she had any children.

See also John K. Standish, "Calamity Jane Often Traveled over Cheyenne and Deadwood Stage Line; Notorious Character." *Lusk* (Wyo.) *Herald,* 28 May 1936, which reprints Conway (186).

190. Lockley, Fred. "Impressions and Observations of the Journal Man." (Portland) *Oregon Sunday Journal,* 12 September 1931.

The indefatigable interviewer Fred Lockley speaks here to Mrs. Grace Norvell. Now living in Oregon, she resided in Deadwood for six years as a young married woman, beginning in 1877. Calamity worked as a "hired girl" for "several months" for Norvell and "for quite a number of women at Deadwood." She was a good housekeeper, quiet and hardworking. On other occasions, she dressed like a man and acted in a "way that was not considered ladylike."

191. "10 Years Ago." *Lander* (Wyo.) *State Journal,* 13 January 1932.

"A. J. Mokler was preparing a history of Calamity Jane, who at the age of 13 was at Miner's Delight in 1869. After a notorious career she came back to Lander. She was placed under arrest by Sheriff Arthur Sparhawk but released when she married and left the city." Martha Canary may have been at Miner's Delight in 1869, but she did not marry in Lander. Her one legal husband was

William Steers of Rawlins, Wyoming, whom Calamity married in 1000 in Pocatello, Idaho. See Mokler's account (299).

192. Deadwood (S.Dak.) *Black Hills Weekly*, 28 July 1933.

A letter from Miss Jessie E. Oakes of Los Angles to the Adams Memorial Hall in Deadwood requests information on her grandmother, Calamity Jane. Actually the daughter of Calamity rather than her granddaughter, Jessie Elizabeth Oakes (Murray) speaks of a brother and her possible father. Later, after Jean Hickok McCormick claimed to be Calamity's daughter (198–99), Jessie referred to Calamity as her aunt. Several newspapers in the 1930s carried similar stories. See, for example, the *Cody* (Wyo.) *Enterprise*, 28 March 1934.

193. *Billings* (Mont.) *Gazette*, 11, 29 March, 4, 5, 6 April 1934.

This series of stories deals with Jessie E. Oakes (later, Murray) and her quest for information about Calamity Jane, whom she calls her grandmother. Jessie also wanted to locate Jack Oakes, her half-brother. Some sources quoted here mistakenly state that Calamity's real name was Jane Dalton and that she had no daughter. The most telling information comes from one Olive McDaniels, who knew Calamity and her daughter. McDaniels says Jessie "was at the time [early twentieth century] married." She kept in touch with Calamity and her daughter, Jessie, after they left Billings, but the letters between them indicated "that no granddaughter was born during the years of their correspondence" (6 April 1934). Here are the first Jessie Elizabeth Oakes Murray letters asking for information about her family heritage; they continued for nearly twenty years.

194. Newcom, W. H. (Wirt). "Quick Exit from City Recalled When Order to Move Out Was Issued." *Miles City* (Mont.) *Daily Star*, 24 May 1934. Reprinted as "Calamity Jane Once Took Possession of Shack Behind Grey Mule Saloon in Miles City; Was Soon Ordered to 'Move On.'" *Ismay* (Mont.) *Journal*, 28 June 1934.

Wirt Newcom, who had come up the trail as a cowboy and settled in Miles City, Montana, met Calamity Jane there in the mid-1890s. She was camping out in a shack behind the old Grey Mule Saloon. When Calamity told Wirt she was married to Clinton Burke, he commented on Burke's youth. Calamity replied: "Yeah, I never had a fellow with a h—— of a lot of money; [but] I always did pick a looker." Not too long afterwards, Calamity burst into Wirt's abode and hurriedly asked him to drive her to Deadwood. The sheriff had thrown her in jail for being a "celebrity," and the judge, fining her $100, had let her out on bail to raise that amount. But she wanted to dash out of town. On the way out of Miles City, they stopped by Calamity's place to gather up her "war bag" and "a cheap suit case," "good old Jane's 'forty years' gatherings." Before Wirt left, Calamity told him to inform the cop who arrested her that she was coming back to Miles City to "whip h— out of him."

Later, in 1901, Newcom happened into the Pan-American Exposition in Buffalo, New York, where Calamity was performing as a Wild West star. Newcom's relatives were Sunday- and Wednesday-night churchgoing folks, so he had to ask Calamity to tone down her language after she gave him a hug of surprise at the exposition grounds. Calamity proved to be the perfect gentlewoman with his relatives, leading Wirt to remember that she "was as polite as any one of the party and entertained them all royally."

195. Walker, Tacetta B. "Calamity Jane and Other Quaint Characters." *Wyoming Stockman Farmer*, August 1936.

The author rides consistently the two mounts of the best-known Calamity legends—as a Wild Woman "character of the West" and as "generous or kind" frontier woman. Walker contends, however, that it was not the latter legend that made "her stand out." Rather, she had a "Hollywood complex"; she loved "her stage settings and always played to an audience." The author lists Calamity among the rambunctious, publicity-conscious western characters who grabbed headlines with their controversial actions. Generally provocative but based on skimpy evidence.

196. Taylor, Walter Ed. "Refusal to Make Vaudeville Tour of East Coast Cost Calamity Jane a Husband." *Judith Basin County Press* (Montana News Association insert), 7 September 1936.

Taylor, drawing on the memories of reporter Jerome Williams, a Big Timber, Montana, reporter who knew Calamity, recounts several stories about Calamity that no one else provides. For example, Taylor says that when Calamity's unnamed husband (Robert Dorsett?) urged her to go on a vaudeville tour speaking of her fantastic western experiences, she refused. When she did so, he left. Other sources do not confirm that this was the reason Dorsett split from Calamity—if indeed this reference is to Dorsett. Taylor also dismisses the story of the Livingston log cabin often said to be Calamity's. It was not her home; she stayed but a few days in the cabin with its "negress" resident The reporter speaks, too, of Calamity's lively days in Gardiner, a hamlet near Yellowstone National Park, when soldiers stationed nearby came to town to whoop it up with Calamity. In addition, a few Calamity trips to Big Timber ended abruptly when Calamity became embroiled in a fight with a Mrs. Dooly, who lived there.

197. "Calamity Jane Not Romantic or Admirable, Pioneer Says." *Cheyenne* (Wyo.) *Tribune*, [n.d.] 1937.

Drawing on the memories of no-nonsense Wyoming pioneer trader John Hunton, this story presents the "devil-may-care-female" Calamity as a much-flawed woman. She was, Hunton asserts, a "sporting character" (prostitute) at the E. Coffey and Cuny road and hog ranch. She was, he adds, "among the commonest of her class." True, Calamity was part of military expeditions, but she went surreptitiously, not as a scout or soldier. Most writers have falsely depicted Calamity as a romantic, appealing character. Not true, contends Hunton. He also doubts (wrongly) that Wild Bill "had ever seen" Calamity. Hunton's comments here square with the much more extensive treatment in Hunton's published diaries (264)

198. Meldrum, Helen. "Daughter of 'Calamity' Jane Interviewed; Recollects Mother." *Sheridan* (Wyo.) *Press*, 13 May 1941.

This longish story about Jessie Hickok McCormick appeared just one week after she startled a nationwide audience on the radio program *We the People* (broadcast 6 May 1941) by declaring she was the daughter of Calamity Jane and Wild Bill Hickok. The first extensive news report following McCormick's announcement, this article summarizes her story, that of her reputed mother Calamity Jane, and the content of the letters and diary she claimed were Calamity's. All these details were exposed as specious in James McLaird's key article fifty years later (376). This 1941 article also states that McCormick "has written a book which is now at the publishers called 'Calamity Jane Exposed.' McCormick is said to be headed off to Hollywood where "a movie based on her story of Calamity Jane" is planned. Neither project ever came to fruition.

199. Chaffee, Oscar. "Billings Woman Announces That She Is Daughter of Famed Calamity Jane." *Billings* (Mont.) *Gazette*, 15 June 1941.

On 6 May 1941, Jean Hickok McCormick announced on the national radio program *We the People* that she was the daughter of a Calamity Jane–Wild

Bill union. Five weeks later this story summarized the incredible details of Mrs. McCormick's off-track claim. This writer summarizes some of the letters and diary entries that McCormick fraudulently claimed to be those of her reputed mother Calamity Jane. The heart-wrenching tale captured many readers, especially those yearning for mother-daughter stories. Hickok McCormick's narrative captivated general readers—and scholars—for a half-century before James McLaird proved her contentions were lies (376). See a very similar account in the *Rapid City* (S.Dak.) *Journal*, 12 September 1941.

200. "Calamity Jane Had a Daughter Says Niece." (Lander) *Wyoming State Journal*, 2 April 1942.

Calamity's daughter, Jessie Elizabeth Oakes Murray, has now changed her story: she is the niece, not the granddaughter, of Calamity. Jessie probably revised her story after 1941 when Jean Hickok McCormick appeared and used her fraudulent letters and diary to try to prove Calamity was her mother. Jessie says, too, that she is the daughter of another Hickok, not the famous Wild Bill. In 1908 Jessie had stated that she was the daughter of Martha Canary, in the 1930s the granddaughter, and in the 1940s the niece.

201. "James Reagan Recalls Calamity Jane." *Lander* (Wyo.) *State Journal*, 14 May 1942.

Reagan, a Wyoming stockman, recalls that in Fort Bridger and Piedmont Mrs. Ed Alton "mothered" Martha until she was about fourteen. He also later remembers Calamity's working like a man chopping wood and whacking bulls along the Union Pacific Railroad. He knew her as "Martha Jane Kanealy, rather than Canary."

202. Shevlin, Nellie M. "Packsaddle Ben." (Denver, Colo.) *Rocky Mountain Empire* magazine, Sunday, 15 October 1950.

Ben Greenough came west from Brooklyn as a sixteen-year-old greenhorn and met Calamity Jane in Billings, Montana. She lived outside town on Canyon Creek and cut wood, selling it to hoteliers and other buyers in Billings. Greenough retells the often-narrated story of Calamity's being pelted with a lemon in a pool hall and her picking up billiard balls and flinging them, some with near deadly accuracy, at prime targets in the saloon.

Such stories are misleading, the author contends. Calamity, according to Greenough, "was a very beautiful woman, with dark brown eyes, wavy red hair and moods as variable as the desert winds." Ben and Calamity became warm companions. "No one," says Greenough, "could have a more loyal friend than Calamity Jane."

203. (Rawlins, Wyo.) *Daily Times,* 17 December 1952.

Demonstrating how off-track later reports were, this piece mistakenly states that Calamity died "at age 73," and that "'Squint' Squires of Salt Lake City" was one of her later husbands. The reporter could be right, however, in stating Calamity "married" a "man from Montana named King," and that she became known for a time in Rawlins, Wyoming, as Mattie King.

204. Thompson, Doris. "Final Chapter in Life of Calamity Jane, Famous Character, Ended 50 Years Ago." *Princeton* (Mo.) *Post-Telegraph,* 30 July 1953.

A lengthy story by a thorough investigative journalist, this piece is based on extensive interviews with older residents of the Mercer County area. The story adds information on Martha's birthplace and residences near Princeton, Missouri, and speculates on other possible happenings. The latter section of the piece, based on sources outside Missouri, is much less satisfactory.

205. Morrell, Sarren. "Thru the Hills." *Rapid City* (S.Dak.) *Daily Journal,* 1 November 1953.

"The most famous woman ever to live in the Black Hills was . . . Calamity Jane." To substantiate this assertion, the writer interviewed several old-timers who knew Calamity. His stories illustrate the two best-known legends surrounding Calamity: the Wild Woman of the Old West and the Angel of Mercy. Like this one, several other sources simultaneously advanced both legends.

206. "Oldtime Nebraskan Explodes Theory Calamity Was Rootin' Tootin' Jane." *Sioux City* (Iowa) *Journal,* 25 January 1954.

Octogenarian Charles Andrews of Scottsbluff, Nebraska, stiff-arms outrageous rumors that Martha was a rootin' tootin' young teenager about 1870 or 1871. He states his mother, Emma Alton, fired Martha when she misbehaved and dressed up as a soldier, but she never was a bullwhacker, Wild Bill's companion, or a superb shootist. When Andrews ventures away from these interesting ideas, he falls into the quicksand of misinformation. Author Ned Buntline did not write a book about Martha and give her the name Calamity Jane, and Martha did not work at Mrs. Alton's boardinghouse for several years. One must remember, too, that if the eighty-four-year-old Andrews were born in 1870, he could not have remembered much, if anything, about Martha.

207. "A Smear on 'Calamity's' Reputation." *Kansas City Star*, 5 February 1954.

This news story, repeating much of the previous newspaper article, speaks of eighty-four-year-old Charles Andrews, then a resident of Scottsbluff, having lived in Piedmont, Wyoming, "about 1871 [1870?]." Martha Canary was his babysitter, he claims. She was not a bull team driver nor a special friend of Wild Bill's, and Andrews was convinced she never "fired a rifle in her life." These contentions about young Martha are revealing, but keep in mind that Andrews would have been born about 1870, meaning he was a babe when Martha tended him. The article refers to Edward Alton and his wife, Andrews's stepfather and mother; their names appear with that of Martha in the special Wyoming census of 1869 (41). An important bit of evidence.

208. *Santa Cruz* (Calif.) *Sentinel*, 14 May 1954.

This brief story announces the final rites of Robert Harrison Dorsett, age seventy-nine, in Santa Cruz, California. It names among his acquaintances Calamity Jane and Charlie Russell. Dorsett, born in Union Villa, Missouri, on 28 July 1874, was frequently named as Calamity's final "husband." They were rumored to be together about 1898–1900. Dorsett may have removed Calamity's daughter, Jessie, and taken her to live with his mother in Livingston, Montana (see 65–68).

209. Thompson, Doris. "Princeton Claims Fame as Calamity Jane Birthplace." *Princeton* (Mo.) *Post-Telegraph*, 25 July 1957.

Journalist Thompson's thoroughly researched piece is one of the best sources to appear on Martha Canary's early years since the publication of Aikman's account in 1927 (230). Thompson interviewed several families, dug into local land records, and pulled together other valuable sources in the first half of her essay. The second part of the piece, because it relies almost entirely on Calamity's marred autobiography (241), is of much less value. The essay appeared as Princeton was dedicating Calamity Jane Roadside Park, just north of town. That act indicated the town was becoming more accepting of being known as the hometown of Calamity Jane.

210. Holbrook, Stewart. "A Lively Lady Was Calamity Jane." (Portland) *Oregonian*, 17 August 1957.

Drawing on Holbrook's essay in *American Mercury* (February 1947)—which was later expanded in Holbrook's *Little Annie Oakley and Other Rugged*

People (271)—this newspaper article must not be relied on heavily. Holbrook touches on several known events in Calamity's life, but his account is so error-ridden and out of chronological order that it confirms Holbrook's limited research and careless storytelling.

211. "Calamity Jane Left an Impression on Annals of History of the West." *Buffalo* (Wyo.) *Bulletin*, 21 August 1957.

This retrospective piece, caught as it is between the few facts the writer has uncovered and the misbegotten tales of Jean Hickok McCormick (198–99), must be avoided. It overflows with false information. For one, it is wrong from the start in asserting that Lander, Wyoming, was Calamity's home. Calamity spent much more time in Deadwood and the Billings and Livingston areas of Montana, and even in Rawlins, Wyoming, than in Lander. Nor did she know Wild Bill Hickok before their trip to Deadwood in June–July 1876. The author fails, too, to mention that Bill Steers, Clinton Burke, and Robert Dorsett were companions of Calamity's for much longer than her five-weeks' acquaintance with Wild Bill. Not to be taken as a serious, dependable piece.

212. Harmon, J. R., "Memories of 'Jane'" (letter to the editor). (Portland) *Oregonian*, 25 August 1957.

Harmon, son of 22 Ranch owner Captain William Harmon, recalls his youthful experiences with Calamity in this letter to the *Oregonian* editor. In 1894–95 Harmon was fourteen and living on the 22 Ranch nearly ten miles east of Ekalaka in southeastern Montana. Calamity and "Jack" [*sic*, Clinton] Burke worked on the ranch while living in a tent nearby, and evidently stole, on the sly, milk and chickens from Captain Harmon. Calamity dressed as man, was exceedingly profane, chewed tobacco, and often won wrestling matches with her much younger "husband." Captain Harmon had known Calamity earlier, in her pre-Deadwood days.

213. *Newcastle* (Wyo.) *News Letter Journal*, 18 June 1959.

An elderly settler, Mrs. May Dow, recalls her first sight of Calamity. May and her mother were shopping at a store when Calamity pulled her team up front, dropping down from the seat with her brown skirt hiked up enough to show her "heavy laced boots." May recalled Calamity as "over medium in height, and rather raw-boned with large hands and skin so tanned and weather beaten that it looked like leather." Calamity spied, on a shelf, "some pink China silk" and "exclaimed, 'My, how pretty that would be for a wrapper!'" Calamity quickly bought fifteen yards of the material and explained how she would want the wrapper made with "Matteau Pleats," then gloriously in fashion. After purchasing the silk, Calamity climbed back to her perch on the freight wagon, cracked her long whip, and drove off. An intriguing, bifurcated image of Calamity as a veteran bullwhacker who has not lost her desire for stylish feminine apparel.

214. Connolly, Mary C. "Calamity Jane Rough, Tough, but Not Much Different from Folks in Present Generation" (letter to the editor). Livingston (Mont.) *Park County News*, 8 December 1960.

Connolly speaks of her connections with Calamity and her daughter in Billings. "Her daughter [Jessie] attended the same grade school I did in Billings and we all played hopscotch and jumped rope on the same playground." True, Calamity drank and smoked cigars at times, but she also minded her "own business . . . [and in] a lot of undercover charity . . . [helped] the sick and downtrodden." She worked hard, was not afraid to help, and did not expect pay in return.

215. Dils, Lenore. "Calamity Jane Spent Happy Years in El Paso." *El Paso* (Texas) *Times*, 24 May 1964.

This may be the most fabricated and off-the-wall of all newspaper stories about Calamity Jane. The author betrays her inaccuracies in the second sentence when she writes that Calamity "came to El Paso in 1884 and spent the five happiest years of her life there." Only one bit of evidence would support that assertion, and that evidence is whole-cloth malarkey. In her highly inventive autobiography (241), Calamity claimed that she went to El Paso in the mid-1880s, but dozens of newspapers and other references prove her to have been in Montana, Idaho, and Wyoming during nearly all of the period from 1884 to 1889. Unfortunately, Dils is mistaken in most of what she contends, even giving Calamity's death date as 1905. A demanding fact-checker would have quickly killed this catalog of errors and falsifications.

216. Whithorn, Doris. "Jane Could Cop the Headlines." *Billings* (Mont.) *Gazette*, 16 August 1964.

A superb local historian, Whithorn gathers here several of the Livingston, Montana, newspaper stories that headline Calamity. These stories were reprinted in Whithorn and Whithorn, *Calamity's in Town* (339). The author moves chronologically from Calamity's first appearance in Livingston in the early 1880s to her death in 1903.

217. Peterson, Lucy Lytton. "Lines from Long Ago—Calamity Jane." *Belle Fourche* (S.Dak.) *Bee*, 4 December 1964.

Most of this retrospective story is wide of the mark. It opens with the off-track Jane Dalton yarn, lists Calamity as a mule skinner for Custer, and asserts she came to the Black Hills on 14 May 1876 with Al Swearninger's [*sic*] theater group. Calamity is sanitized, with no mention of her possible prostitution, chronic drunkenness, or several "husbands." Not to be followed.

218. *Mercer County* (Mo.) *Pioneer Press*, 1 October 1966.

A special issue celebrating Calamity Jane Days, this newspaper carries a story about a new marker being placed at the reputed birthplace of Martha Canary/Calamity Jane east of Princeton, Missouri. Other stories deal with the Canary family's residences in Mercer County and the truth or fiction of her autobiography of 1896 (241).

219. "Calamity Jane, Symbol of the Old West." *Mercer County* (Mo.) *Pioneer Press*, 7 October 1967.

Summarizing briefly much of what is already known about the Wild West heroine Calamity Jane, this piece adds no new information. Unhappily, equal numbers of factual errors subtract from the story's contributions. Another piece written for the annual Calamity Jane days.

220. *Mercer County* (Mo.) *Pioneer Press*, 5 October 1968.

This special issue of the local newspaper features a front-page story on "Calamity Jane and Deadwood" by Camille Yuill of Deadwood. Although its specific facts are not all trustworthy, the short piece nonetheless furnishes a good general summary of Calamity's varied life over her time in the Dead-wood area. Another piece in this issue, "Environment the Key to Calamity," treats Martha's early years in the Princeton area, drawing largely on the account in Aikman (230).

221. "Calamity Was No Angel." *Mercer County* (Mo.) *Pioneer Press*, 30 December 1970.

This brief story includes a good deal of information about Martha's earliest years in Missouri. Most of the information is taken from Aikman's *Calamity Jane and the Lady Wildcats* (230), although rumors said to emanate from earlier county residents speak of Martha's having attended school with their ancestors. Quite positive impressions of father Robert; exceedingly negative of mother Charlotte.

222. Mathison, Art. "Calamity's Mom Resides over Ghost." *Spearfish* (S.Dak.) *Queen City Mail*, 11 July 1979.

The author summarizes the research of Montanan Les Barton concerning the Montana ghost town of Blackfoot City, located about thirty miles west of Helena. Barton contends that Martha Canary's mother, Charlotte, died and was buried in the Montana boomtown about 1866. This piece, although including no new information, conveniently summarizes the little information known about Charlotte Canary and her short stay in Blackfoot City.

223. Brainard, Wendell. "Calamity Jane Brought Her Girls to Murray." *North Idaho Sunday*, 27 July 1986. Reprinted from *Shoshone County* (Idaho) *News-Press*, 27 July 1986.

The author speaks of Calamity's coming with "eight girls" to put on "a big social event" in boomtown Eagle City, Idaho, in February 1884. He quotes pioneering journalist Adam Aulbach in the *Coeur d'Alene Sun* (no date given) about Calamity's experiences in Eagle City. She "did a monologue of her life." The other girls—"more feminine"—lined up, danced, and entertained the miners. Other information here on Calamity's life is off-track, but this is one of a handful of sources on Calamity's two trips to and brief stay in the Coeur d'Alenes during the mineral rush era in northern Idaho.

224. *Mercer County* (Mo.) *Pioneer Press*, 20 September 1986.

A Calamity Jane Days special issue, this newspaper reprints the affidavit report from Hannibal Armstrong, administrator for the James Canary estate. Dated 30 June 1862, the report lists Grandpa James's children and their residences. It says James died without a will, but Armstrong will inventory the estate and "faithfully administrate" it. The document derives from Administrations, Executives and Guardians Books, Book A, p. 230, in the Mercer County Courthouse in Princeton (20, 38).

225. "Historians Debunk Western Heroes." *Rapid City* (S.Dak.) *Journal*, 29 October 1989.

The reporter deals with the debunking of Calamity and other western "heroes" that has captured the attention—and perhaps the minds—of the general public. In a session at the annual Montana History Conference

entitled "Speaking Ill of the Dead: Jerks in Montana History," a presenter
pooh-poohs Calamity as a self-advertiser "who fed lurid stories to newspapers that didn't care if they were true." "Much of the legend of Calamity
Jane can be flatly disproved," the speaker continued. True enough, but what
are the verifiable facts among the many myths, and why did so many of
Calamity's contemporaries and later aficionados of a lively Old West buy her
exaggerated stories? Those larger—and perhaps more significant questions—
remain unaddressed here.

226. *Princeton* (Mo.) *Overland Courier*, 4 September 1991.

This news story details the preparation of a skit entitled "Calamity Jane's
Return, Who Says You Can't Go Back Home?" to be performed in Princeton,
Missouri, on 22 September 1991. A local historian and actress have prepared
the skit. The essay's biographical details are untrustworthy because they are
based primarily on Calamity's faulty autobiography (241) and other misleading sources. The piece refers to the skit's being part of the 29th annual
Calamity Jane Days.

227. "Forty-Five Years Ago." *Ekalaka* (Mont.) *Eagle*, 4 October 2002.

The Ekalaka newspaper refers to both the Stewart Holbrook essay, "A Lively
Lady Was Calamity Jane" (210) and a letter to the *Portland Oregonian* editor by J. R. Harmon, a former resident of Ekalaka (212). The son of Captain
William Harmon, who owned the 22 Ranch near Ekalaka where Calamity
resided briefly, J. R. recalled Calamity as a sturdy, unorthodox woman. After
nearly a half century, J. R. misremembered Calamity's husband as "Jack"
rather than Clinton, Burke, and the year as 1896 rather than 1894–95.

228. Kershover, Jim. "Calamity Jane: Part Cheers, Mostly Booze." (Spokane,
Wash.) *Spokesman Review*, 26 February 2006.

This retrospective piece relies almost entirely on a 6 August 1903 story in
the *Spokane* (Wash.) *Post* about Calamity's brief stay in Spokane in 1884.
The author also draws on McLaird's superb biography of Calamity (290) to
provide substantiation and evaluations about widely circulated information
concerning Calamity's character and actions. A well-written overview of
little-known incidents in Calamity's life.

Books and Pamphlets

This section contains books on Calamity herself and on the western context in which she lived, listed alphabetically by author. On occasion, I cite specific chapters of particular relevance. There are also a few unpublished dissertations and theses. Numbers in parentheses cross-reference other entries in this guide.

229. Abbott, E. C. ("Teddy Blue"), and Helena Huntington Smith. *We Pointed Them North: Recollections of a Cowpuncher*. Norman: University of Oklahoma Press, 1954. Originally published 1939.

Although Teddy Blue's brief memories of Calamity are rife with errors, they also overflow with poignant observations. Blue mistakenly recalls meeting Calamity in 1907 (four years after her death), but he also remembers borrowing money from her and attempting to pay it back, an act Calamity casually dismissed. Most revealing of all, Blue asks Calamity how the East treated her when she went there to take part in the Pan-American Exposition, and to be "reformed and civilized." Calamity retorts, the cowboy recalls, "Blue, why don't the sons of bitches leave me alone and let me go to hell my own route" (p. 76)? Blue and Calamity were photographed together in the late 1890s in Utica or Gilt Edge, Montana (527–28).

230. Aikman, Duncan. *Calamity Jane and the Lady Wildcats*. New York: Henry Holt. 1927. Reprint, Lincoln: University of Nebraska Press, 1987.

This book, with 125 of its 350 pages devoted to Calamity Jane, was the first extended story of her. In addition to Calamity, Aikman furnishes other chapters on "wildcats" such as Cattle Kate, Belle Starr, Lola Montez, and Pearl Hart.

Regrettably, the accounts of Calamity and the other women of the Old
West are a curious mish-mash of unique facts and outrageous imagined or
incorrect assertions. This imbalance is particularly true of the opening and
longest section on Calamity. The most valuable of Aikman's findings are the
interviews he conducted in the 1920s with persons who had known Calamity, especially individuals in Princeton, Missouri. These interviews provided
information no other early biographer discovered. Aikman was also the first
to uncover land and other legal records disclosing important information
about the Canary families in Mercer County, Missouri (36, 38). Conversely,
Aikman imagined other scenes so outrageously as to make a creative nonfic-
tionist blush. The conclusions based on the interviews, and particularly Aikman's conjured-up scenes, must be used with caution or abandoned entirely.

The major limitation of Aikman's book is that well more than half of its
pages—perhaps as much as 70 to 80 percent—are filled with the author's
gushy, vernacular contrived scenes rather than hard facts about Calamity.
Clearly, the author's limited, hit-and-run research kept him from turning up
much more than the few informal interviews and newspaper clippings he
revealed. Aikman is also guilty of dozens of small and large errors. Plus, the
coverage after the 1870s is skimpy and bereft of detail.

231. Ames, John. *The Real Deadwood: True Life Histories of Wild Bill Hickok,
     Calamity Jane, Outlaw Towns, and Other Characters of the Lawless West.*
     New York: Chamberlain Bros., 2004.

This collection of essays, written for a popular audience and probably building on the widespread following of the HBO series *Deadwood* and certainly
on Wild West fascination, is a disappointing source on Calamity. The author
has done minimal research (his list of further readings contains no major
works on Calamity) and repeatedly shies away from making statements on
facts that other stronger writers had substantiated by 2004. He seems not to
have read Sollid (326) or any of the major essays by McLaird (373–78). The
chapter "Deadwood's Cussin' Angel: Calamity Jane" (pp. 126–38) is deriva-
tive, error-ridden, and evasive. The author claims Calamity was born in 1852
but more likely 1847 (the actual date was 1856), was "nearly six feet tall," and
was the West's "greatest bullshit artist ever." The following section on Wild
Bill Hickok (pp. 139–51) is even less valuable. Not a source to be trusted.

232. Baker, D. F., as told by Bill Walker. *The Longest Rope: The Truth about the
     Johnson County War.* Caldwell, Idaho: Caxton Printers, 1940.

Walker's tale includes incorrect details, but also adds what he claims are firsthand observations. He met Calamity fairly late in her life. "She wasn't bad looking," he says, "but she always dressed like a tramp" (p. 200). Walker adds that Calamity was pointed in the wrong direction early on, when an "old wren . . . got hold of her . . . [and] taught the kid [Martha Canary] everything she shouldn't know" (p. 200). Others have told similar stories of wrongful early influences, but no one names this bad woman.

233. Bankson, Russell A. *The Klondike Nugget*. Caldwell, Idaho: Caxton Printers, 1935.

Bankson, a Spokane journalist, adds a small bit of evidence to substantiate that Calamity was indeed in the Klondike in 1898. He cites a June 1898 news item that places Calamity in Dawson (142). Yet the off-kilter account states, wrongly, that "on more than one occasion she [Calamity] has been forced to take human life in defense of her own" (p. 151). No evidence exists that Calamity killed anyone. The reporter is also off base in calling Calamity "one of Wells-Fargo's most trusted detectives" (p. 151). She never worked for that company.

234. Bennett, Estelline. *Old Deadwood Days*. Lincoln: University of Nebraska Press, 1982. Originally published 1928.

This is a valuable memoir/history of Deadwood from a girl who grew to womanhood in the early years of Deadwood's history and knew Calamity firsthand. Bennett, the daughter of a federal judge in Dakota Territory, was in Deadwood when Calamity returned in 1895, intending to find employment and enroll her daughter Jessie (then about eight) in an area school. The author describes Calamity as shabbily dressed and showing clear signs of a hard life; but, overall, the portrait is sympathetic to Calamity, then nearly forty years of age.

Bennett, writing in the 1920s, also speaks of Calamity's historic role in the shaping of Deadwood in 1875–77, drawing on the memories of her father and uncle, who were there during parts of those years. The author links those stories with her personal observations of Calamity in 1895, and then provocatively shows how Calamity revisits a Deadwood a generation removed from its swaddling-clothes days of lawlessness, frenzy, and chaos. Deadwood has moved on, but Calamity still represents the inchoate, older days. As Bennett puts it, "Calamity Jane came back to Deadwood after her name had become a tradition" (p. 217).

Bennett's twenty-five-page chapter entitled "When Calamity Jane Came Home" is most useful for the disparity it demonstrates between Calamity's Old West Deadwood and the newer, more capitalized and socially stratified Deadwood. Indeed, the author mixes up the chronology of Calamity's life and gets facts wrong (occurrences in Calamity's early life, the exact events of 1875–76, and the date of Calamity's death), but her contention that Calamity's return to Deadwood showed her to be "an anachronism, a bit of an alien even in her old haunts" (p. 242) is dead center.

235. Briggs, Harold E. *Frontiers of the Northwest: A History of the Upper Missouri Valley.* New York: D. Appleton-Century, 1940; see, esp., "The Calamity Jane Myth," pp. 75–82.

Briggs, a historian, is explicitly negative in "The Calamity Jane Myth." He uses Calamity's undependable autobiography (241) both to trace and to discredit her account of her life in the northern West. Mostly, the author suggests that Calamity cannot be trusted as a source on her own life. He dismisses the possibility of Calamity's having served as an army scout but does not deal with her as ranch worker, entrepreneur, or laundress. The chronology of Calamity's roles as dancer, entertainer, and traveling performer is out of whack, and nothing is said about Calamity as a possible prostitute.

Briggs is more valuable when he speaks of how frontier exaggerators— Calamity clearly among them—transformed her into a romantic heroine, which she was not. Most of the author's quotes are decidedly critical and dark.

236. Brown, Larry K. *The Hog Ranches of Wyoming: Liquor, Lust, and Lies under the Sagebrush Skies.* Glendo, Wyo.: High Plains Press, 1995.

Brown's study of Wyoming hog ranches (rural houses of prostitution) details the shadowy lives of residents of and visitors to these controversial institutions. Rumors from several sources place Calamity Jane in one or two of these infamous places early in her life. Brown says she "plied her trade" (p. 32) at the Six-Mile Hog Ranch, six miles southwest of Fort Laramie. He does not mention her possible connection with the Three-Mile Ranch, halfway to the fort.

237. Brown, Mark H. *The Plainsmen of the Yellowstone: A History of the Yellowstone Basin.* Lincoln: University of Nebraska Press, 1969. Originally published 1961.

Brown deals mainly with Calamity's activities in Montana as the Northern Pacific pushed through the region in the early 1880s. He describes Calamity as a "kind hearted, amoral woman." For Brown, most writings about her were "sentimental nonsense" and a large part of the "exciting adventures" "in her autobiography are impossibilities" (p. 350). She was certainly a bullwhacker but also "a chronic alcoholic, frequently an inmate of hook shops, and often disorderly to the point of being obnoxious—when in her cups" (p. 350). Brown then cites several significant newspaper accounts from the Livingston and Billings areas, depicting Calamity's life and rambunctious actions in the early 1880s.

238. Brown, Mark H., and W. R. Felton. *The Frontier Years: L. A. Huffman, Photographer of the Plains*. New York: Bramhall House, 1955.

The brief account of Calamity (pp. 146–48, 246) in a book on the noted western photographer L. A. Huffman provides a predominantly negative portrait of her. The authors quote the well-known Black Hills poet and frontier writer Badger Clark, who bluntly states that Calamity was a "shabby old lady with nothing romantic about her. She had no sexual morals, was a reckless and heavy drinker, and she undoubtedly was a cheerful liar when it came to her own life and exploits" (p. 146). The authors are "doubtful," too, that "Calamity ever had any of the hair-raising adventures which legend attributes to her" (p. 147). They do admit, however, following Estelline Bennett (234), that Calamity had a big heart for the needy. They likewise accept that she may have traveled with General Crook's troops. The authors reprint the famous Huffman photo, "Only and Original 'Calamity Jane.' Taken in 1880" (519). That photo was probably taken about 1882, when Calamity was indeed in Miles City, and not before.

239. Brown, Thomas Henderson. *The Romance of Everyday Life*. Mitchell, S.Dak.: Educator Supply, 1923.

Brown, first a miner and then a businessman in South Dakota, devotes a chapter (pp. 41–45) to Calamity Jane. Too bad that Brown's interesting comments are done in by mistakes. He estimates her age at twenty to twenty-two in 1865 in Montana, when she was actually nine to eleven. Then Brown tells a story of her pulling her guns and robbing a store to help sick miners. Was he perhaps confusing Calamity with her mother, Charlotte, who was in her mid-twenties then? Later, when the author encounters Calamity at a dime museum performance in Chicago in the late 1890s or 1900, he thinks of her as "now nearly 60 years of age, athletic and well preserved" (p. 43). She was actually in her early forties. Brown also creates conversations with Calamity concerning her days in Montana and on the road. Calamity, in Brown's opinion, had "no blushes, real or painted, but she was not a disgrace to her sex" (p. 43). Errors and intriguing insights jostle one another in this source.

240. Brownlee, Claudia J. *Colonel Joe, the Last of the Rough Riders.* Hicksville, N.Y.: Exposition Press, 1978.

The brief section on Calamity (pp. 77–80) describes Colonel Joe's memories of her in Montana. He met her in the small towns of Kendall, Gilt Edge, Harlowton, and White Sulphur Springs. The reminiscences state Calamity had a sweetheart in Gilt Edge (Robert Dorsett?) and that the couple would ride out on high, huge horses for their lively "doin's." The colonel is convinced that Calamity, although "not exactly of a prudish nature," "was not a sportin' gal . . . [or] a professional [prostitute]" (p. 79). There are interesting bits here about Calamity's dress, riding, and high jinx.

241. [Canary, Martha]. *Life and Adventures of Calamity Jane by Herself.* N.p. [1896].

This seven-page pamphlet was probably prepared to serve as a publicity and sales item for Calamity's tour with the Kohl and Middleton group in 1896. Since Calamity was illiterate, she must have had a good deal of help in producing this come-on. After the tour, Calamity continued to sell the pamphlet up until her death in 1903.

The autobiography mixes valuable facts and outrageous falsehoods. The important details include information about her birth in Princeton, Missouri, the six Canary children, the trip to Montana and death of her parents, and her early years in Utah and Wyoming. Also helpful are mentions of her whereabouts in South Dakota, Wyoming, and Montana.

Conversely, there are numerous overstatements. Despite what Calamity claims, she never served with General Custer, was probably not a hired scout, did not apprehend Wild Bill's assassin, and did not rescue a stage after John Slaughter was killed. She likely did give birth to a daughter on 28 October 1887, as she relates, but the father of the child was probably William Steers (not mentioned) rather than "Mr. Clinton Burk."

Generally, the dramatic—even sensational—parts of Calamity's career are overemphasized. Understandably so, since she was trying to sell the pamphlet at touring museum shows, where Calamity was billed as *The* Wild West woman. Not surprisingly, no hints of Calamity's problems with alcoholism, likely prostitution, or other "husbands" are given here.

242. Casey, Robert J. *The Black Hills and Their Incredible Characters.* Indianapolis: Bobbs-Merrill, 1949; see, esp., "Lady in Buckskin Pants," pp. 175–83.

Casey devoted one chapter to Calamity, but several errors limit its value. He has Calamity born in 1850, married to a George White at age sixteen in 1866, and living for some time in Hays City, Kansas—all mistaken assumptions. Casey is also over the top in stating Calamity appeared in sixty-four Deadwood Dick books, instead of about half that number. The discussions of the Calamity–Wild Bill relations are also shaky and indecisive. These flaws lessen the importance of Casey's otherwise rather balanced treatment of Calamity.

243. Clairmonte, Glenn. *Calamity Was the Name for Jane.* Denver: Sage Books, 1959.

This is not the worst biography ever written, as one disgruntled critic claimed. Still, it is a disappointing life story for any serious student of Calamity Jane. As Duncan Aikman did in his early book *Calamity Jane and the Lady Wildcats* (230), Clairmonte invents scenes, conversations, and characterizations throughout her book with scant proof for many of these imaginings. This work is obviously creative nonfiction, more biographical novel than biography.

Even more detrimental, Clairmonte enthusiastically embraced the Jean Hickok McCormick story and thus had to create incidents to fit those tall tales of Wild Bill and Calamity bedding down and producing a baby girl. More than half of the 215-page biography is distorted in order to narrate Calamity's life after age eighteen according to the false McCormick yarn. In her desire to understand Calamity, Clairmonte creates a contrived, imagined world at odds with facts; she is driven to do so in order to embrace a desired mother-daughter story that never existed.

In another equally outrageous, whole-cloth invention the author places Calamity's young brother Elijah (Lige) among the dead and mutilated soldiers at Custer's Last Stand in June 1876. To complete this totally false sub-story, Clairmonte sends Calamity to the battlefield to locate the decapitated Lige. None of this is true; there is no basis for any of it. Lige did not fight with Custer, and he was not killed there. Indeed, two to three decades later he was imprisoned for illegal actions in Wyoming and Idaho (48, 50).

Reluctantly, one must warn readers away from this book. Errors of fact and imagined events and people—both enemies of acceptable biography and history—lurk here.

244. Cloud, Barbara. *The Business of Newspapers on the Western Frontier*. Reno: University of Nevada Press, 1992.

This well-researched and clearly written study of frontier newspapers supplies important cultural, social, and economic backgrounds for understanding the western journalists who were the first to write accounts of Calamity Jane from 1875 forward. A professor of journalism at the University of Nevada, Las Vegas, Cloud covers important topics, such as newspaper markets, income sources, advertising, and circulation, among others. Her discussions of "pressures on the presses," including what approaches journalists used on readers, how they wrote lively if not controversial stories, and in what ways they hyped people and happenings—all were and are important for understanding the sensational stories about Calamity that circulated widely in the final thirty years of her life. Although a major goal of many frontier newspapers was to "obliterate the frontier"—that is, to civilize it— readers and reporters alike were fascinated with Calamity and wrote nonstop about her unorthodox behavior.

245. Clowser, Don C. *Deadwood . . . The Historical City*. Deadwood, S.Dak.: Fenwyn Press Books, 1969.

This eighty-page booklet contains chapters on the "Deadwood Gold Rush," "Wild Bill Hickok," "Guns of Wild Bill," "Calamity Jane," and "The Life and Adventures of Calamity Jane." The sections on Calamity are very brief, with the final part adding three pages alongside her reprinted autobiography of 1896 (241). Much of the biographical section, which contains numerous errors, is headlined "as remembered by Percy Russell," an old-timer in the Deadwood area. Discussion of the pre-Deadwood years is particularly unreliable. Disappointing source.

246. *Copies of Calamity Jane's Diary and Letters*. N.p.: Don A. and Stella A. Foote, 1951.

These are the diary and letters that Jean Hickok McCormick (who claimed she was the daughter of Calamity and Wild Bill) asserted were Calamity's writings. Don and Stella Foote, who hired Mrs. McCormick to work in their Wonderland park in Billings, Montana, purchased the diary and letters and began publishing parts of the purported Calamity documents in 1951. Over the years, perhaps as many as 100,000 copies, or more, of this small-sized, red-cover pamphlet of twenty-six pages may have been sold. Expanded versions of the documents appeared earlier in Nolie Mumey (302) and later Stella Foote (265), and in Great Britain were published, with an introduction by Bryony Lavery, as *The Letters of Calamity Jane to Her Daughter* (Hounslow: Battle Axe Books, 1984).

This publication appeared nearly ten years after Jean McCormick made her startling announcement about her parentage and birth. The McCormick falsehoods and the publication of this little booklet of forgeries threw stories about Calamity off-course for the next two or three decades. Many serious and popular biographers alike bought the false account, probably because it provided a much-cherished mother-daughter story and pretended to reveal Calamity's inner life. Smitten by what seemed a breakthrough in understanding Calamity, biographers accepted the invented yarn before carefully scrutinizing its credibility. Not until James McLaird's (376) point-by-point study of McCormick's falsehoods reduced them to fraud did the contrived subterfuge fade in popularity. But, for those who have failed to consult McLaird's work, the McCormick story remains an inviting but unreliable story.

247. Crawford, Lewis F. *The Exploits of Ben Arnold: Indian Fighter, Gold Miner, Cowboy, Hunter, and Army Scout.* Foreword by Paul L. Hedren. Norman: University of Oklahoma Press, 1999. Originally titled *Rekindling Camp Fires*, 1926.

Arnold, who crisscrossed the West in the late nineteenth century, encountered Calamity in North Dakota, but he may also have met her earlier in Virginia City, Montana, in the mid-1860s. The author mixes up details: he names her Calamity Jane Somers from Princeton and says her mother died in Blackfoot, Idaho, and her father in Piedmont, Wyoming. Yet Crawford's rendering of Arnold's two-sentence description of Calamity comes close: she "was a strange mixture of the wild and the wayward, the generous and unselfish. . . . She never posed; her personality was her own" (p. 273).

248. Crutchfield, James A., Bill O'Neal, and Dale L. Walker. *Legends of the Wild West.* Lincolnwood, Ill.: Publications International, 1995; see, esp., "Calamity Jane," pp. 124–27.

When a brief chapter opens with a fallacious statement   "Calamity Jane
was born Martha Jane Cannary in 1844, according to the census of 1860"
(p. 124)—one immediately wonders about the veracity of what follows. In the
next paragraph errors pop up one after another. Perhaps not surprisingly,
the authors mix up the content of Calamity's autobiography of 1896 with the
spurious Calamity diary that Jean Hickok McCormick (265, 302) foisted on
the public a half century later. Calamity did not claim to have married Wild
Bill in her 1896 autobiography, for example. Disappointing.

249. Cullen, Thomas P., comp. *Rock Springs—A Look Back.* Portland, Ore.:
Thomas P. Cullen, 1991.

This rather amateurish collection of oral histories and reminiscences
includes "Calamity Jane in Rock Springs," by Effice Widdop (103–105) and
other remembrances by other authors. Widdop reports that Calamity rarely
associated with women; instead, she was seen with men "riding buck-
ing horses, [participating in] horse races, [and] target shooting." While in
Rock Springs, Wyoming, she lived in a dugout "on what is now M. street"
(p. 104). She was always dressed as a man but also helped "the poorer class
of people, giving liberally of money and accepting no thanks" (p. 105). She
harmed no one, but "was her own worst enemy" (p. 105). Another pioneer, a
Mr. Dankowski, recalled that Calamity, while living in Rock Springs, visited
a saloon in nearby Green River. When the bartender failed to pay quick
attention to her wants, "she proceeded to throw things about and give the
bartender a piece of her mind."

250. Dary, David. *Red Blood and Black Ink: Journalism in the Old West.* New
York: Alfred A. Knopf, 1998.

Dary, a former journalist and later a professor of journalism, supplies a
first-rate history of frontier journalism. His lively study helps historians
and biographers understand the sociocultural contexts of reporters and
newspaper editors who did so much to bring Calamity Jane onto regional
and national stages in the 1870s and 1880s. An excellent source on frontier
newspapers.

251. DeBarthe, Joe. *Life and Adventures of Frank Grouard.* Edited by Edgar I.
Stewart. Norman: University of Oklahoma Press, 1958.

This source lists Calamity among the persons Grouard hired to scout for
General Crook in 1876 on his march into the Black Hills. No one else has

provided solid evidence for this assertion. In fact, editor Stewart doubts Grouard's contention, as he states in an editorial footnote: "This is somewhat doubtful because she [Calamity] had been sent back earlier, and when she arrived in camp at a later date, she was immediately placed under arrest" (p. 147). The book is, however, a good source on Crook's movements in 1876.

252. Dee, D. [Dora Du Fran, pseud.]. *Low Down on Calamity Jane*. Edited by Helen Rezatto. Stickney, S.Dak.: Argus Printers, 1981. Originally published 1932.

Dora Du Fran, a widely recognized brothel madam in South Dakota, writes here as D. Dee. Her account provides helpful personal information, but her recitation of other so-called facts is not to be followed. Du Fran says of Calamity: "This ignorant, uneducated, untamed, unmoral, iron-hearted woman, who had been thrown among unfit associates from babyhood, played the part of a ministering angel in the life of the frontier" (p. 3). The two women first met in 1886, Du Fran writes, and again later in the last year of Calamity's life. Calamity worked as a cook in Du Fran's "joy palace," in Belle Fourche, but Dora calls her place, instead, "a dance hall and boarding house" (p. 10). After a few weeks of excellent work, Calamity went on a blow-out, and ran drunk and howling up the street like a wild coyote.

Too many of the author's other statements are clearly wrong. Du Fran mistakenly follows the Jane Dalton origins story of Martha Canary near Fort Laramie. She misdates Crook's battles with Indians, misspells Wild Bill's name "Hicock," and misplaces Calamity in Chicago in 1893. The 1981 reprint includes additional photographs and a valuable introduction by Helen Rezatto.

253. Dolph, Jerry, and Arthur Randall. *Wyatt Earp and Coeur d'Alene Gold!: Stampede to Idaho Territory*. 2nd ed. Post Falls, Idaho: Eagle City Publications, 2000. Originally published 1999.

The two authors incorporate considerable detail about Calamity's trip to the Coeur d'Alene boomtowns of Idaho in 1884, and a bit of information on stops in Spokane Falls in 1883 and 1884. Unfortunately, the writers' sources are not clear, and several of their discussions contain suspect if not bogus information. For example: "Everyone [in Spokane] knew that she had killed men in open duels (gunfights) before and nobody evinced the desire to be next. She shot her last husband's arm off in a duel the two had to decide which of them should be leader of the family" (p. 102). All nonsense.

The authors provide several descriptions, again without citing specific sources, of Calamity's meetings with Maggie Burdon (Molly b'Damn), the notoriously pretty and articulate prostitute of the mining camps, and Calamity's famous dance with eight recruited dancers from Spokane in a jerry-built barroom/dance hall in February 1884. Dolph and Randall overlook Calamity's return to Eagle City the next month. Interesting tidbits on brief, revealing Calamity ventures, but suspect in research and conclusions.

254. Drago, Harry Sinclair. *Notorious Ladies of the Frontier*. New York: Dodd, Mead, 1969.

A widely recognized author of popular western history, Drago undertakes here a collection of biographical vignettes of lively ladies of the Old West. His profile of Calamity appears alongside portraits of Lola Montez, Cattle Kate, Baby Doe Tabor, and several others. Regrettably, his chapter entitled "Calamity Jane in Fact and Fiction" (pp. 208–22), mixes fact and fiction. He rightly discounts the false story of Jean Hickok McCormick, but wrongly asserts that Calamity legally married Clinton Burke, a one-legged man with a ten-year-old daughter, on 25 September 1891. All incorrect claims. Dozens of mistakes follow, and Drago provides very little information about Calamity after 1878. Not a valuable source.

255. Du Fran, Dora. *See* Dee, D. (252).

256. Etulain, Richard W. *Beyond the Missouri: The Story of the American West*. Albuquerque: University of New Mexico Press, 2006.

This overview of western history furnishes considerable context for the Calamity Jane story. Chapter 8 explains the struggles and conflicts that led to difficult circumstances for women like Calamity in the late nineteenth century. Chapter 10 adds information on how dime novels and other writings promoted exaggerated and romantic yarns about Calamity from the 1870s forward.

257. Etulain, Richard W. *The Life and Legends of Calamity Jane*. Norman: University of Oklahoma Press, 2014.

Except for McLaird's definitive biography of Calamity (290), this is the most thorough life story of the subject. Like all volumes in the Oklahoma Western Biographies series, the book does not carry footnotes, although the author provides a thorough listing of his sources and has deposited fully footnoted copies in the Montana and South Dakota Historical Societies (21, 23). The work is based on thorough research in all major sources: newspapers, manuscript collections, and published books and essays.

Although the author deals with all the major controversies of Calamity's life, unlike McLaird, he does not provide extensive discussion of the competing interpretations of those controversies. Rather, this account follows the one or two interpretations of these questions that the biographer considers the most defensible. He does not, for example, label Calamity a prostitute because irrefutable evidence that she sold sex is lacking.

The sections discussing the treatments of Calamity by journalists, historians and biographers, novelists, and moviemakers are particularly extensive. Even before her death in 1903, Calamity had become a legend in her own time. The major legends about her were three: (1) a Wild Woman of the Old West; (2) a Florence Nightingale–like Angel of Mercy helping the sick and needy; and (3) a Pioneer Woman hoping to marry, become a mother, and establish a stable home. The first legend was established, particularly, in newspaper articles and in the Deadwood Dick dime novel series of the 1870s and 1880s (404–37), the second in the writings of frontier journalists, and the third in interviews with Calamity and other writings about her before her death.

The final four chapters divide the interpretations of Calamity into four periods: up to 1930, 1930 to 1960, 1960 to 1990, and 1990 to the present. The author stresses the historical accuracy—or inaccuracies—of histories and biographies, novels, and films. He also deals extensively with Calamity's "husbands"; Calamity's daughter, Jessie; and the false claims of Jean Hickok McCormick that she was the daughter of Calamity and Wild Bill Hickok. The writer also points out how a New Gray Calamity emerged in the 1960s and afterward, following the revisionist interpretations of U.S. and western American history during those years.

258. Etulain, Richard W. *Re-imagining the Modern American West: A Century of Fiction, History, and Art.* Tucson: University of Arizona Press, 1996.

The author examines the fictional, historical, and artistic treatments of the American West from the mid-nineteenth to the end of the twentieth centuries. Although this book contains little on Calamity Jane, it treats the dime novelists, regionalists, and post-regionalists who did write about Calamity. The volume includes commentary on writers Henry Nash Smith, Mari

Sandoz, and Larry McMurtry, who have written about Calamity, and on Old West figures such as Buffalo Bill Cody, Billy the Kid, General Custer, and Wild Bill Hickok.

259. Etulain, Richard W. *Telling Western Stories: From Buffalo Bill to Larry McMurtry*. Albuquerque: University of New Mexico Press, 1999, see, esp., pp. 41–51, 148, 149.

In this brief overview of western storytelling, Etulain uses, in one chapter, the life and legends of Calamity Jane to illustrate what he calls the "Untold Stories" of the American West. The author argues that the blizzard of Wild West stories stretching from the dime novels through the early Westerns of Owen Wister and Zane Grey overlooked or misshaped stories of a more domestic and feminine West, as told by Mary Hallock Foote, and stories about female characters such as Calamity Jane. In Calamity's case, she was transformed into "one of the boys" in the earliest newspaper stories and dime novels, which too often forced her into the image of a mannish woman without feminine desires or dreams. Calamity's identity as a pioneer woman was smothered or even lost in the powerful fictive needs of the hundreds of masculine adventure stories written in the generations before and after 1900.

260. Faber, Doris. *Calamity Jane: Her Life and Her Legend*. Boston: Houghton Mifflin, 1992.

This well-written and handsomely packaged biography of sixty-two pages is intended primarily for "young readers." Faber, the author of nearly fifty volumes, attempts "to write a dual biography: the life of the real Martha Jane Cannary [*sic*], and that of the legendary heroine whom she became, Calamity Jane" (back flap).

   For the most part a realistic account that includes Calamity's rough and uncouth behavior, the polished narrative combines good facts, unnecessary errors (following the Jean Hickok McCormick distortions [246]), and mistaken claims (e.g., that Calamity served with General George Custer). The author admits to Calamity's nude bathing among the soldiers, her overindulgences with whiskey, and her many "husbands" (including, wrongly, a marriage to Wild Bill). Faber, regrettably, gets the details of Calamity's travels as a Wild West show woman all mixed up. Still, despite the miscues, this is a significant work on Calamity for young adult audiences.

261. Fellman, Michael. *Inside War: The Guerrilla Conflict in Missouri during the American Civil War*. New York: Oxford University Press, 1989.

The most informative book on ordinary Missourians under the extraordinary stresses of the Civil War, Fellman's volume spotlights what people like Martha Canary's family might have felt in such uncertain times. No one has yet proven that Martha's family left Missouri because of Civil War conflicts, but bits and pieces of evidence reveal that some members of the family—including Martha's mother, Charlotte, and her uncle James T. Canary—may have had strong inclinations toward the South and the Confederacy that their pro-Northern Missouri neighbors did not share. A notable examination of Missouri in the early 1860s.

262. Fielder, Mildred. *Silver Is the Fortune*. Aberdeen, S.Dak.: North Plains Press, 1978.

The author relates the story of Calamity's wanting to bury a dog killed on the streets of Deadwood. Men paid no attention to her request. But when Fred Borsch buried the dog for her, she paid him five dollars. He remembered the happening not so much for Calamity's actions as that this was his first five-dollar gold piece.

263. Fisher, Vardis, and Opal Laurel Holmes. *Gold Rushes and Mining Camps of the Early American West*. Caldwell, Idaho: Caxton Printers, 1990.

Idaho novelist and historian Vardis Fisher and his wife, Opal Laurel Holmes, devote much of a chapter entitled "Camp Angels" in their oversize, richly illustrated book to Calamity. The authors move through much of the important writing on Calamity (following and often quoting Sollid [326] especially), pointing out obvious errors and exaggerations, countering unproven statements (that Calamity was often a "whore"), and embracing the ambiguities of most of Calamity's complex stories. Fisher and Holmes are also adamant in their praise of Calamity as a nursemaid of sick miners, pest-ridden sojourners, and poor and needy frontier families. In these kind and helpful actions, the authors argue, Calamity served as a "camp angel."

264. Flannery, L. G. ("Pat"), ed. *John Hunton's Diary*. 6 vols. Vols. 1–5, Lingle, Wyo.: Guide- Review, 1956–64; vol. 6. Glendale, Calif.: Arthur H. Clark, 1970.

The entries and comments in the six-volume diaries of tradesman and road ranch operator John Hunton provide valuable information on the northern plains, events of the 1870s and 1880s, and Calamity. Hunton, situated on the Cheyenne-Deadwood stage route, knew Calamity firsthand and did not like her. His unvarnished comments are realistic, uncomplimentary, and mostly factually correct. In "My Recollections of Calamity Jane" (vol. 2, pp. 109–10), Hunton places Martha (later Calamity) at the E. Coffey and Cuny post, close to Fort Laramie. She had come as one of the "sporting girls" and "was among the commonest of her class." Writers that Hunton read had "greatly magnified . . . her achievements." He probably saw her first in 1875 when she was with the Newton-Jenney Expedition (335).

In a later section of volume 2, "Wild Bill and Calamity Jane" (pp. 115–16), Hunton mixes up the details of the Wild Bill–Calamity connection on the way to Deadwood. Hunton also states that "at the time of [Wild] Bill's death Jane was in the hands of the military authorities" (p. 116). What he means by the latter comment is not clear. Still later, in sections of volume 6—"The Return of Calamity Jane" (pp. 178–81) and "Calamity Jane Back Again" (pp. 199–200)—editor Flannery adds other information about Calamity from newspapers and letters.

265. Foote, Stella. *A History of Calamity Jane: Our Country's First Liberated Woman*. New York: Vantage Press, 1995.

Stella Foote was a supporter of and a believer in the stories of Jean Hickok McCormick. Here she draws extensively from the diary and letters that McCormick claimed Calamity Jane authored (and which Foote and her husband had purchased). When Professor James McLaird proved those documents to be frauds (376), then the value of this volume crumbled. Sadly, Foote undermines the value of her other research by larding her narrative with information and quotations from the false McCormick documents.

Foote's research is spotty. She reprints important land records of the Canary family in Princeton but overlooks census records and thus does not know the best source for documenting that Calamity was born in Princeton, Missouri, in 1856. In addition, the author's treatment of the Princeton years is too often a very close paraphrasing of Duncan Aikman's shaky account (230).

Much of Foote's narrative consists of long block quotations from newspaper accounts and published books and essays. Also, the narrative is jumbled chronologically and rent with authorial intrusions. Worse are such inaccurate statements as, "Only six books were written about Calamity before 1900 and these included two dime novels." Thirty-three dime novels alone appeared in the Edward L. Wheeler Deadwood Dick series, most of which featured Calamity as a lead or major supporting heroine (404–37).

Foote obviously did due diligence as an amateur researcher, but the publisher and editors of this volume failed to supply the author with needed editorial guidance. Also, the author's unacceptable reliance on counterfeit sources doomed her book from the beginning.

266. Frackelton, Will. *Sagebrush Dentist*. Ed. Herman Gastrell Seely. Chicago: A. C. McClurg, 1941; see, esp., pp. 123–27.

Frackelton provides a thoughtful, balanced, but very brief portrait of Calamity and her visit (probably in 1896) to his dentist's office. Residents of Sheridan, Wyoming, warned him about her tirades and profanity, but he found her talkative, restless, and willing to pay for his work. He said she had "lived with a man named Frank King on a ranch on Powder River" (p. 125). One old packer reported that Calamity worked like a man but also was willing to head off into the brush with any willing man. Then, embarrassed by what he had implied about Calamity, the packer told Frackelton to forget his statement: "Jane was a perfect angel sent from heaven when any of the boys was sick and gave them a mother's care till they got well" (p. 125). Reflecting on these conflicting comments concerning Calamity, Frackelton wondered if the rosy notions of "romantic writers and railroad press agents" hadn't overlooked the facts of her life in their rush to circulate sensational stories about her.

267. Freeman, Lewis R. *Down the Yellowstone*. New York: Dodd, Mead, 1922. See 362.

268. Furlong, Leslie Anne. "Gold Dust and Buckskins: An Analysis of Calamity Jane as a Symbol of Luck and Womanhood in the Black Hills." Ph.D. diss., University of Virginia, 1991.

This six-hundred-page study, the only doctoral dissertation completed on Calamity Jane, examines economic and gender-related cultural values in Deadwood from 1876 to 1903. Theoretical in nature and heavily loaded with academic jargon and analytical-evaluative comments, the dissertation carefully examines the changing newspaper coverage of Calamity during her lifetime and the transformations in her reputation after her death. The author is convinced that complex and shifting attitudes toward womanhood, gender roles, and respectability led to the often-twisting, kaleidoscopic interpretations of Calamity. For example, when the early "luck economy" of Deadwood moved "toward an emphasis on permanence, respectability, and the market economy" (p. 23), the earlier, relatively favorable attitudes toward Calamity shifted into less accepting ones. Strangely, the author is less interested in examining the authenticity of the sources she utilizes than in the shifting images of Calamity they reveal. The study is based almost entirely on newspapers and other published sources, with few or no references to documentary materials such as census, marriage, and birth records or manuscripts.

269. Hickok, Martha Jane Cannary. *Calamity Jane's Letters to Her Daughter.* Berkeley, Calif.: Shameless Hussy Press, 1976.

This booklet reprints essentially the same contents, the Jean Hickok McCormick materials, which appeared in Mumey (302) and in *Copies of Calamity Jane's Diary and Letters* (246). But this edition does not contain the so-called confession Calamity ostensibly wrote on 3 June 1903, in which she overturned many of the claims appearing earlier in the diary and letters. This version also includes a one-page introduction by one "alta" that, because of its vague generalizations, must be used with caution.

270. *History of Harrison and Mercer Counties, Missouri. . . .* St. Louis: Goodspeed, 1888. Reprint, Princeton, Mo.: Mercer County Historical Society, 1972.

The second section of this weighty tome, pp. 385–476, furnishes a helpful chronology and description of Mercer County. It provides changing population figures, city and town organizations, and the establishment of schools and churches. The Canary family is not mentioned. A biographical index of Mercer County appears on pp. 661–758.

271. Holbrook, Stewart H. *Little Annie Oakley and Other Rugged People.* New York: Macmillan, 1948.

Holbrook, a well-known journalist-historian, includes an eight-page biographical vignette of Calamity in this collection of twenty-eight sketches. Among other figures profiled are Annie Oakley, outlaw Luke Short, Kit Carson, and several loggers and woodsmen. The author's approach is decidedly popular—and rather superficial. He has not read or studied Calamity extensively (he knows of only two of her twenty-five or so photos) and mixes up her chronology by placing her in Buffalo, New York (1901), before she traveled with the Kohl and Middleton museum group (1896). A very negative and dismissive treatment of Calamity.

272. Holmes, Burton. *Travelogues.* Vol. 12. Chicago: Travelogue Bureau, 1918.

Holmes, a well-known traveler and tourist guide, takes readers of this volume on a tour of Yellowstone National Park, the Grand Canyon, and southwestern Indian villages. While traveling to and from Yellowstone Park, the passengers pass through the small town of Gardiner, near which they meet Calamity standing close to Larry Matthews's "canvas palace" café. Although the text does not mention the fact, Calamity often visited Yellowstone and Gardiner in the late 1890s to sell her photos and pamphlet autobiography. She had a license to sell these items in the park. A unique photograph of Calamity (529), nicely attired in a rather stylish dress, appears on p. 38, next to her familiar photo as a buckskin-clad "scout."

273. Homsher, Lola M., ed. *South Pass, 1868: James Chisholm's Journal of the Wyoming Gold Rush*. Lincoln: University of Nebraska Press, 1975. Originally published 1960.

Chisholm's revealing diary of his 1868 visit to the South Pass and Miner's Delight areas in Wyoming does not refer to Martha Canary. In fact, he says only three women were in Miner's Delight in 1868, and Martha was not one of them. This omission has led some biographers and historians to conclude she must not have been in the area at that time. Perhaps, but other good sources (114, 290) contend she was there, or came a bit later. Excellent for descriptions of terrain, early mining efforts, and life in pioneer, primitive mining camps. Strong editorial apparatus.

274. Hooker, William Francis. *The Bullwhacker*. Ed. Howard R. Driggs. Yonkers-on-Hudson, N.Y.: World Book, 1940.

Hooker's account provides helpful information on the lives and roles of bull-whackers in the transportation systems of the northern frontier West. The author speaks of the group as a hardy, very masculine fraternity of men who often spent their wages in riotous living once they reached a boomtown like Deadwood, with all its beckoning dance halls and saloons. Calamity's clear links with "the guys" in these frontier areas suggests that she would have—and probably did—fit well into this lively coterie of men.

275. Horan, James D. *Desperate Women*. New York: G. P. Putnam's Sons, 1952; see, esp., "Calamity Jane: White Devil of the Yellowstone," pp. 171–200.

In this lively collection of biographical chapters treating "wild women" of the Civil War and Old West years, Horan devotes one extensive chapter to Calamity Jane. His coverage of Calamity's first years relies heavily on Duncan Aikman's (230) exaggerated account and Calamity's suspect autobiography (241). Although Horan doubts many of Calamity's tall tales, he repeats others without having consulted the legal records in Princeton, Mo.; the two U.S.

census reports of 1860 and 1869 listing Martha Canary; and the records of
the Jenney and General Crook marches into the Black Hills in 1875 and 1876.

Horan makes much of the Calamity–Wild Bill story without reaching
any conclusion. And he devotes more attention to Calamity as nursemaid
to the smallpox patients than do most other writers. To his detriment,
Horan relies too heavily on dozens of sensational newspaper stories that
detail Calamity's controversial antics without checking parallel sources that
challenge or counter the journalistic accounts. Plus, the author's chronology
frequently falls into a jumble, and he gets dates wrong. Like so many others,
for example, he alters the date of Calamity's death to make it twenty-seven
years to the day after the demise of Wild Bill.

Horan ends his fact-filled chapter with a discussion of Jean Hickok
McCormick's falsehoods, which first appeared about a decade before
this essay. Horan rightly concludes that the contrived diary "seems highly
improbable," but he hedges by stating "it cannot be flatly labeled spurious"
(p. 199). Fortunately, James D. McLaird provides that necessary proof (376).

276. Hughes, Richard B. *Pioneer Years in the Black Hills.* Ed. Agnes Wright
Spring. Glendale, Calif.: Arthur H. Clark, 1957; 3rd ed. Rapid City, S.Dak.:
Dakota Alpha Press, 2002.

Hughes arrived in Deadwood in 1876, making him a contemporary with
Calamity Jane in the Black Hills. As a reporter, the author kept a daily diary
and put it into book form in the 1920s. Agnes Wright Spring, an authority
on early Deadwood and the Black Hills, edited the typescript for publication in 1957. Hughes's two pages on Calamity describe her dramatic entry
into Deadwood in July 1876, along with Wild Bill, the Utter brothers, and
"Bloody" Dick Seymour. Hughes's descriptions of life in Deadwood, including work patterns, social life, and legal-political actions, are invaluable.

277. Huntington, Bill. *They Were Good Men and Salty Cusses.* Billings, Mont.:
Western Livestock Reporter Press, 1952.

This anecdote-filled narrative includes a description of Calamity when the
author met her in Lander, Wyoming. She and "her man" (unnamed) were
drinking straight whiskey in Coulter's Saloon. "Every time I saw her," Huntington avers, "she acted like a lady and was treated like one." Dressed like a
man, "she was a tall, dark, striking looking woman, not much of a mixer but
tended to her own business" (p. 46).

278. Jennewein, J. Leonard. *Calamity Jane of the Western Trails*. 4th ed., Rapid City, S.Dak.: Dakota West Books, 1991. Originally published 1953.

A professor and journalist, Jennewein collected materials on Calamity Jane for many years and produced a brief, realistic study. He reluctantly decided not to expand his publication beyond this work of about forty pages of text. The author's approach is topical, but he does move chronologically—except for the curious opening section on the controversies surrounding the date of Calamity's death. He also deals with the contentious disagreements about Calamity's birthplace and agrees that Princeton, Missouri, was the most likely site of her birth. Evidently, the author had not traveled to Princeton to look at local manuscript records there or consulted the U.S. census rolls.

Jennewein had strongly negative and dissenting opinions on the McCormick story that she was the daughter of a Wild Bill Hickok–Calamity union and that Calamity had kept a diary and written unknown letters to the daughter (246). The author asserts that "the package is a hoax from start to finish" (p. 29). The good research of Jennewein and his defendable conclusions seem to have markedly influenced his later colleague at Dakota Wesleyan University, James D. McLaird.

279. Johnston, Elsie P., ed. *Laurel's Story: A Montana Heritage*. Laurel, Mont.: Artcraft, 1979.

This collection of materials, a grab-bag town history of Laurel, Montana, includes a brief piece "Calamity Jane" (pp. 43–45), by T. J. Giles. The errors in Giles's essay are primarily in chronology and specific facts; the valuable contributions are the few comments about Calamity's time in the Laurel area. The collection also reprints some of Calamity's spurious diary and letters (pp. 45ff).

280. Jucovy, Linda. *Searching for Calamity: The Life and Times of Calamity*. Philadelphia: Stampede Books, 2012.

There is much to salute in this recent biography of Calamity Jane. Extraordinarily well written, smoothly organized, and encompassing in approach, Jucovy's life story of Calamity is a pleasure to read. It also contains useful maps, helpful explanatory footnotes, and the usual run of important photographs. Unfortunately, however, limitations undermine some of these strengths. Jucovy is too skeptical of previous strong research, including the

best we have on Calamity by James D. McLaird (290). She dissents from his
convincing argument that Calamity was born in 1856, instead standing on
Calamity's false assertion of 1852; dismisses the very important 1896 M. L.
Fox interview in the *Illustrated American* (361); and tosses aside accounts
of Calamity's having been in Spokane, Washington, the Coeur d'Alenes of
Idaho, and Dawson in the Yukon as old men's tales told much later. Had
the author cast her research net much wider and deeper, she would have
discovered that census reports, marriage and birth records, and obscure
newspaper accounts counter her skepticism. In the end, this is a good but
nonetheless flawed source.

281. Kime, Wayne R., ed. *The Black Hills Journals of Colonel Richard Irving
Dodge*. Norman: University of Oklahoma Press, 1996.

These published journals of Colonel Dodge, the most extensive account
of the Newton-Jenney Expedition to the Black Hills in 1875, do not
mention Calamity. Although Dodge reportedly dismissed Calamity from
the expedition once her gender was discovered, he did not write about
her. Editor Kime, however, notes her presence with the expedition in
his introduction, calling her "Jane Dalton, alias Jane or Martha Canary,
better known as Calamity Jane." (p. 21). Later, Kime adds, she was
allowed "to remain [with the expedition], helping about the camp and
proving a valuable member of the party" (p. 22). The editor also identifies A. Guerin as the photographer of the first extant photograph of
Calamity (p. 96).

282. Klock, Irma A. *Here Comes Calamity*. Deadwood, S.Dak.: Dakota Graph-
ics, 1979.

This thirty-two-page pamphlet, including text, photos, and bibliography,
much resembles the Muller pamphlet on Calamity (301). But this work is
more meaty, analytical, and thorough. The author has reviewed much of the
writing about Calamity, including the Jean Hickok McCormick diary and letters, which she comments on without accepting or rejecting. Several familiar
photos of Calamity and other news of scenes and people are included. A
brief bibliography lists about thirty items, but even more helpful is a five- or
six-page timeline, a chronology of Calamity's full life, and mention of the
sources on which these happenings are based. A modest and somewhat
dated source but nonetheless still useful.

283. Lamar, Howard Roberts. *Dakota Territory, 1861–1889: A Study of Frontier Politics.* New Haven, Conn.: Yale University Press, 1966. Originally published 1956.

Although Lamar's excellent volume makes but one fleeting reference to Calamity Jane, it remains the best study of the Dakota territorial politics that surrounded her. The author's thorough, balanced, and insightful examination furnishes important background for understanding political meanings behind the Black Hills, Deadwood, and wider Dakota happenings. A first-rate contextual study of Dakota territorial politics.

284. Lee, Wayne C. *Wild Towns of Nebraska.* Caldwell, Idaho: Caxton Printers, 1988.

Historian-journalist Lee reports Calamity was in Crawford, Nebraska, proximate to Fort Robinson, in the mid-1880s. The author states that Calamity lived in a tent and was in the area to recruit girls for the dance halls and saloons of Deadwood. She was usually successful in her recruitment since "Crawford in its early days was seldom short of this commodity." Here is one of the few sources placing Calamity in western Nebraska. Her time there more likely occurred during the 1870s, however, if she was recruiting women for Deadwood entertainment centers.

285. Livingston Enterprise. *Centennial Scrapbook: A Collection of Stories Celebrating the 100th Anniversary of the Founding of Livingston, Montana.* Livingston, Mont.: Livingston Enterprise, 1982; see, esp., "Notorious Calamity," by Karen Straus, pp. 61–64.

Author Straus attempts to provide a middle-of-the-road portrait of Calamity, balancing wildcat and Florence Nightingale images. Straus shows Calamity's drunkenness and possible prostitution but also her aid for others. Unfortunately, the author's parallel mistakes—several large and small ones—undermine her attempt at a balanced study. Among other miscues, she is mistaken on Calamity's husbands, children, and relationship with Wild Bill Hickok.

286. Maguire, Horatio N. *The Black Hills and American Wonderland: From Personal Exploration. . . .* Chicago: Donnelley, Loyd, 1877.

Maguire's two-paragraph physical and personal description of Calamity (p. 304) caught the attention of writers across the country. Newspapermen and other writers in the northern West, and dime novelist Edward L. Wheeler in the East, were among those who stole ideas and exact words from Maguire for their own writings. Maguire's Calamity, dressed like a young man, sits astride a "fiery horse," and is electric with energy. "Throwing herself from side to side," she goads her steed "up the gulch, over ditches and through reservoirs and mudholes . . . [,] giving as good an imitation of a Sioux war-whoop as a feminine voice is capable of" (p. 304).

Mistaken though many of Maguire's biographical assertions were, they became widely quoted. Calamity did not hail from Virginia City, Nevada, and she did not come from a "family of respectability and intelligence." And she had not begun her cross-dressing in Nevada, nor "rendered good services as a scout in an Indian campaign" (p. 304).

Still, Maguire caught much of Calamity's essence in referring to her "career of ruin, disgrace and recklessness." She would be a woman of independent character who would "stand alone" and not rely on others. Then, there were the ending lines of his paragraphs, primarily stolen from poet Lord Bryon: "She is still in early womanhood, and her rough and dissipated career has not yet altogether 'Swept away the lines where beauty lingers'" (p. 304).

287. Maguire, Horatio N. *The Coming Empire: A Complete and Reliable Treatise on the Black Hills, Yellowstone and Big Horn Regions. . . .* Sioux City, Iowa: Watkins and Smead, 1878; see, esp., pp. 63–65.

Journalist Maguire quotes Calamity as criticizing the press for abusing her. She has been depicted, she says, as a "horse thief," "highwaywoman," "three-card monte sharp," and "minister's daughter." These sharp attacks are false, she says, "the last especially" (p. 64). She admits to having dressed in buckskins, and to serving as a scout and a bullwhacker. After all, she asks, "Has n't a poor woman as a good a right to make a living as a man?" Besides, if she has done anything wrong, society is more to blame than she because she has been starving to death trying "to support herself in a more womanly way" (p. 65).

Maguire includes a wonderfully illuminating illustration of Calamity, mounted, dashing through a challenging western landscape. It is titled "Miss Martha Canary, ('Calamity Jane'), The female Scout" (p. 50). A brief, revealing description of Calamity.

288. McClintock, John S. *Pioneer Days in the Black Hills: Accurate History and Facts Related by One of the Early Day Pioneers.* Foreword by Wayne R. Kime. Norman: University of Oklahoma Press, 2000. Originally published 1939.

McClintock was one of the early Deadwood pioneers, coming in April 1876. He knew all the early arrivals, including Calamity Jane, and lived in Deadwood until his death in 1937. Most observers consider his account as dependable as any of the pioneer memoirs of early Deadwood.

The author devotes a brief chapter to "Calamity Jane" (pp. 115–19), but also scatters comments about her through other sections of his book. Generally, McClintock helpfully evaluates Calamity's autobiography (241), agreeing or disagreeing with its contents and adding other information from written or oral sources. As McClintock puts it, "It is difficult to cull from this mass of fiction the real facts" (p. 115).

McClintock, who was in Montana during the early mineral-rush era, disputes some of the tales told about Martha Canary when she lived there as a girl, about 1864–65. Since McClintock was in Deadwood during the few weeks Wild Bill lived there, he gives his valuable views about Hickok's actions in the summer of 1876 and adds information on the Calamity–Wild Bill relationship. Of Calamity, whom he knew, McClintock says: "She dressed, after her first appearance in Deadwood, as other women dressed, and although she was the last word in slang, obscenity, and profanity, her deportment in the streets, when sober, was not worse than that of others of her class" (p. 118).

McClintock's book is a very helpful source on Calamity and her Deadwood sociocultural and economic contexts. The author also adds useful information on Calamity's longtime "husband" Clinton Burk[e].

289. McGillycuddy, Julia B. *McGillycuddy, Agent: A Biography of Dr. Valentine T. McGillycuddy.* Stanford, Calif.: Stanford University Press, 1941. Reprinted as *Blood on the Moon: Valentine McGillycuddy and the Sioux.* Introduction by James C. Olson. Lincoln: University of Nebraska Press, 1990.

Dr. Valentine T. McGillycuddy wore several different hats on the late-nineteenth-century frontier. He was, by turns, Indian agent, peace negotiator, and medical doctor. He became acquainted with several well-known frontiersmen and women, including Indian leaders Sitting Bull and Red Cloud, Generals George Crook and George Custer, Buffalo Bill, and Calamity Jane.

McGillycuddy, repeating stories he had heard at Fort Laramie, argued that Calamity was born as Jane Dalton to the infantryman and later settler Dalton and his wife, Jane. Indians killed Dalton, but his wife escaped with their infant daughter (Jane/Calamity) to Fort Laramie, where the mother died from her injuries. Baby Jane was adopted by Sergeant Bassett and raised as a "child of the regiment." McGillycuddy heard this story from several members of the Fourteenth Infantry in 1875 and spoke assertively (as he did on most issues) in defense of the story, even after others, including Calamity herself, pointed out her birth in Princeton, Missouri. McGillycuddy also related information about Calamity's being with George Crook's soldiers and in Deadwood.

Harry "Sam" Young also spoke vociferously for the Jane Dalton and Fort Laramie lineage of Calamity. Some think McGillycuddy borrowed his information from Young (342; see also Sollid [326], pp. 5ff). Others, including Jennewein (278), conclude the opposite.

290. McLaird, James D. *Calamity Jane: The Woman and the Legend.* Norman: University of Oklahoma Press, 2005.

This book is by far the single best source on the life and legends of Calamity Jane. If a reader were limited to one volume on the subject, this is it. Clearly written and diligently researched, this thorough study is the product of years of careful research in a wide variety of published primary and secondary sources. The book also exhausts all known sources in manuscript collections. McLaird is particularly thorough in his use of newspaper sources, turning up dozens of obscure, unknown facts from his painstaking reading of important newspapers of the northern Rockies. Adding much to McLaird's first-rate work are his extensive footnotes, lengthy bibliography, and impressive run of photographs.

McLaird provides judicious comparisons between sound interpretations and misguided conclusions about Calamity's life and actions. In addition to tracing Calamity's life through its mysterious twists and turns, he clears away mistaken notions about her having served as a scout, participated in Custer's and Buffalo Bill's activities, and written the diary that Jean Hickok McCormick claimed was hers. Readers who carefully scrutinize McLaird's systematic findings will be forced to abandon wrong information about Calamity so widely scattered throughout the United States and Europe.

291. McLaird, James D. *Wild Bill Hickok and Calamity Jane: Deadwood Legends.* Pierre: South Dakota Historical Society Press, 2008.

This compact, smoothly written dual biography of Wild Bill and Calamity is of first importance to the study of these two legendary Old West figures. McLaird greatly expands his earlier essays on these two characters (373, 374–77), draws on his recent definitive biography of Calamity (290), and utilizes information from his forthcoming biography of Wild Bill. No one is better suited than this author to write this joint biography. Here is the beginning place to decipher the realities and myths that encrust these two Wild West demigods.

McLaird devotes two chapters to Wild Bill, two to Calamity, and one, entitled "United in Legend," to both figures. The 160-page study provides the best examination we have of these Old West characters and the legends that often surround and distort them. McLaird furnishes what we need: concise, factual biographies of both figures and then a searching scrutiny of how and why mythic characters like Wild Bill and Calamity emerged from the marriage of facts and legends.

292. McPherren, Ida. *Imprints on Pioneer Trails.* Boston: Christopher, 1950.

McPherren, a local historian of the northern Rockies, includes numerous lively anecdotes about Montana small towns at the turn of the twentieth century. Her treatment of Calamity, especially the early years, contains interesting but unsubstantiated stories about how Calamity made her way in Montana hurdy-gurdies (combination dance halls–saloons). The author likewise thoroughly castigates one unnamed writer for suggesting Calamity became an easy mark sexually: "it is a damn lie," she asserts. Her take on the Wild Bill–Calamity story is mistaken, and she is off base in stating that Calamity died on 2 August 1906, thirty years to the day after Wild Bill cashed in his chips. McPherren met Calamity on the Fourth of July in the small town of Cinnabar, north of Yellowstone Park. She describes Calamity as "dressed in buckskin trousers, fringed buckskin jacket and a man's wide brimmed hat." Calamity was at "the height of her glory," the author adds, "because she was creating a sensation" (p. 273).

293. *Mercer County, Missouri History and Genealogy.* [Compact disk]. Joplin, Mo.: Hearthstone Legacy Publications, n.d. Available from hearthstone legacy.com/mercer-county-Missouri.htm.

An extensive compendium of family biographies, maps, and other county information appears on this CD. It also includes a copy of *Rogers' Souvenir History of Mercer County, Missouri* (315).

294. *Mercer County Pioneer Traces.* Vols. 1–2. Princeton, Mo.: Mercer County Genealogical Society, 1997.

Part of a three-volume set totaling more than 1,700 pages, these huge resources are notable reference guides to large amounts of information on

Mercer County. The most extensive sections deal with families. Several other sections deal with Martha Canary/Calamity Jane; and Norma Slack, a descendant of Martha's younger sister, Lena, contributes a brief piece on her ancestor (vol. 1, pp. 150–51). But the Slack account also contains incorrect information the Canary-Borner family evidently passed on to their children. The author also misdates Lena's birth year as 1856 rather than 1858 or 1859. Another entry, "Martha Canary" (vol. 1, pp. 151), by researcher William R. Whiteside, furnishes a valuable, dependable sketch of the Canary family, including information on Martha's grandparents, parents, aunts and uncles, and siblings. An important if abbreviated source. "Norma Slack" (in vol. 2), an autobiographical piece by Calamity's great-great-niece, deals with Slack becoming a Calamity impersonator in Wyoming and elsewhere in the 1990s and thereafter. It too includes incorrect information on the lives of Martha and sister Lena's parents.

295. *Mercer County Pioneer Traces*. Vol. 3. Princeton, Mo.: Mercer County Genealogical Society, 1997; see, esp., "Calamity Jane Days" (pp. 197–98), "Calamity Jane Melodrama" (p. 198), "Calamity Jane Roadside Park Is Dedicated" (pp. 198–99).

"Martha Jane Alias 'Calamity Jane,'" by Harry B. Robinson (vol. 3, pp. 207–208) is a curious piece. It opens, "Calamity Jane was not born in Princeton nor did she ever live there or elsewhere in Mercer County, Missouri." Then, most of Robinson's essay proceeds to accept Martha's residence in Mercer County up to about 1863. Generally, the entry is a mishmash of important details and misinformation. Use with caution.

Several sections in this volume address events revolving around Calamity Jane Days in Princeton, Mo. In November 1960, Princeton merchants organized the first Calamity Jane Days, a celebration that included costumed gatherings, special sales at businesses, and other festivities. The success of the initial event led to an annual celebration. Later, a Miss Calamity Jane contest became part of the annual gathering. A trail ride, a barbecue, a melodrama, and an annual "shootout" were later additions. Still other augmentations were music and artistic events and a large parade. The Calamity Jane Days celebration continues to attract large audiences. The melodrama pioneered in 1962 and continues to the present. The section on the dedication of the Calamity Jane Roadside Park is taken from the story in the Princeton *Post-Telegraph* of 25 July 1957 (209). The launching of Calamity Jane Days served as a coming-out party, signifying that Princeton accepted its history as the birthplace of the notorious Calamity Jane.

296. Miller, Ronald Dean. *Shady Ladies of the West.* Tucson, Ariz.: Westernlore Press, 1985.

Miller's account of dozens of prostitutes in the American West focuses on California and Nevada, but also includes a brief section (pp. 112–17) on Calamity Jane. The author has not studied Calamity thoroughly, relying too heavily on her suspect autobiography (241) and failing to examine the sturdy, dependable works of Jennewein (278) and Sollid (326) available to him. He does not know enough about the subject to discount the autobiographical miscues of Calamity or many other romanticizers. Nor should readers accept uncritically Miller's blanket conclusion that "Calamity Jane was mourned by all who loved her. This was almost every one who had ever met her" (p. 117).

297. Mills, Anson. *My Life.* Edited by C. H. Claudy. Washington, D.C.: Byron S. Adams, 1918.

Mills, a captain with General Crook, says Calamity slipped into the Crook command and went along until she was discovered and "placed under guard" (p. 401). Calamity greatly embarrassed the married, conservative Mills when she enthusiastically declared, "There is Colonel [*sic*] Mills, he knows me." Despite Mills's strong protestations, along with resultant laughter, onlookers seemed to doubt Mills. This account gives strong credence to Calamity's having been with Crook a second time in June 1876, a few days before she rode into Deadwood with Hickok and Charlie Utter.

298. Milner, Joe E., and Earle E. Forrest. *California Joe: Noted Scout and Indian Fighter.* Foreword by Joseph G. Rosa. Lincoln: University of Nebraska Press, 1987. Originally published 1935.

Following the earlier views of V. T. McGillycuddy (289) and Harry Young (342), this book points to the Dalton story of Calamity's origins. The authors quote a McGillycuddy letter (p. 230) supporting that Calamity spent her first years as Jane Dalton in the Fort Laramie area. They are convinced that Martha degenerated in a quick downward cycle: from "a dance hall girl, then a camp follower, and finally a common prostitute" (p. 231). They add, however, that she was generous, courageous, and a camp angel in times of sickness. The authors also cite the Missouri origins story, but do not comment on it.

Milner and Forrest tell an unverified tale that on one occasion Calamity evidently stole California Joe's dog. After finding out what Calamity had done, Joe grabbed her and hoisted her up feet first several times, warning her not to steal the dog again. Later, when Calamity bothered Joe in Deadwood, he whipped out his pistols to make her dance and made her promise "to keep away from him unless she wanted to dance every time they met" (p. 248). Unsubstantiated, lively stories in a book profiling a well-known frontier figure.

299. Mokler, Alfred James. *History of Natrona County, Wyoming, 1888–1922*. Chicago: R. R. Donnelley and Sons, 1923.

A local historian well known for his writing on early Wyoming, Mokler clearly mixes up his information on Martha/Calamity (pp. 431–35). Where he is undoubtedly right is in saying that young Martha was a "poor, neglected little girl, who did not know right from wrong, and whose associates were the rough men of that country" (p. 431) near Miner's Delight in the late 1860s; he is obviously wrong in stating that a woman of that time took young Martha to New York City, where she lived for several years. Mokler then retells the story Calamity includes in her autobiography about being named "Calamity" after she rescued Captain Egan. In subsequent paragraphs the author attempts to balance the Wild Woman and Angel of Mercy stories that clustered around Calamity after the late 1870s. Her lively life and the rumors about her, Mokler concludes, "brought her into the limelight more than any other woman who has ever lived in the Middle West" (p. 435).

300. Monro, Gregory. *Calamity Jane: Mémoires de l'Ouest*. Paris: Éditions Hoëbeke, 2010.

Written in French, Monro's attractive and splashy life-and-times biography is a pictorial feast. In 120 pages of text and dozens of photographs (many oversized) of Calamity, places she lived and visited, and frontier life in general, the author serves up an eye-catching background of Calamity's western wanderings. Monro is also fascinated with the documents that Jean Hickok McCormick claimed were Calamity's. He now owns these documents and he devotes his final chapter to the mysteries and controversies still surrounding them. Not able to extricate himself completely from these fraudulent materials, the author includes information and questionable photographs from them. Monro has just released a major movie documentary of Calamity's life (487).

301. Muller, Ellen Crago. *Calamity Jane*. Laramie, Wyo.: Jelm Mountain Press, 1981.

This twenty-four-page pamphlet by a local historian relies too heavily on Calamity's suspect autobiography. In her discussions of Calamity's story, the author fails to sort out misinformation from useful facts. She falls victim, too, to the Jean Hickok McCormick (246) tall tales. In addition, the authorial intrusions of Muller's own personal and family information detract from her third-person narrative. But her apt utilization of newspaper stories and interviews with descendants of Calamity's younger sister, Lena Pauline Canary Borner (1859?–88) adds valuable information, balancing the limitations of the pamphlet.

302. Mumey, Nolie. *Calamity Jane, 1852–1903: A History of Her Life and Adventures in the West*. Denver: Range Press, 1950.

This 146-page book by a Colorado physician and local historian contains about eighty pages concerning Calamity's complex life; about forty-five pages of the diary and letters that Jean Hickok McCormick claimed were Calamity's; and pages devoted to photographs, an index, and other information. The study reflects the state of research and writing about Calamity in the late 1940s. Rich and thorough in terms of newspapers and diligent in other kinds of sources, Mumey's brief biography nonetheless chooses to follow the spurious McCormick documents, which seem to have dazzled so many biographers and historians up to the 1960s. Mumey's research, especially in newspapers, was much more extensive than Aikman's a quarter century earlier (230). Also, Mumey avoided the flights of imagination that undermined Aikman's account. Still, Mumey bought into the McCormick bogus documents.

Generally, Mumey summarizes varied opinions—for example, the conflicting views of Martha's birth and early years—without explicitly stating his own conclusion. He seemed wary about advancing determinations, pointing out instead that Calamity's life was "a strange mixture of fact and fiction, full of imaginary accounts. Separating the true from the false is a difficult task" (p. 38). Mumey includes most of the tallest tales about Calamity's having served as a scout and become an entrepreneur and an entertainer without evaluating which stories are the most and least persuasive. The author's approach, primarily topical, becomes too anecdotal and often muddles chronology. Sometimes his narrative is little more than long, stitched-together, block quotations from primary sources. Without saying much about Wild

Bill Hickok, Mumey nonetheless follows the McCormick story introducing her and reprinting her spurious diary and letters (pp. 83–126). Mumey prints portions of the diary and letters omitted in later publications (246, 265). The final chapter is a mishmash of Calamity's performances, her last days, her death (misdated), and her funeral.

303. Nelson, Bruce. *Land of the Dacotahs*. Minneapolis: University of Minnesota Press, 1946.

In a chapter entitled "The Spoilers" Nelson provides a five- or six-page discussion of Calamity. He frames well the huge disparity between the reality and romanticism of Calamity's life in one apt sentence: "The true story of her life is a drab caricature of the glamorous career invented by herself and fitted with trappings by numerous biographers" (p. 162). Nelson gets much of Calamity's early years correct except when he relies too much on her embellished autobiography. He is much closer to historical fact when he asserts "virtually every adventure related by this bedraggled creature in her 'autobiography' was nothing more than a figment of her imagination" (p. 166). Nelson's conclusion is provocative but not quite right: "In the imperishable story of the West, legend has made her [Calamity] what she most desired to be, but never was, in real life" (p. 167). There is strong evidence, instead, that Calamity likewise wished to be a typical pioneer woman, a wife and mother, which her tumultuous life never vouchsafed to her. A few pages of this account of Calamity appeared earlier in Bruce Nelson, "The Myth of Calamity Jane," *Adventure* 110 (December 1943): 108–11.

304. Newson, Thomas McLean. *Drama of Life in the Black Hills*. St. Paul, Minn.: Doge and Larpenteur, 1878.

This brief drama of "3 Acts, 26 Scenes, 30 Characters," with forty engravings, provides important information about Calamity while she was in the Black Hills about 1876–77. The ninety-two-page play features several scenes with Calamity and also includes sketches and an important early photograph of her now lost (518).

Newson, a journalist from Minnesota who spent time in the Black Hills, evidently knew and interviewed Calamity. Yet the author's information must be sorted out, the notable facts separated from the mistaken notions. For instance, Newson gathered information from Calamity and others (and followed the incorrect story of her origins in a military family), but got her age right as about twenty-one or twenty-two. He portrays her as a woman of tender emotions, aloof from most other women entertainers, perhaps "married" to a "husband," and dressed, alternatively, as both a man and a woman. Newson is the earliest source to reveal Calamity as a cross-dresser, not only in women's clothes but also in mannish buckskins.

Very pertinent is what the author portrays about Calamity's actions and personality. Dressed as a woman, she gambles with the men, sometimes dances with them, and usually drinks wine rather than whiskey. In another scene, she is "dressed in a plain black dress—[with a] comely figure" (p. 35). She is "quiet, with an occasional remark; [and] dances modestly" (p. 37). When an inquirer asks Calamity "ain't you tired of this way of living?" (p. 37) she breaks down in tears.

Most revealing of all is the factual pen portrait the author provides just below the authentic photo now missing. He speaks of her having been thrown into the world without parental guidance and having to make her own way so early in life. She has a "rather pleasant eye, but when in passion, emitting a greenish glare. . . . Her conversation is animated, her language good, and her heart warm and generous. . . . [W]hen dressed in her own garments she looks comely; when equipped as a man she has all the characteristics of the sterner sex" (p. 39).

In short, Newson provides a more complex, balanced, and revealing portrait of Calamity in the Black Hills than most depictions of her as solely a drunken, profane prostitute. Newson's comments take on larger significance because they appeared at the same time that Calamity was being turned into a sensational dime novel heroine. A major, revealing source on Calamity in her early twenties.

305. O'Connor, Richard. *Wild Bill Hickok*. Garden City, N.Y.: Doubleday, 1959.

O'Connor, a journalist and author of several lively biographies, provides a speedy narrative of Wild Bill that, because it is long on action and short on interpretation, should appeal to general readers interested in the frontier West. The author adopts an episodic approach, using the high points of Hickok's brief but action-filled life to power his narrative. The book is without footnotes or bibliography but includes in-text references to some of the author's sources.

In a very brief section, O'Connor deals with Calamity. He attempts to demythologize her, dismissing much of her self-advertisements as fables and the exaggerations of journalists as falsehoods. The author frequently cites Duncan Aikman (230) but betrays his lack of information about Calamity.

He is right, however, in dismissing the rumored romance of Wild Bill and Calamity and in pointing out they knew one another for only a few short weeks in 1876. (O'Connor errs in getting Hickok and Calamity to Deadwood in the spring of the year rather than the summer.) A mixed bag of speedy narrative without much analysis or hard information on Calamity.

306. Parker, Watson. *Deadwood: The Golden Years.* Lincoln: University of Nebraska Press, 1981.

Parker probably knew more about Deadwood than any other historian. His diligence as a researcher, his skills as a narrative historian, and his knowledge of the surrounding physical and socioeconomic settings were unsurpassed and abundantly showcased in this valuable volume. But his perspective on Calamity Jane is decidedly negative. His Calamity is a "boozy old bawd." Worst of all, Parker unfairly claims that "her name, Calamity, perhaps came from the various venereal calamities which may have afflicted those who patronized her charms" (p. 198). In a moment of truth, the author admits this scurrilous charge "is entirely my own invention" (p. 260)—in other words without substantiation.

   In some ways, Calamity is victimized in this account because of Parker's tendency to corner, copy, and quote nearly every lively story he's heard about Deadwood and its exceptional characters. That means the womanly and motherly instincts Calamity displayed at some moments in Deadwood are not mentioned here. Even though Parker praises J. Leonard Jennewein's work on Calamity (278), calling it "as even-handed an account of her as I know of" (p. 260), he does not achieve that balance himself.

307. Parker, Watson. *Gold in the Black Hills.* Lincoln: University of Nebraska Press, 1981. Originally published 1966.

A leading authority on the Black Hills, Deadwood, and the gold rush of the 1870s, Parker was largely negative in nearly all of his writing about Calamity. In his view, she was "the notorious harlot" (p. 64), was a "notorious bawd" (p. 167), and got her nickname because her paramours were generally visited by some venereal "calamity" (p. 167). There is no evidence for the last, particularly unkind comment, save the author's cynical opinions. In several of his writings, Parker quotes references to Calamity's appearance as being "built like a busted bale of hay" and "about the roughest looking human being" (p. 168) in the area. Although admitting Calamity helped with nursing smallpox victims, Parker ends his brief treatment of her with more negative comments. Parker's works overflow with dark descriptions of Calamity.

308. Pence, Mary Lou, and Lola M. Homsher. *The Ghost Towns of Wyoming.* New York: Hastings House, 1956.

Several anecdotes about Calamity are scattered through the pages of this popularly written work on Wyoming ghost towns. The authors exaggerate Martha's wildness and wrongly send her to New York while still in her teens. Of minimal use for diligent scholars.

309. *Pioneer Footprints.* Sioux Falls, S.Dak.: Black Hills Half Century Club of Belle Fourche, 1964.

This local history of the Bear Butte country includes a brief, half-page biographical portrait of George Cosgrove (p. 217), said to be one of Calamity's husbands. A Canadian by birth (1853), Cosgrove immigrated with his family to the United States and rode into the Black Hills with the Hickok-Utter wagon train in midsummer 1876. Calamity claimed she had "married" George; they may have been together about 1876–78. Later, Cosgrove admitted that he had lived with Calamity.

310. Ray, Grace Ernestine. *Wily Women of the West.* San Antonio, Texas: Naylor, 1972.

In her five-page account of Calamity, Ray provides a fact-filled and mainly dependable discussion. The author has obviously read extensively—she understands and deals with the conflicting treatments of Calamity's early years and relationship with Wild Bill, for example—and embraces the complex Calamity that the best studies offer. Most of this discussion handles the sensational and masculine sides of Calamity; little is said about her feminine or maternal sides. Generally, a helpful, abbreviated piece, proving that an account may veer toward the romantic without being factually inaccurate.

311. Reece, Amy L. "Annie Oakley, Calamity Jane, and the Myth of the West." Master's thesis, University of New Mexico, 2011.

The author offers three sections each on Calamity and Annie Oakley: (1) a literature review, (2) background information, and (3) an analysis of their myths. The thesis of seventy-seven pages is generally helpful on Calamity but is wrong on Calamity's being with Custer rather than with Crook. And Reece is reductive and vague on "the western myth." But, utilizing McLaird (290) thoroughly, the author's chronology is instructive. The writer also makes good use of many films that deal with the two western heroines.

312. Rezatto, Helen. *Mount Moriah: "Kill a Man—Start a Cemetery."* Rapid City, S.Dak.: Fenwyn Press, 1989.

Rezatto focuses on the Deadwood "Big Four"—Wild Bill, Calamity Jane, Potato Creek Johnny, and Preacher Smith—in her book on the Mount Moriah Cemetery and its most vaunted residents. The section entitled "Calamity Jane[,] Queen of the Wild West" (pp. 58–74) is surprisingly full, balanced, and more than adequately researched. The author is certain that Calamity was a prostitute, but that she was also an Angel of Mercy. Why did Calamity become a celebrity? For two reasons: (1) she was an adept liar and self-appointed publicity agent; and (2) dime novelists and other popularizers early on made her the heroine of their sensational western stories. Informal footnotes, "footsies" the author calls them, indicate that Rezatto's account of Calamity is based primarily on newspapers, Deadwood memoirs, and a few more recent and strong secondary sources.

313. Rezatto, Helen. *Tales of the Black Hills*. Rapid City, S.Dak.: Fenwyn Press, 1989. Originally published 1983.

The author describes her book as "an informal history of the Black Hills." She admits to gathering and retelling many popular stories but also attempting "to write from an honest and objective viewpoint" (pp. 11, 12). After long sections narrating Indian and "white man" legends, Rezatto devotes an even longer section to the first settlements in the Black Hills. A final section, "Pioneers and Personalities," includes a section on Calamity, "'That's No Man—That's Calamity Jane'" (pp. 200–207).

Rezatto dismisses much of Calamity's tale-telling as lies, including the claimed romance with Wild Bill. But she accepts the dubious claim that Calamity scouted for General George Crook. She also misfires on Calamity's never having married and wrongly claims that the little girl who accompanied Calamity back to Deadwood in 1895 "was actually [Clinton] Burke's stepdaughter" (p. 206). Even more egregious, she states that Edward L. Wheeler was a "pseudonym for Ned Buntline" (p. 207) and that Buntline began to write dime novels about Calamity in the 1880s. The naming is wrong, and the dating of the dime novels off by several years.

Finally, Rezatto makes much of Calamity's kindheartedness, her nursing, and her aid to the down-and-outers. Why remember Calamity, the author asks? Well, she became a very good self-publicist, spawned bold headlines, fit Wild West stereotypes, and captured attention as "a Diamond in the Rough" (p. 207).

314. Robinson, Doane. *Encyclopedia of South Dakota*. Pierre, S.Dak.: Doane Robinson, 1925.

    Robinson's very brief entry on Calamity Jane opens with the false Jane Dalton hypothesis, thus giving Calamity the life dates of 1860 to 1903. Calamity was, in Robinson's words, "coarse, hard, but kindhearted and when sober enough frequently nursed miners" (p. 106). Too much romantic and sentimental nonsense has been written about Calamity, Robinson continues, although he would admit "the best that can be said for her is that 'there is some good in the worst of us.'" (p. 106). Privately, Robinson was much harsher in denouncing Calamity as a notorious prostitute.

315. Rogers, W. B. *Rogers' Souvenir History of Mercer County*. Trenton, Mo.: W. B. Rogers, 1911.

    This lengthy volume provides very useful but general historical background for about eighty years of Mercer County history. The account furnishes helpful contexts for the Canary family experiences in the Princeton area in the 1850s and 1860s. Regrettably, the very brief portrait of Calamity (pp. 286–87) is so riddled with errors that it must be dismissed.

316. Rosa, Joseph G. *They Called Him Wild Bill: The Life and Adventures of James Butler Hickok*. 2nd ed. Norman: University of Oklahoma Press, 1974. Originally published 1964.

    In the strongest of the biographies of Wild Bill, Englishman Rosa clearly and decisively shows that most stories about a Hickok-Calamity romance are far afield or pure nonsense. Even though the author's information about Calamity contains errors, he demonstrates that Hickok did not meet Calamity until they were on their way to Deadwood in June–July 1876. He also cogently undermines the Jean Hickok McCormick yarn by pointing to the several errors of fact and unbelievability of the so-called Calamity diary (246). This account is the best source of information on the limited Wild Bill–Calamity connection—from the Hickok perspective.

317. Ross, Nancy Wilson. *Westward the Women*. New York: Alfred A. Knopf, 1944.

    Ross, a novelist, journalist, and author of a regional study of the Pacific Northwest, *Farthest Reach* (1942), deals here with women who took part in migrations to the Pacific Northwest. The author utilizes the lives of several women to illustrate her lively contentions about women's central participation in the westward movement. Many of the women are virtually unknown. Better known examples include Narcissa Whitman, Eliza Spalding, Mrs. Jason Lee, and several other missionaries and nuns; Sacajawea and other Indian women; Asa Mercer's "girls," the brides-to-be; Jane Barnes with the overland fur traders; the hurdy-gurdy girls and prostitutes; Bethina Owens-Adair, a doctor; and maybe the sister and brother of Calamity Jane. No other writer has been able to confirm or deny Ross's provocative comments about these possible siblings of Calamity. A thought-provoking, well-written study with minimal information about Calamity but helpful contextual discussions of women in the Pacific Northwest.

318. Ryan, Ed. *Me and the Black Hills.* Custer, S.Dak.: Ed Ryan, 1951.

Ryan asserts, with undoubtedly a bit of leg-pulling involved, that it was he who named Calamity. When she would slap down her cards in a poker game, she would often yell, "What a calamity." After one game when Ryan called her hand and she lost to him, he told her it was a calamity—"and ever since that game she was known as Calamity Jane" (p. 47). Clearly, the story is more fiction than fact.

319. Sabin, Edwin L. *Wild Men of the Wild West.* New York: Thomas Y. Crowell, 1929.

As a nod to gender balance, Sabin includes a chapter on "Wild Women" (pp. 309–42) in his overly dramatic book. After a few paragraphs on the likes of doña Tules, Madame Moustache, and Rose of Cimarron, and a longer section on Belle Starr (pp. 318–28), Sabin devotes the rest of the chapter (pp. 328–42) to a breezy discussion of Calamity. He points out the shortcomings of Calamity's autobiography, but he himself falls for the false Jane Dalton story of Calamity's origins that Harry (Sam) Young had initiated in 1915 in his book *Hard Knocks* (342). Sabin has Calamity's birth date as 1848, buys into her trumped-up story of Captain Egan's first naming her, depicts her as an Indian killer, and claims she "married a dozen times [with] . . . several children" (p. 340). The author tries, with limited success, to balance the Wild West woman and Florence Nightingale legends that clustered around Calamity.

320. Sanford, William R., and Carl R. Green. *Calamity Jane: Frontier Original.* Legendary Heroes of the Wild West. Springfield, N.J.: Enslow, 1996.

This forty-eight-page minibook is intended for juvenile readers. The authors make good use of a modicum of important sources, even though they also cite the suspect sources of Clairmonte (243) and the McCormick forgery (246), and falsely state Calamity was married to Wild Bill who "was the great love of . . . [her] life" (p. 18). Conversely, Sanford and Green point out the stretchers in Calamity's autobiography, note her service in smallpox epidemics ("an angel of mercy"; p. 23), explain Calamity's transformative depictions in dime novels, and discuss her touring with Wild West shows. A better than adequate biography for young readers based on decent research. The authors avoid mentioning prostitution or other sex-related matters.

321. Seagraves, Anne. *Soiled Doves: Prostitution in the Early West.* Hayden, Idaho: Wesanne, 1994.

This study of frontier prostitution, by an author who has written several books for general readers about women in the early West, utilizes several pen portraits of red-light ladies to illustrate her general contentions. Among these are mini-biographies of Lola Montez, Mattie Silks, Julia Bulette, "Chicago Joe," Mary Ellen Pleasant, and Calamity Jane (pp. 124–26, 130–33). Unhappily, the author follows much too closely the exaggerations of Duncan Aikman (230) and has not thoroughly researched more recent, strong publications on Calamity, particularly those discussing her possible experiences as a prostitute at hog ranches.

322. Secrest, William B., ed. *I Buried Hickok: The Memoirs of White Eye Anderson.* College Station, Texas: Creative Publishing, 1980.

"White Eye" Anderson's memoir provides important information on the Wild Bill Hickok and Colorado Charley Utter trip to the Black Hills in June–July 1876 and Calamity Jane's presence with the group. As Anderson's remembrances make clear, Calamity joined the wagon train to Deadwood at Fort Laramie and spent nearly two weeks with the group on the journey north. This account concludes that Wild Bill and Calamity had not met before this trip, that Wild Bill paid scant attention to Calamity, and that she imbibed more than a few drinks from his whiskey keg. Anderson also says Calamity and several other women threw flowers on the coffin of Wild Bill before the grave was filled. Finally, Anderson adds that soon after the trip to Deadwood Calamity married George Cosgrove, one of the men who traveled to the Black Hills with the Wild Bill–Colorado Charley train. This is a source of central significance on Calamity's journey to the Black Hills. White Eye's memory seems to confirm the other limited information on the story, and the editor's very full notes add much depth to the account.

323. Senn, Edward L. *"Deadwood Dick" and "Calamity Jane": A Thorough Sifting of Facts from Fiction*. Deadwood, S.Dak.: Edward L. Senn, 1939.

Despite the author's ambitious subtitle, this brief pamphlet is much less than a "thorough sifting" of all the facts about Deadwood Dick and Calamity Jane. Indeed, Senn promises much more than he delivers. A Deadwood newspaperman, Senn failed to do the necessary homework. Of the nine pages devoted to Calamity (pp. 7–15), nearly a third is long quotations from Calamity's unreliable autobiography (241) and Dora Du Fran's uncertain account (252). Even though Senn discounts some of Calamity's exaggerations, he mistakenly accepts most of what she says about serving with Custer in Arizona and is incorrect in thinking no one mentioned that she served as a scout (Frank Grouard [251] does so) and that she had not been in the Black Hills in 1875. Senn is very critical of Calamity's actions, saying that the "one womanly trait in the otherwise wanton woman, was kindness of heart toward the sick and needy" (p. 11). Surprisingly for a journalist, Senn makes almost no use of newspapers and overlooks Aikman (230) as the best—albeit deeply flawed—source on Calamity's life published before 1930.

324. Shadley, Ruth. *Calamity Jane's Daughter: The Story of Maude Weir: A Story Never Before Told*. Caldwell, Idaho: Caxton Printers, 1996.

This abbreviated volume follows an unreliable thesis: Maude Weir was Calamity's unacknowledged daughter by an unnamed man. About forty pages in length, this small book is more about the author and her family (Shadley is Maude Weir's daughter, and by her contention, Calamity's granddaughter) than about Calamity. Sadly, the numerous errors of fact and the weak writing undercut the strength of the author's conclusions. Actually, the book contains little information on Calamity. Overall, Shadley's argument remains unproven.

325. Sherlock, James L. *South Pass and Its Tales*. Basin, Wyo.: Wolverine Gallery, 1978.

Although this modest, informal account says little about Martha Canary, it provides useful backgrounds on South Pass City, Atlantic City, and Miner's Delight, Wyoming. All three were sites Martha was supposed to have visited—and perhaps stayed in for a short time—in the late 1860s or early 1870s. Sherlock views Calamity positively: "Calamity Jane was very warm-hearted and kind, in spite of her rough and unladylike actions, and a real workhorse whenever help was needed" (n.p). The author praises her nursing help in Miner's Delight and her aid elsewhere. She seemed to be available whenever help was needed. This positive availability "is what earned for her the sobriquet of Calamity Jane" (n.p.). The author correctly notes that Calamity's sister Lena/Lana was in the area before marrying and moving with John Borner to Borner's Garden, near Lander, Wyoming; but he is off-track in stating that Calamity was the niece of Major Patrick A. Gallagher, though Martha may have stayed with his family for a time.

326. Sollid, Roberta Beed. *Calamity Jane: A Study in Historical Criticism.* Introduction by James D. McLaird. Afterword by Richard W. Etulain. Helena: Montana Historical Society Press, 1995. Originally published 1958.

Sollid's book was a turning point in the interpretations of Calamity Jane. Straightforwardly written and based on more thorough research than earlier studies of Calamity, this volume is realistic in tone—almost muckraking at times. Sollid bluntly tells readers in her preface, "No career is so elusive to the historian as that of a loose woman. Calamity Jane was that sort of woman" (p. xvii). Adopting a topical organization, the author provides chapters on Calamity's birth and appearance followed by discussions of her scouting, nickname, "husbands," nursing, work as a bullwhacker, time as a jail resident, "gunman," and death.

Sollid's valuable study was based on her revised master's thesis at the University of Montana. She dove deeper into regional newspapers than previous biographers. She also probed many other sources about Calamity, interviewed old-timers in the northern West who knew Calamity, and examined manuscript sources. Sollid used these sources critically, thereby providing the first analytical book on Calamity Jane.

But Sollid did not locate all the important sources that other strong studies have turned up in the past half century. She overlooked census records and several other significant primary sources and was guilty of a few erroneous conclusions. Still, hers was and remains the first significant study of Calamity Jane, furnishing useful information for general readers and scholars. More than twenty plates, several accompanied by revealing explanatory notes, enhance the value of this pioneering work.

327. Spring, Agnes Wright. *The Cheyenne and Black Hills Stage and Express Routes*. Lincoln: University of Nebraska Press, 1967. Originally published 1948.

Spring's thoroughly researched and pleasingly written account of the Cheyenne and Black Hills stagecoach route remains *the* source for this subject. Drawing on regional newspapers, the diaries of John Hunton, and other valuable sources, Spring provides glimpses of Calamity as a bullwhacker, a possible stagecoach driver, and probably a sex worker at a hog ranch or two. This important source exhibits wide research, cautious assertions, and balanced conclusions. It is a model for other scholars. It is all the more surprising, then, that Spring always argued for the authenticity of a photo (plate 14 in her book) of C. S. Stobie (Mountain Charley) and Captain Jack Crawford, ostensibly with Calamity. The comely woman in the photo's center is obviously not our Calamity, but she may be another Calamity (Mattie Young), who died in a carriage accident in Denver in 1878 (94–95). Spring provides one of the best one-line quotations from a manuscript diary written by Isaac N. Bard in February 1876: "Calamity Jane is Hear going up with troops. I think there is trouble ahead." (p. 86).

328. Spring, Agnes Wright. *Colorado Charley, Wild Bill's Pard*. Boulder, Colo.: Pruett Press, 1968.

Spring expresses doubts that Calamity accompanied Wild Bill and Colorado Charley from Fort Laramie to Deadwood in June–July 1876. The memoirs of White Eye Anderson (322) show however that she did.

329. Steckmesser, Kent Ladd. *The Western Hero in History and Legend*. Norman: University of Oklahoma Press, 1965.

This straightforwardly written book about the evolution of notable western figures into legendary heroes, now a half-century old, is still a valuable study. Steckmesser's well-organized and thorough examination, along with Henry Nash Smith's *Virgin Land* (402) and Richard Slotkin's *Regeneration through Violence* (1973), remains the best treatment we have of the evolution of western historical characters into larger-than-life mythic heroes. Steckmesser uses Kit Carson, Billy the Kid, Wild Bill Hickok, and George Armstrong Custer as illustrations of the transformations occurring through the molding impact of sensational biographies and histories, novels and poems, and films.

Steckmesser writes little about Calamity, except in regard to her alleged connection with Wild Bill Hickok. The author does not accept the Wild

Bill–Calamity romantic relationship often featured in popular fiction and Western films. But he demonstrates how that false history, once introduced, has remained a part of most popular images of Wild Bill and Calamity Jane.

More important, Steckmesser provides a very useful model for studying the evolution of Martha Canary into the legendary Calamity Jane. Following Steckmesser's outline and methods would allow one to trace how the daughter of a Missouri farmer became the most-written-about woman of the Wild West.

330. Stevenson, Elizabeth. *Figures in a Western Landscape: Men and Women of the Northern Rockies.* Baltimore, Md.: Johns Hopkins University Press, 1994; see, esp., pp. 146–72, 199–200.

A smoothly written piece by a skilled stylist, this chapter provides a capsule biography of Calamity; deals even more extensively with interpretations; and focuses, most of all, on the supposed Calamity diary and letters. Stevenson, for the most part, gets the facts right, and her balance and willingness to understand diverse interpretations add value to her chapter on Calamity (pp. 147–72). Emphasizing books published from the 1940s onward (she does not deal with Aikman [230] or Mumey [302]), the author discusses both secondary and primary sources. She was the first to deal extensively with the letters and other writings of Will Lull (378), who befriended Calamity in Deadwood. About half of the chapter discusses the Jean Hickok McCormick story and rumored Calamity diary and letters, which Stevenson seems to believe confirmed the McCormick tale. After careful and thoughtful examination of the McCormick story and the diary, Stevenson concludes "the consideration must be one of a judicious suspension of final judgment" (p. 171).

331. Stokes, George W. *Deadwood Gold: A Story of the Black Hills.* Yonkers-on-Hudson, N.Y.: World Book, 1926.

Stokes, an early-arriving miner in the Black Hills, describes Calamity in a Deadwood gathering as "under a ten-dollar Stetson with a cowman's purple handkerchief around her neck." In the "scene of wild merrymaking," she "danced with everybody and promenaded to the bar, as was the custom, after every dance" (p. 61). Later, Stokes tells us, Calamity "reformed," learning to make dresses but refusing to go to prayer meetings. She also "married a wood contractor on Bald Mountain," but "it proved too quiet . . . for her out in the woods," so she repaired to Swearingen's Gem Theater and joined his "Lady Entertainers" (p. 77). Was Stokes's unnamed wood contractor a reference to Calamity's first reputed "husband," George Cosgrove, or to the later Clinton Burke or Robert Dorsett? The evidence is not clear.

332. Thane, Eric [Ralph C. Henry, pseud.]. *High Border Country.* New York: Duell, Sloan and Pearce, 1942; see, esp., 191–99.

Thane/Henry writes with the flair and verve of a superb stylist and story-teller. He also gathers false facts and imagines fabricated tales like a practiced yarn-spinner. Most of what he writes—particularly about Calamity's male companions, her children, and her relationship with Wild Bill Hickok—is dead wrong. Likewise, he is off the mark in dealing with her early years in Montana and in his argument that she scouted for General Custer. Even information close to being factual loses out to the romance of the author's zingy style. Calamity is caricatured: "A sloppy slattern, she went her lonely way, happy only when alcohol was singing through her veins" (p. 199). Nary a hint here of Calamity's desire to be a typical pioneer woman with a home and family.

333. Tippets, Susan Thomas, comp. *Piedmont, Uinta County, Wyoming: Ghost Town.* N.p.: n.p., 1995.

This privately published book of fifty-four pages provides genealogical and local history information for Piedmont, a small railroad town in western Wyoming where Martha Canary resided in 1869. Most of the hodgepodge of material concerns the Moses Byrne and Charles Guild families, who lived in the town and on nearby ranches for many years. Piedmont was the site of a potentially explosive incident when railroad officials from the East on their way to celebrate completion of the transcontinental Central Pacific–Union Pacific Railroad in Promontory, Utah, found the rail line blocked. Unpaid construction workers stopped the train until funds were sent to pay them. The 1869 census lists Martha Canary as living in Piedmont when the incident took place.

Local tradition and four contributors to this collection state that Joseph [*sic*] Canary, Martha's father, was gunned down in a local saloon and buried in an unmarked grave. No research has confirmed this probably false oral story.

334. Trexler, H. A. *Missouri-Montana Highways.* Columbia: State Historical Society of Missouri, 1918.

Since the route the Canary family followed in coming west from Missouri to Montana between 1863 and 1865 has never been revealed, this study of Missouri immigration to Montana suggests possible routes Robert, Charlotte, and their family could have taken. The carefully researched monograph, reprinted from the *Missouri Historical Review*, focuses on the 1860s but covers later trails as well.

335. Turchen, Lesta V., and James D. McLaird. *The Black Hills Expedition of 1875.* Mitchell, S.Dak.: Dakota Wesleyan University Press, 1975.

This helpful collection brings together several sources important to an understanding of the scientific Newton-Jenney Expedition of 1875 and its military escort led by Colonel Richard Irving Dodge. Gathered here are Jenney's dispatches to the commissioner of Indian Affairs, the journal of Colonel Dodge, and stereoscopic views of the expedition.

These materials are important for comprehending Martha Canary's first trip to the Black Hills. Although she is not mentioned in these documents, the volume editors place her with the expedition through references to her in other sources about the trip. It is most likely that Martha became Calamity Jane during this journey in the summer of 1875. Members of the expedition also named a mining area they encountered "Calamity Bar" and a nearby mountain "Calamity Peak."

336. Waite, Walter. *Silver Dollar Tales: Old Utica.* Conrad, Mont.: Marilyn and Walter Waite, 1994.

Waite tells a delightful tale about Calamity in Utica, Montana. A bartender, an ancestor of the author's, stole some of Calamity's underwear and hung it above the bar in his saloon. Hearing what had happened, Calamity strapped on her guns and went after the bartender. To avoid a shooting, the bartender bargained with an offer of free drinks for Calamity for the week. Calamity and Robert Dorsett, one of her steady "husbands" in the 1890s, lived together in Utica for up to a year.

337. Walker, Dale L. *The Calamity Papers: Western Myths and Cold Cases.* New York: A Forge Book, 2006. Originally published 2004.

This collection of eight topical sections includes essays on, among others, Lewis and Clark, Sam Houston, Thomas Francis Meagher (Montana territorial governor), Pat Garrett, Calamity Jane, and Walker's longtime interest, Jack London. Popularly and appealingly written, the essays treat unresolved incidents—"cold cases"—that have intrigued western historians and biographers for several decades.

The first part of the section on Calamity (pp. 195–208) avoids most of the errors in the short piece that follows and places major emphasis on Jean Hickok McCormick's claim to be the offspring of Calamity and Wild Bill. Revealingly, although Walker cites secondary sources that provide brief but dependable overviews of Calamity's life, he seems reluctant to accept the latter findings.

Some errors mar Walker's account of Calamity. He misdates Crook's major encounters with the Sioux (the military expeditions Calamity joined on two occasions in the winter and spring of 1876) as occurring in 1875. Following too closely Duncan Aikman's flawed account (230) and paying too little attention to James McLaird's scholarship, the author misses the significance of Calamity's life in Deadwood leading up to Hickok's murder on 2 August 1876. The author is wrong, too, about Clinton Burke's being "a one-legged Civil War veteran" (p. 215) and about the child Calamity had with her in Deadwood in 1895 being Burke's and not hers. He also badly jumbles Calamity's appearances in books written about her in the 1870s and 1880s.

A second section (pp. 221–38) deals with McCormick's falsehoods. Curiously, Walker gives about as much space to this hoax as to the entire life of Calamity Jane. He mainly agrees with Professor McLaird that the McCormick documents are fraudulent, but he is convinced there is more to the story than anyone has revealed. In the end, the McCormick story superbly illustrates Walker's lively purpose of illuminating "western myths and cold cases."

338. Watkins, John McClain. "Calamity Jane: A Pageant-Drama in Three Acts." Master's thesis, Montana State University, 1961.

The historical background portion of this pageant-drama is a cut-and-paste account of Calamity drawn from published primary sources (especially newspapers) and secondary sources. The author relies heavily on Sollid's important book (326). Many of the long, block quotations, though they add useful raw information, are not interrogated; the author fails to provide needed analysis and evaluation of his sources. Surprisingly, Watkins, although drawing much from Sollid, on the same pages quotes from the spurious Calamity Jane diary and letters, suggesting the two are of equal value as sources. The quotations from and about Montana are particularly extensive. At one time Watkins hoped to direct a pageant on Calamity in Livingston, but could not secure the needed support from the town. This account is more useful for the sources quoted than for its limited evaluations of Calamity and the utilized sources.

339. Whithorn, Bill, and Doris Whithorn. *Calamity's in Town: The Town Was Livingston, Montana.* Livingston, Mont.: [Enterprise], n.d.

This very useful forty-eight-page pamphlet is a testament to the diligent research of the Whithorns into the local history of Livingston, Montana, and the surrounding areas. The pamphlet reprints forty-one full or partial newspaper stories dealing with Calamity, mostly from the *Livingston Daily Enterprise* (later *Livingston Enterprise*) and adds a wealth of details about Calamity's activities in the area from 1884 to her death in 1903; a few post-1903 stories are also reprinted. Some of the newspaper articles merely repeat well-worn and exaggerated sources, but others contain new factual information and interviews that contribute unique reports about Calamity's life in south-central Montana. The sixteen photos of Calamity and the Livingston environs enhance the value of this modest but invaluable source.

340. Williams, Albert N. *The Black Hills: Mid-Continent Resort.* American Resort Series No. 4. Dallas, Texas: Southern Methodist University Press, 1952.

The decidedly negative account on pages 107–14 reduces Calamity to a "drunken harlot" (p. 108) or an "alcoholic old harlot" (p. 113). The author speaks for the Missouri origins of Calamity rather than for the Fort Laramie beginnings that Dr. McGillycuddy (289) and Doane Robinson (314) advocated. Williams also warmly recommends Nolie Mumey's account of Calamity (302). The facts in this source are so mixed and the chronology of Calamity's life so tangled that the account is reduced in value. Not to be relied on.

341. Wilstach, Frank J. *Wild Bill Hickok: The Prince of Pistoleers.* Garden City, N.Y.: Doubleday, Page, 1926.

In this early, foundational biography of Wild Bill, Wilstach denounces any serious relationship between Calamity Jane and Wild Bill as "wholly moonshine" (p. 254). Following the testimony of Ellis T. "Doc" Pierce and disagreeing with the view of another early Deadwood resident, John S. McClintock (288), Wilstach states that the two notorious Westerners were acquaintances—and no more than that. Still, Wilstach speaks highly of Calamity as "quite a remarkable person. Hers is one of the most amazing lives among the men and women who lived through the romance of the plains" (p. 260).

The author adds, mistakenly, that Calamity was a scout for General Custer and a pony express rider. She was "a most kind and generous heart," but "had no more use for skirts than an owl has for the Book of Common Prayer" (p. 263). Wilstach advances here the bifurcated view of several Wild Bill biographers: Calamity and Wild Bill were obviously neither sweethearts nor lovers, but Calamity was nonetheless a notable Wild West woman with kindly intentions for the needy.

342. Young, Harry ("Sam"). *Hard Knocks: A Life Story of the Vanishing West.* Introduction by James D. McLaird. Pierre: South Dakota State Historical Society, 2005. Originally published 1915.

Sam Young's greatest claim to fame in the Old West was his having been the bartender at Saloon No. 10 in Deadwood when Jack McCall assassinated Wild Bill Hickok on 2 August 1876. Young had spent more than a dozen previous years on the frontier as a teamster, bullwhacker, and in other jobs. This account narrates Young's active life in the northern West up to October 1876, when he left Deadwood.

Young knew Calamity Jane well and includes important firsthand information about her in his autobiographical volume. They rode together in a wagon as part of the Newton-Jenney Expedition into the Dakota Country in 1875, and he knew her later in Deadwood as an entertainer at Al Swearingen's Gem Theater. She was also, Young indicated, the boss of the girls at the Gem. Young is mistaken, however, in asserting that Calamity was born in Fort Laramie (pp. 169–70) and died on 2 August 1906—or thirty years to the day after Wild Bill's assassination (pp. 206–207). The correct date was 1 August 1903.

343. Zupan, Shirley, and Harry Owens, eds. *Red Lodge: Saga of a Western Area.* Red Lodge, Mont.: Carbon County Historical Society, 1979.

An abbreviated account of Calamity's stay in Red Lodge, Montana (pp. 238–39), that deals with her later days. When Calamity took sick, town residents, including some of its leaders, offered to support her. They would brook no criticism of Calamity because she had helped others in need, never turning "her back to a friend or stranger in want" (p. 238). The writers mention Calamity's friendship with Ben Greenough (202) and her tendency to sleep in a stable and dress, illegally, in men's attire.

Essays

This section contains a mix of book chapters, magazine and journal articles, conference papers, online postings, and other relatively brief pieces. All are arranged alphabetically by author. Numbers in parentheses cross-reference other entries in this guide.

344. Abild, Ethel Dowell. "Calamity Jane—Woman of Mystery." In *Papers of the 14th Annual Dakota History Conference, April 2–3, 1982*. Compiled by H. W. Blakely. Karl E. Mundt Historical and Educational Foundation Series. Madison, S.Dak.: Dakota State College, 1983, pp. 419–24.

    Abild tells a young girl's story of her encounter with Calamity Jane early in the twentieth century. Her provocative generalization—that Calamity did not gain her famous name "because she caused calamity, but because where calamities were, Jane arrived to care for those in need" (p. 420)—is worthy of additional consideration. Unfortunately, many other statements by the author are wrong: Martha Canary's parents were not missionaries, Calamity was not unmatched in shotgun accuracy, and her mother Charlotte was illiterate, not "well educated." At the end of Abild's brief essay, when she falls into the clutches of the Jean Hickok McCormick falsehoods, her story stumbles off-track. The author's memories illuminate, but her statements are often mistaken.

345. Blewitt, Andrew. "Calamity Jane." *English Westerners' Brand Book* 5 (January 1963): 1–9.

    A thoroughly footnoted piece (152 notes in less than ten double-spaced pages), this essay by a British writer provides a very useful, but brief introduction to Calamity Jane, Blewitt, primarily, makes strong, systematic uses of secondary sources, mostly the best ones. He moves chronologically through Calamity's life, pointing out competing interpretations of major events in her career. He also shows how the facts are at odds with what Calamity claimed about her life. This was the best abbreviated overview of Calamity into the 1960s and remains a helpful, compact treatment of the subject. Overall, the author's realistic, no-nonsense approach is the major strength of his appealing work.

346. Borner, Tobe. "Stories of the Early Life of Calamity Jane." *Wind River Mountaineer* 5 (October–December 1989): 33–34.

Reprinted from issues of the *Basin Republican Rustler* newspaper in 1941 and later in 27 October and 3 November 1983, this brief piece summarizes the Canary family history from the perspective of Calamity Jane's nephew Tobe Borner, the son of sister Lena. This story is greatly at odds with the Martha Canary/Calamity documents and should not be accepted. The Canarie father and mother (Tobe's spelling) did not die in an Indian attack in 1864 or 1865, and Martha and Lena's father was not named Elijah, not a Methodist minister, and not studying the Mormons, as far as we know. Other details are, by and large, more acceptable. Tobe says he learned his story from his mother, Lena Canary Borner.

347. Brink, Elizabeth A. "Clothing Calamity Jane: An Exercise in Historical Research." *True West* 37 (November 1990): 20–24.

This essay contributes new information. It details a historical researcher's endeavors to verify as Calamity Jane's three items of clothing found among artist Frederic Remington's collection given to the Buffalo Bill Historical Museum in Cody, Wyoming. After diligent study and comparisons of the coat, vest, and trousers at the Buffalo Bill Museum with several portraits of Calamity, Elizabeth Brink confidently concludes the articles of clothing are indeed Calamity's. How Remington came to have the clothing remains a mystery. Here are some—perhaps the only ones—of Calamity's personal items still in existence. A sidebar entitled "A Brief History of Myth Calamity Jane" (pp. 22–23) provides a very brief biographical overview of Calamity. The then-editor of *True West*, John Joerschke, comments on the preparation of the Brink essay in his "From the Editor" (p. 5).

348. Britz, Kevin. "Deadwood's Days of '76: The Wild West Show as Community Celebration." *South Dakota History* 40 (Spring 2010): 52–84.

The late Kevin Britz, a skilled student of tourism, historical memory, and community celebrations, describes how the Deadwood Days of '76 commenced in 1924 and have continued to the present. Anti-vice crusader and newspaper editor Edward L. Senn did not want the big doings to be a celebration of a Wild West Deadwood but rather a strong salute to the town's gradual maturation into something more than a frenetic frontier. But those sensing the tourist draws of such figures as Wild Bill, Calamity Jane, and a boomtown Deadwood won out. The Days of '76 became and remain more of an Old West blowout than a touting of Deadwood's economic and socio-cultural development. A valuable, thoughtful essay.

349. Burke, John. "The Wildest Woman in the West." *True West* 1 (June 1967): 12–13, 44–45.

In the initial issue of this Wild West popular magazine, Calamity is presented as the wildest of all western women. The author follows the discounted Dalton story of Martha's origins—that she was born at Fort Laramie and raised there after the deaths of her father and mother following an Indian attack. He also accepts the line that Captain Egan gave her the nickname "Calamity Jane" after she rescued him from a band of Indians. Obviously, Burke also follows the Jean Hickok McCormick yarn (246) that Calamity and Wild Bill met, consorted, and produced a daughter. He also includes an outrageous tale of a drunken Calamity, on a bet, almost choking Wild Bill with her errant whip in a Deadwood saloon. As might be expected, the author ends his error-marred piece with the wrong date for Calamity's death. Not to be trusted.

350. Burkholder, Edwin V. "Calamity Jane." *Argosy* 346 (May 1958): 30–33, 86–88.

Early in this essay the author declares that Calamity's actions at Wild Bill's assassination raised a "two-bit whore to . . . honored glory" (p. 32). That is, newspapermen snatched up Calamity's actions in Deadwood and transformed them into a romantic, sensational story of love, violence, and high drama. Burkholder's general point is well taken: Martha Canary was converted into Calamity Jane in the Black Hills events of 1875–78.

But the author misspells so many names and so often claims Calamity told stories she never did that his valuable thesis is undermined and thrown partially off track. For example, Calamity never bragged of being the offspring of royalty or of being the daughter of General Custer. And she did speak of Princeton, Missouri, as her birthplace, contrary to what the author states here. Nor did she travel to New York City to help sell dime novels featuring her as a heroine or take a trip to England to advance her career. The value of Burkholder's tenable thesis of the important shift from reality to myth in Calamity's life is greatly reduced via his many errors and mistakes.

351. Burkholder, Edwin V. "Love Life of Calamity Jane." *Real: The Exciting Magazine for Men* 7 (November 1955): 10–11, 58–60. Also printed in *Real West*, November 1955.

Most of this assertive, pretentious essay is off the mark. The author gets both Calamity's birth and death dates wrong, he is mistaken about the dime novels that featured her, he also sends her on trips to New York City and England that she never made, and the chronology of her life is all awry. More exasperating still are the falsehoods the author puts in Calamity's mouth. She never claimed to be the daughter of a military leader and a beautiful belle, and she did not plan revenge on Indians for killing her parents. What Burkholder does get right is the importance of sensational and incorrect newspaper and dime novels in transforming a Calamity who had trouble with alcohol, physical cleanliness, and sexual promiscuity into a beautiful, romantic heroine of a Wild West.

352. "Calamity Jane as a Lady Robin Hood." *Literary Digest* 87 (14 November 1925): 46, 48.

This curious piece is primarily a summary of Seymour Pond's essay (185) that appeared a month earlier. The information is nearly all the same but in a different order.

353. "Calamity Jane Was Lady Wildcat from Missouri." *Missouri Historical Review* 48 (October 1953): 49–50.

This little-known essay contains one of the first references to Martha Canary's being listed in the 1860 census. Her birth date is given as 1856, the most dependable date we have for her birth. The account is mistaken, however, in describing her father and mother; they were hardly "improvident parents" (p. 49), and Wild Bill was not her "long-time friend" (p. 50). Other mistakes include numbering Calamity among a Wild Bill drama group and stating that she died on 2 August.

354. Croy, Homer. "Calamity Jane's Romantic Diary." *American Weekly* (1 June 1958): 20–22.

Well-known magazine writer Homer Croy accepts the Jean Hickok McCormick story and enthusiastically embraces the phony diary and letters said to be Calamity's. The author really goes awry in creating conversations, imagining thoughts of his characters, and inventing an intimate Calamity–Wild Bill relationship. Croy's unacceptable essay ends by misdating Calamity's death.

355. Etulain, Richard W. Afterword to Roberta Beed Sollid, *Calamity Jane: A Study in Historical Criticism*. Helena: Montana Historical Society Press, 1995, pp. 149–63.

This brief afterword in the new edition of Sollid's important early study (first published in 1958) focuses on secondary writings about Calamity rather than on her. In brief compass, the author deals with the major biographies, novels, and movies treating Calamity Jane in the twentieth century. Most of the material presented here was utilized in Etulain's later writings (see 357–59).

356. Etulain, Richard W. "Calamity Jane," *Cowboys and Indians* 1 (July 1993): 30–33.

This brief piece, Etulain's first on Calamity Jane, appeared in the premier issue of this increasingly popular and slick western magazine. Unfortunately, a few misspellings and erroneous facts crept into this abbreviated account. Later publications by the same author corrected the mistakes. Nicely illustrated with well-produced photo reproductions.

357. Etulain, Richard W. "Calamity Jane: A Life and Legends." *Montana: The Magazine of Western History* 64 (Summer 2014): 21–45, 92–94.

This long essay draws heavily on the author's full-length study of Calamity (257). The first half of the essay provides a brief biography of Calamity, the second half summarizes, chronologically, the interpretations of her from the late 1870s to the present. This account touches on the major controversies of Calamity's story: her birth date and place, "husbands," motherhood, ramblings, alcoholism, possible prostitution, and decline and death. These sections are built on archival and published research.

The second section moves from the earliest newspaper and dime novel interpretations of Calamity to the most recent biographical, novelistic, and cinematic treatments. The author outlines the three major legends that have congealed around Calamity: (1) her image as a Wild Woman of the Old West; (2) her legend as an Angel of Mercy treating the sick and needy; and (3) her desire to be a typical Pioneer Woman who married, had children, and

established a stable home. The essay also includes a good deal of informa-
tion on Calamity's male partners; her daughter, Jessie; and the woman, Jean
Hickok McCormick, who falsely claimed to be the daughter of Calamity and
Wild Bill Hickok. Heavily illustrated.

358. Etulain, Richard W. "Calamity Jane: Independent Woman of the Wild West."
In *By Grit and Grace: Eleven Women Who Shaped the American West*,
edited by Glenda Riley and Richard W. Etulain. Golden, Colo.: Fulcrum,
1997, pp. 72–92.

This twenty-page essay is a brief interpretive biography of Calamity Jane.
Based on published and manuscript sources, the essay clarifies the controversies surrounding Calamity's birth, early years, and whereabouts in the
wandering times from the 1870s through the 1890s. Etulain also provides
a brief evaluation of the biographies, novels, and films that helped shape
the legend of this woman of the Old West. The essay is without footnotes,
but a two-page bibliographical discussion lists and comments on the major
sources for Calamity's life and legends. Five photographs accompany the
essay.

359. Etulain, Richard W. "Calamity Jane: The Making of a Frontier Legend." In
Wild Women of the Old West, edited by Glenda Riley and Richard W. Etulain.
Golden, Colo.: Fulcrum, 2003, pp. 177–95, 209–11.

This chapter provides a brief summary of Martha Canary's transformation
into the mythic Old West woman Calamity Jane. The major emphasis in the
piece is on the life stories, novels, and movies that helped mold the legendary woman. Included in these discussions are influential dime novels, biographies, and films such as *The Plainsman* (1936); *Calamity Jane* (1953); and
Buffalo Girls—the novel by Larry McMurtry (1990) as well as the movie by
the same name starring Anjelica Huston (1995). Footnotes are omitted, but
an essay on sources evaluates the most notable fiction and nonfiction dealing
with Calamity. Five photographs illustrate major points of the essay.

360. Forney, Gary. "Montana's Pioneer Editor." http://mtpioneer.com/2011-june
-pioneer-editor.html.

An immensely helpful piece of investigative journalism, this essay briefly
traces the life and writing career of journalist Horatio N. Maguire (286–87).
His two books, *The Black Hills and American Wonderland* (1877) and *The
Coming Empire* (1878) provided early, revealing paragraphs about Martha/

Calamity that became widely utilized sources for biographers, historians, and novelists dealing with Calamity.

361. F[ox], M. [L.]. "Calamity Jane." *Illustrated American*, 7 March 1896, p. 312.

Although only one page in length, this is one of the most significant published pieces of writing about Calamity. Perhaps this female journalist reveals that if, early on, more women, rather than mostly men, had written about Calamity, her first images might have been quite different. Here, the writer takes a decided feminine tack in interviewing Calamity, just before she embarked on her tour with the Kohl and Middleton museum group.

Calamity reveals much in telling Fox "I'd like to be respectable, but nobody'll notice me; they say 'There's old Calamity Jane,' an' I've got enough woman left bout me so that cuts to hear them say it." In the conversation, Calamity clarifies her Missouri birth, the early death of her parents when she "was nine year ole." When her young daughter Jessie returns from school during the interview, Calamity tells the journalist "She's all I've got to live for; she's my only comfort. I had a little boy, but he died."

The picture of Calamity that emerges here is of a mother—and perhaps a wife—who wants to be like other pioneer women. She hopes to provide for her daughter and educate her so that she will "be honest an' respectable." A revealing source on Calamity, much at odds with the usual run of Wild West female portraits.

362. Freeman, Lewis R. "Calamity Jane and Yankee Jim: Historic Characters of the Old Yellowstone." *Sunset Magazine* 49 (July 1922): 22–25, 52, 54.

This essay became part of Freeman's book *Down the Yellowstone* (1922). A journalist and baseball player, young Freeman came to Livingston, Montana, in 1901. There, he encountered Calamity in what he described as "one event that transcends all others in the bigness with which it" bulked in his memory (p. 25). Well written and spiced with humor, this piece is nonetheless depressing in its depiction of Calamity deep into drunkenness in her final years. Unable to find her room in a besotted state, Calamity accosts Freeman—"Short Pants," she calls him, because of his checkered knickers—to aid her. He does.

The next morning Freeman checks on Calamity and finds her smoking a cigar and cooking breakfast. She asks him to bring her a "can of suds," and primed with that libation, she proceeds to give him her Wild West spiel delivered for dime museums. When he breaks in to ask a question,

she swears and begins again. When he questions her account and those
in popular fiction, she grows angry and starts over again. Finally realizing what is happening, Freeman stops breaking in and gets Calamity's full
story and other intriguing facts, some of which unfortunately the journalist never put to paper. A lively account that includes two unique Calamity
photos (532, 533).

363. "The Girls of the Gulch: Calamity Jane Was Part of the Overhead." *Deadwood Magazine* 11 (July–August 2001): 10, 15–16.

This very general piece summarizes several popular notions about Calamity at the turn of the twenty-first century. She was, first of all, a very heavy
drinker, lived her life primarily in bars, and wore buckskins most of the time.
And some of the misinformation appears too: she had never married (or better yet a marriage license had never been found), was not a mother, and was
likely born well before 1852. All of these statements are errors, of course. The
writer has not moved beyond at-hand sources to burrow below the surface
and counter incorrect details. A companion essay in the same issue, "Here
Comes Calamity!" (367) describes Dianne Gleason's work as a Calamity
impersonator.

364. Hacecky, Kerry. "Calamity Jane, We Hardly Knew You." *South Dakota Magazine* 22 (May–June 2006): 36–40.

Primarily an essay review of James McLaird's then newly published biography, *Calamity Jane* (2005 [290]), this brief piece provides a capsule overview
of Calamity's life. Nothing new is presented, but in following McLaird closely
the author furnishes an abbreviated, realistic overview of Calamity so often
missing in popular magazines. A small sidebar discussion of Wild Bill, Charlie Utter, and Calamity clarifies bits of those complicated relationships.

365. Hart, Ernest H. "Deadlier Than the Male." *Real West* 16 (November 1973):
22–26.

This brief essay discusses well-known Wild West women such as Belle Starr,
Mattie Silks, Madame Moustache, Big Nose Kate, Rose Dunn ("Rose of the
Cimarron"), Madam Vestal, Cattle Kate Watson, and Calamity Jane. Hart's
abbreviated treatment of Calamity adds nothing new and is rather reductive,
calling her "a drunken prostitute consorting with rough and tough bull-
whackers, teamsters, cowboys, soldiers, and hardcases of the frontier West"
(p. 23). A minor essay containing small errors.

366. Hart, George. "Who Was Calamity Jane?" *Real West* 17 (January 1974): 28–31, 68–69.

The first half of this essay reprints Calamity's 1896 autobiography (241), and the second half takes issue with the falsehoods in this brief life story. Unfortunately, Hart misses Calamity's Canary family in the 1860 Missouri census, mistakenly identifying her as M. J. Conarray (a mistake duplicated in several other sources). Compounding the error, Hart tries to force the known facts of Calamity's adult life into the Conarray story, even though the Canary family, with her parents' correct names, is just a few pages away from Conarray in the census report. The author's incorrect thesis undermines the value of this essay.

367. "Here Comes Calamity." *Deadwood Magazine* 11 (July–August 2001): 4–5.

This brief essay attempts to paint Dianne Gleason as a realistic portrayer of Calamity—in fact, as like her in many ways. True, Gleason describes herself as an independent woman, a skilled gunwoman, and a person with alcoholism—the last problem now in the past. Unhappily, the unnamed author introduces too many errors. Calamity, for instance, was not six feet tall and of a "big-boned physique" but a woman of about five feet, six inches with a sinewy, compact build. The author is wrong, too, in asserting "there's no record of her ever having been lawfully wed" (p. 5). Records in Pocatello, Idaho, show she legally married William P. Steers on 30 May 1888 (43). On the other hand, the writer wisely refrains from calling Calamity a whore because there are indeed no "records of Calamity Jane ever being arrested as prostitute" (p. 4). In fact, no one has incontrovertible proof—only rumors and unconfirmed claims—that she was a prostitute.

368. Hiatt, Diane. "Calamity Jane: Her True Story." *True Frontier* 41 (February 1975): 11–13, 64–65.

Beware. This essay advances as truth much we have no factual proof of, especially about Calamity's family. Hiatt argues that Calamity's mother, Charlotte, wanted to stay in Princeton, Missouri, and her father, Robert, wanted to go west. The author adds that Charlotte "felt no particular loyalty to either side" in the Civil War (p. 12). The one tidbit we have on the subject suggests Charlotte was a "secesh," siding with the Confederates. Hiatt also provides created conversations with little or no supporting evidence and a depiction of Martha working on the railroad like a male worker when she was but twelve years old.

The author misreads the chronology in 1876 and buys the idea that Wild Bill wanted Calamity to be part of his theatrical group. Hiatt has not read much on Calamity (certainly not Sollid's book [326], which was available to her). Nor does she do much with the post-Deadwood days. And certainly Calamity did not claim to be married to Wild Bill. Not a compelling piece of work.

369. Hope, B. W. "Joe Elliott's Story." *Annals of Wyoming* 45 (Fall 1973): 143–75.

Bits of good information about Calamity and her "husband" Clinton Burke appear in these reminiscences of frontier lawman and wanderer Joe Elliott. He saw Calamity and Burke, with a "little girl, that I assumed was theirs" (p. 167) in eastern Montana. Calamity was cooking in a logging camp, and "she behaved herself. She looked and acted just like a big German housewife."

370. Hunter, J. Marvin, Sr. "The Real Calamity Jane." *Frontier Times* 29 (November 1951): 31–33.

Hunter, one of the founding fathers of popular western historical writing, badly misfires in this, a pioneering journal of Wild West history. The brief essay overflows with errors and unproven assertions. Hunter contends Calamity "likely made several killings," was an army scout in battles against the Apache in Arizona, and "got into many an Indian battle" (p. 32)—all conclusions that minimal research would have overturned. The "drink-sodden wretch," Hunter adds, early on "teamed up with Wild Bill Hickok" (p. 32), another exaggeration. And the author gets Calamity's death date wrong. Misleading and superficial essay.

371. James, Al. "Calamity Jane: Hottest Gun of the West." *Man's Adventure* 1 (August 1958): 30–31, 67–70.

A disposable Wild West piece, this essay opens with Calamity killing a man, which never happened. The author proceeds to describe Martha/Calamity as "a tigress in tight britches with morals as loose as a jar of marbles" (pp. 31, 67). Next comes a girl—all of ten—who can "blast the eye out of a buzzard at fifty yards" (p. 68). Then a sexpot with "shapely legs" and a "bosom that was hard to hide" (p. 68). Most egregious, the author manufactures a coupling between Calamity and a man she never met and a scene between Calamity and Wild Bill that never occurred. The untrustworthiness of the author descends to its worst when he states Calamity had "twelve husbands. They all died from unnatural causes" (p. 70). More than half of this essay is unverifiable fiction or provable lies. A travesty of a publication.

372. Mays, Carleton. "The Real Calamity Jane." *Real West* 3 (January 1960): 26–29, 48–50.

    This "double length feature" essay fails to depict the promised "real" Calamity. It is doubly bad, pretending to be something it is not and adding outrageous false stories for which there is no substance of truth. Author Mays has Calamity going east at the behest of publisher Beadle, one of the "Dime Novel boys" (p. 48), and also making a trip to England, where she visited and alienated Queen Victoria. Why the author should peddle such lies is beyond kenning; there is no proof for such stories, and no one else has tried to foment them. The author dismisses the nonsense that Calamity was a veteran scout and discounts exaggerations about Wild Bill but then misdates Calamity's birth and death and mixes up the timeline of major events in her life. Mays seems to conclude that the "real" Calamity was little more than a "tobacco chewing whore" (p. 28).

373. McLaird, James D. "Calamity Jane: The Development of a Legend." In *Papers of the 15th Annual Dakota History Conference, April 7–9, 1983*. Compiled by H. W. Blakely. Karl E. Mundt Historical and Educational Foundation Series. Madison, S.Dak.: Dakota State College, 1984, pp. 384–405.

    A pathbreaking essay, this little-known piece of McLaird's attempts what no one had undertaken at that time: to provide a brief overview of the Calamity Jane legend-making process. The author reviews the importance of the Paine (380–82), Jennewein (278), and Sollid (326) essays and books and addresses the memoirs of Calamity's Deadwood contemporaries, the dime novels of Edward L. Wheeler, and a few other works of fiction and nonfiction. The influences of American Studies scholars Henry Nash Smith (402) and Kent L. Steckmesser (329) are also evident here. Undoubtedly McLaird, the author of the definitive biography of Calamity Jane, would in retrospect appreciate the irony of two of his statements in this pioneering essay: "The real person who was known as Calamity Jane really doesn't deserve a biographical study" (p. 384), and "Calamity Jane was not historically significant" (p. 400). McLaird's own invaluable later works overturn the validity of these two statements. Several of the ideas put forth here are prominent in McLaird's more recent essays and books.

374. McLaird, James D. "Calamity Jane: The Life and Legend." *South Dakota History* 24 (Spring 1994): 1–18.

    This piece provided the most thorough account of Calamity's last months, her funeral, and early postmortem evaluations of her life—until McLaird updated and expanded this information in his later, first-rate biography (290). McLaird bases his narrative on a thorough reading of newspaper and ephemeral sources in South Dakota, Wyoming, and Montana. At this point McLaird did not know of Calamity's marriage to William P. Steers in May 1888, the birth of her two children, or the full story of her daughter, Jessie. Especially revealing is his tracking of the whereabouts of Calamity in 1902–1903, which changed almost weekly.

375. McLaird, James D. "Calamity Jane and Wild Bill: Myth and Reality." *Journal of the West* 37 (April 1998): 23–32. Reprinted in Richard W. Etulain, ed. *Myths and the American West.* Manhattan, Kans.: Sunflower University Press, 1998, pp. 23–32.

This fine essay introduces the information McLaird greatly expanded in his later book, *Wild Bill Hickok and Calamity Jane* (291). McLaird correctly notes that the notorious pair knew one another for only five weeks—from late June to early August of 1876. They were acquaintances, not close friends, and no romantic relationship evolved from the contact, as the author makes clear. A brief section on Wild Bill traces his life up to the summer of 1876, and a longer section details the weeks of Calamity's life in Deadwood leading up to Hickok's assassination on 2 August.

The second half of this valuable essay traces the Wild Bill–Calamity connection in American popular culture. McLaird clearly and succinctly shows how false stories and rumors shaped the falsities of love and romance in such movies as *The Plainsman* (1936) and *Calamity Jane* (1953). Jean Hickok McCormick's wild claim of being the daughter of Wild Bill and Calamity helped launch a new generation of fiction and films featuring fresh falsehoods about Calamity. A gullible public in love with a mythical Wild West and a Hollywood bent on reviving and starting stretchers have kept the Wild Bill–Calamity fantasy before readers and viewers. So it has been and is likely to continue.

376. McLaird, James D. "Calamity Jane's Diary and Letters: Story of a Fraud." *Montana The Magazine of Western History* 45 (Autumn–Winter 1995): 20–35.

In one of the most important essays ever written about Calamity Jane, scholar James D. McLaird demolishes Jean Hickok McCormick's claim to be the daughter of Calamity Jane and Wild Bill Hickok. He also proves the diary and letters Calamity purportedly wrote to Jean to be frauds. Ransacking all the pertinent evidence, McLaird shows that Calamity, unable to read and write, could not have written the diary because it exhibits the diction and syntax of a well-educated writer. In addition to the internal evidence proving forgery, McLaird points out the numerous factual errors—wrong dates, imagined persons, and incorrect happenings—that spill out from the diary and letters. Unfortunately, too many readers, drawn to the mother-daughter warmth and tragic elements of McCormick's story, have accepted these sources without analyzing their reliability. Sadly, too many biographers and popularizers, especially, continue to build their romantic stories on these fraudulent documents.

377. McLaird, James D. "'I Know . . . Because I Was There': Leander P. Richardson Reports the Black Hills Gold Rush." *South Dakota History* 31 (Fall–Winter 2001): 239–68.

L. P. Richardson, an eastern journalist, traveled to Deadwood for a few days in midsummer 1876. This fact-filled essay sketches in the details of Richardson's trip and describes the people he encountered, including Calamity Jane, Wild Bill Hickok, Charley Utter, Moses ("California Joe") Milner, and Kitty Arnold. Calamity is portrayed as one "who bossed a dancehouse" and often appeared drunk, or nearly so, on the streets of Deadwood. McLaird provides important contextual detail surrounding Calamity's first days in the Dakota mining boomtown in the summer of 1876. Thoroughly and well illustrated.

378. McLaird, James D., ed. "Calamity Jane and the Black Hills Gold Rush in the Writings of William B. Lull." Biographical notes by David J. Lull. *South Dakota History* 28 (Spring–Summer 1998): 1–68.

William B. Lull, a young New Yorker, went west to Deadwood in 1875–76 and remained in the boomtown for nearly two years. This revealing and extensive essay contains several letters Lull wrote to his parents as well as a portion of a later manuscript he wrote, "In Old Deadwood," which includes his firsthand observations of and friendship with Calamity Jane. Lull's account, although including reconstructed conversations and mistaken facts, nonetheless reveals much about the human and warm side of Calamity. Overall, the essay contains several revealing documents about Deadwood and Calamity in 1876–77.

379. Moulton, Candy. "Following Calamity Jane: From Cheyenne, Wyoming, to Virginia City, Montana." *True West* 57 (January 2010): 74–80.

One of the "Renegade Roads" historical travelogues Moulton regularly contributes to *True West* magazine, this brief essay incorporates a good deal of dependable history about Calamity. The author has obviously read the recent, solid writing on Calamity, and she also makes excellent use of her own research on Valentine T. McGillycuddy, about whom she has recently published a strong biography, *Valentine T. McGillycuddy: Army Surgeon, Agent to the Sioux* (Norman, Okla.: Arthur H. Clark, 2011). Sound history in a brief, popular essay.

380. Paine, Clarence S. "Calamity Jane: Man? Woman? Or Both?" In *The Westerners Brand Book, 1945–46.* Chicago: n.p., 1947, pp. 69–82.

Paine, a college and public librarian, worked on a full-length biography of Calamity in the 1940s and 1950s. It was never completed, but three essays were published out of the author's research. This curious piece, repeating some of what appeared a year earlier in a similar outlet (381), advances the entirely speculative theory that Calamity was a hermaphrodite, neither woman or man—perhaps both. Although a half-dozen years into his research on Calamity, Paine evidently had not turned up some of the most important evidence about his subject's early life. He continued, as he did throughout his career, to be mistaken on the identity of Martha Canary's parents and to overlook important facets of her life before 1875. Still, his comments on the necessity of having to unlearn much to understand Calamity remains important guidance for studying her.

381. Paine, Clarence S. "She Laid Her Pistol Down; or, The Last Will and Testament of Calamity Jane." *The Westerners Brand Book 1944.* Chicago: The Westerners, 1946, pp. 9–21.

The first of Paine's three published essays on Calamity, this piece focuses on the supposed diary and letters that Jean Hickok McCormick (246) claimed were those of her mother, Calamity Jane. Thoughtful and cautious, Paine evaluates the controversial documents as possibly authentic but containing crucial errors if not trumped-up conclusions. Paine had interviewed McCormick in 1941, soon after she appeared on national radio to identify herself as the daughter of Wild Bill and Calamity. In the early 1940s, Paine agreed to work with McCormick on a biography of Calamity, but because Paine could not confirm McCormick's story and refused to move ahead until he could, disagreements surfaced and the biographical project foundered.

Five years into his research on McCormick and Calamity, Paine had not uncovered much correct information. Most disturbingly, he identified the Conarray family in the 1860 census from Mercer County, Missouri, as the family of Martha Canary, thereby missing the true parents, Robert and Charlotte Canary, just a few pages away. He admitted, too, that he had no other documents about Martha/Calamity before 1875, even though Montana and Wyoming newspaper stories, the Wyoming census, and other manuscript materials were available. Still, the essay is valuable, especially as an early attempt to assess the value and reality of the supposed Calamity diary and letters.

382. Paine, Clarence S. "Wild Bill Hickok and Calamity Jane." In *The Black Hills*, edited by Roderick Peattie. New York: Vanguard Press, 1952, pp. 151–76.

Paine had been researching Calamity and related subjects for a decade when this essay appeared. Unfortunately, not much of the extensive collection of materials he gathered over the years (which is now on file at Augustana College in Sioux Falls, South Dakota [22]) is worked into this essay. Perhaps he gradually lost interest in the subject; he published only this essay on Calamity after 1947.

Paine did not change his views on key subjects. He remained convinced, for example, that Robert and Charlotte were not Martha's parents even though nearly all the gradually emerging evidence pointed in their direction. Nor had Paine turned up much information on Martha's life before 1875. And he did little with the post-1880 period of her life, perhaps understandable for an essay in a book dealing with the Black Hills. Surprisingly, too, more than a little of this essay repeats what he had written about Calamity in his essays published in 1946 and 1947.

One wishes Paine had completed his book on Calamity. His research was as thorough as anyone's up to 1950. Lacking such a book delayed a larger understanding of Calamity for the next generation.

383. Patterson, W. G. "'Calamity Jane': A Heroine of the Wild West." *Wide World Magazine* 65 (August 1903): 450–57.

This essay, written in Calamity's final days, is a mixed bag of mistaken and helpful information. It contains more errors, imagined scenes, and exaggerations than established facts. Calamity did not kill dozens of Indians, did not lead an attack on the Sioux, did not have twelve husbands who all died violont doathø, and did not ꙅend hꙇꙇ daughtꙇꙇ east to be educated. Perhaps, since this essay was written for an English magazine intended for young readers, some of Patterson's numerous tall tales are understandable, but as a retrospective on Calamity's life just before her death, it is a failure. Conversely, the essay prints several important photographs of Calamity, some for the first time, and includes information gathered from unique interviews, especially with western jailers who knew Calamity. On balance, though, the limitations outweigh the contributions.

384. Repp, Ed Earl. "The Lady Was a Cavalryman." *The West* 10 (January 1969): 22–23, 49–52. Also printed in *Golden West* 8 (June 1972): 12–13, 55–57.

Repp begins with the skimpy facts known about Martha Canary's life, then quickly and egregiously expands on them. He speaks of Calamity learning to drink and charm men even before the Canary family lived in the Mountain West; Martha was then about seven or eight. He accepts the mistaken story about Calamity's getting her nickname by saving Captain Egan and then adds a conversation between that soldier and Calamity that no else has contrived. It gets worse: the author claims that Calamity joined the military, although no one has found any such military records. And Wild Bill and Colorado Charley were headed to the Black Hills to launch a theatrical company; that is why they invited Calamity to join them. She would be a box-office bonanza, they thought. She remained with Wild Bill during his remaining weeks in Deadwood, and she corralled his assassin, Jack McCall, with a cleaver. Balderdash. Calamity's post-Deadwood days are quickly skimmed over. A weak and misleading account.

385. Richardson, Leander P. "A Trip to the Black Hills." *Scribner's Monthly* 13 (April 1877): 748–56.

Richardson, a well-known traveler and writer, visited Deadwood very briefly in the summer of 1876. He writes of Wild Bill Hickok, Charlie Utter, and others, and reports on Wild Bill's assassination, which occurred while he was in Deadwood. Revealingly, he does not mention the flamboyant Calamity, whose controversial actions were already capturing the attention of local journalists.

386. Robbins, Peggy. "'Hellcat in Leather Britches.'" *American History Illustrated* 10 (June 1975): 12–21.

Robbins's piece mixes verifiable facts with too many mistakes. She gets many of the details about Martha Canary correct, but she also falls victim to Duncan Aikman's errors and exaggerations (230). She mistakes Virginia City, Nevada, for its Montana counterpart, and Blackfoot City, Montana, for Blackfoot, Idaho. Robbins also adds to well-known stories details that cannot be proven. Plus, the writer has not done sufficient research to know when Calamity tells the truth in her half-true, half-false autobiography (241). She also confuses Calamity's roles with Generals Crook and Custer in 1875–76. Although Robbins discounts the Jane [*sic*] Hickok McCormick story, she gets Calamity's death date wrong and misdescribes Clinton Burke and his relationship with Calamity. A well-written and decently researched essay that suffers from too many errors, large and small, to be strong.

387. Russell, John C. "Calamity Jane Lived Up to Her Name." *Wild West* 7 (August 1994): 42–48.

Russell uses the Lewis R. Freeman story (267), with its emphasis on her later years, to open and close his essay. Myths need to be countered, the author asserts: "Jane was little more than a drunken prostitute" (p. 44). The author utilizes the strong research and stout conclusions of Roberta Sollid (326) for most of his secondhand observations. Yet the statement that Calamity "spread the rumor that she and Hickok were lovers" (p. 45) is without substantiation. More upsetting, Russell mixes up Calamity's "marriages" and "husbands," and concludes, wrongly, that Calamity toured with Buffalo Bill's Wild West show. An essay with equal measures of fact and error.

388. Russell, Ona. "What's in a Name Anyway? The Calamity of Calamity Jane." *American Studies* 35 (Fall 1994): 21–38.

Author Russell is much more interested in gender theory than in the life and career of Calamity Jane. She also embraces the Jean Hickok McCormick story (246) that she was the daughter of Wild Bill Hickok and Calamity. These two bents lead the writer to examine what Calamity's "name might have signified, what it might have meant in the context of the late nineteenth-century United States, particularly to people of the western region of the country" (p. 22). The author is convinced that it is "possible to read Calamity as a figure for that period's anxiety over the breakdown of gender norms" (p. 23). Little interested in Calamity's biography, Russell wants to show how Calamity and similar female figures threatened a masculine, idealized West with their New Woman behavior. The author's goal is commendable: to examine late-nineteenth-century gender expectations and whether Calamity challenged them. But in quoting from fraudulent texts to substantiate her assertions and in making several large historical and biographical blunders, she dampens down enthusiasm for her endeavor. In extant photographs, Calamity is pictured more often in feminine than in masculine attire. And Calamity claimed in 1896 that she wanted, most of all, to be a mother and wife, to be a traditional pioneer woman, not to bruise accepted gender norms. She did not want to break free, she wanted to be accepted. Russell misses all that.

The author also uses faulty scholarship on the American West. By the mid-1990s, Sandra Myers, Glenda Riley, and Julie Roy Jeffrey, among several others, had produced strong works on women's experiences in the American West. The author cites none of the work of these authors but instead relies on much less satisfactory books on the subject. Overall, then, this is an essay with a worthwhile goal undermined through faulty research, with too many errors and oversights.

389. Secrest, William B. "The Calamities of Calamity Jane." *Wild West* 23 (February 2011): 56–62.

This lively written overview of Calamity's life zeroes in on her last years. Secrest, a well-known writer about the Old West, emphasizes Calamity's drunkenness and her antisocial behavior. He seems little interested in her female experiences—motherhood and marriage—even though she made these urges clear. Strong reliance on McLaird's biography (290). Generally, dependable on facts.

390. Secrest, William B. "Remembering Wild Bill and Deadwood." *True West* 47 (April 2000): 34–43.

This essay summarizes the final weeks of Wild Bill's life on his way to and in Deadwood in 1876. Much of the story is based on the memories of Joseph "White Eye" Anderson, whose autobiography *I Buried Hickok* (1981, edited by Secrest) tells the story from Anderson's perspective (322). Included in the story are several important details about Calamity.

Traveling to Deadwood in mid-June to do business and to mine—and thereby make a bundle—White Eye, Wild Bill, and Colorado Charlie Utter met Calamity at Fort Laramie. She had been on a drunk with soldiers and now was in the post guardhouse with virtually nothing to wear. Charlie's brother, Steve Utter, promised to keep an eye on Calamity on the way to Deadwood.

White Eye remembered that soldiers and travelers furnished Calamity new underclothes and other wear, including buckskins. "When she got cleaned up and sober she looked quite attractive," said White Eye. Then he added, "I believe it was the first time that Wild Bill had met her and he surely didn't have any use for her" (p. 36). Once the group arrived in Deadwood in mid-July, Anderson details Calamity's roles as an entertainer (maybe prostitute), nursemaid, and companion up through Wild Bill's death in early August. Generally, a strong and very useful essay.

391. Thorp, Raymond W. "White-Eye, Last of the Old-Time Plainsmen." *True West* 12 (March– April 1965): 6–10, 46, 48.

This strong essay on White Eye Anderson includes his revealing comments about Calamity Jane in 1876. White Eye, Wild Bill Hickok, Colorado Charlie Utter, his brother Steve Utter, and dozens of others brought Calamity with them from Fort Laramie to Deadwood, on their journey north in June– July 1876.

White Eye states that Calamity and Wild Bill probably had not known one another before this meeting on the way to Deadwood. He also mentions that Calamity often asked for a swig of whiskey from Wild Bill's keg, but he cautioned her "to go slow, others were dry, too" (p. 10). Calamity "tented with" Steve Utter and helped with the camp cooking. Once in Deadwood she borrowed twenty dollars from Wild Bill so that she could dress up and compete with the other lively ladies in the boomtown. After Wild Bill was assassinated and buried, Calamity picked wildflowers to place on his grave. An informative, balanced essay. For more extensive information on White Eye, see the book-length account edited by William B. Secrest (322).

392. Walker, Dale L. "The Calamitous One." *American Cowboy* 10 (July–August 2003): 64–65.

How is one to react to this two-page essay, rife with errors, by a well-known and respected writer of popular western history? Walker says that Calamity was born in 1852 on her grandfather's farm near Princeton, Missouri; that the Canary family went to Virginia City, Nevada; that mother Charlotte died in Blackfoot, Idaho; that Calamity served in the Nez Perce War of 1872; that she scouted for Buffalo Bill and participated in his Wild West show; and that she died on 3 August 1903. All these statements are palpable errors of fact. Use or quote from this piece at your own risk.

393. Weddon, William, and Marion M. Huseas. "Best Little Whorehouse in Wyoming." *True West* 30 (July 1983). 41–45.

    Forts and other military sites on the frontier often had "hog ranches" (houses of prostitution) as nearby neighbors. These authors state that Calamity was "the most famous woman" at the notorious Three-Mile hog ranch located that distance from Fort Laramie. Others support that conclusion. This essay provides a brief, sketchy description of the tenderloin life at hog ranches—for the prostitutes and their patrons.

394. Wright, Kathryn. "The *Real* Calamity Jane." *True West* 5 (November–December 1957): 22–25, 28, 41–42.

    This work tries to make a case for the authenticity of the diary and letters that Jean McCormick claimed were written by Calamity Jane and that Professor McLaird has proven to be frauds (376). Wright gives the basic details of Jean Hickok McCormick's life and some about the content of the documents. The author was a Montana writer with connections to Don and Stella Foote, the Billings couple who hired McCormick to work in their Old West museum and later purchased her document collection. Disappointingly, Wright asks not a single evaluative question about the documents; she accepts their validity on faith. The essay reprints sections of the diary and other materials said to authenticate those documents. Among these supporting documents is a letter from the radio program *We the People*, a program that did much to foster belief in McCormick's manufactured story. That letter was also used to gain welfare support for Mrs. McCormick. This essay also carries a copy of the *La Crosse* (Wisconsin) *Tribune* (15 September 1941), telling of McCormick's meeting with the Hickok family.

DIME NOVELS AND
COMMENTARIES

Entries in this section are arranged alphabetically by author, with the Edward
Wheeler series listed in chronological order. Numbers in parentheses cross-
reference other entries in this guide.

395. Bold, Christine. *Selling the Wild West: Popular Western Fiction, 1860–1960*.
Bloomington: Indiana University Press, 1987.

This valuable, probing study of popular Western fiction covers the topic
from dime novels to Louis L'Amour. The author is particularly interested in
the fictional formulas authors followed in trying to appeal to general audiences. Her comments on the dime novel, author Edward L. Wheeler, and
Calamity Jane are brief and a bit narrow but nonetheless insightful and illuminating. Bold shows how the Calamity figure, a Wild West heroine, fulfilled
the popular fictional need to locate a leading female figure to play opposite
the Deadwood Dick hero. Calamity illustrates the disguises, violence, and
cultural clashes so often apparent in Wheeler's Deadwood Dick series as
well as numerous other dime novels. This important volume illuminates
how Calamity's first fictional appearances—so antihistorical and contrived—
shaped popular conceptions of her from the 1870s onward.

396. Brown, Bill, ed. *Reading the West: An Anthology of Dime Westerns*. Boston:
Bedford Books, 1997.

This anthology of four dime novels includes Edward L. Wheeler's *Deadwood
Dick, The Prince of the Road; or, The Black Rider of the Black Hills* (1877). It
also contains a probing introduction on the history and content of the dime

novel. Brown puts the dime novel in cultural, literary, and historical contexts and adds valuable information on the Deadwood Dick series, the Beadle publishers, marketing techniques, and audience reception as well. Especially revealing, too, are Brown's comments on how the dime novels became outlets of social criticism, vehicles for criticizing bloated capitalists, eastern plutocrats, and arrogant moguls; and, conversely, celebratory voices for frontier democracy, regenerative violence, and western freedom.

Brown says little about Calamity Jane. Still, his provocative comments help readers to understand how dime novels in the Deadwood Dick series portrayed Calamity and why. Consider, for example, one of Brown's statements: "Reading examples of the dime Western . . . is a matter of witnessing not just how fact became fiction but also how popular culture becomes mass culture, how legend becomes mass-mediated memory" (p. 30). Or perhaps even more apt for historians: the Deadwood Dick series is culturally important because Wheeler "so exaggerates both the formula of the Western and elements foreign to it that the genre must abandon any lingering verisimilitude" (p. 36). These two stimulating comments help readers to see more clearly how the historical Martha Canary was transformed into the mythic Calamity Jane.

397. Fielder, Mildred. *Deadwood Dick and the Dime Novels.* Lead, S.Dak.: Bonanza Trails, 1974. Reprinted from "The Forbidden Adventures of Deadwood Dick, or Riders of the Purple Prose." *Empire* (magazine of the *Denver Post*), 22 November 1964.

This brief booklet contains useful information on the Deadwood Dick dime novels. The author, however, mistakenly identifies the author of these novels, stating, "Edward Zane Carrol Judson, sometimes writing under the name of Edward L. Wheeler, sometimes as Ned Buntline, wrote most of the Deadwood Dick dime and half-dime novels" (pp. 7–8). Fielder is also off base in stating there were sixty-four novels about Deadwood Dick in the series (there were thirty-three) and that Wheeler (alias Buntline) wrote one hundred Deadwood Dick stories.

These mistakes aside, the author provides general but useful information about a typical Deadwood Dick dime novel. She also briefly discusses the men claiming to be the original Deadwood Dick, especially Dick Clark of Deadwood. The author does not deal with Calamity; rather, she speaks of the type of dime novels in which the mythic Calamity appeared in the 1870s and 1880s.

398. Gard, Wayne. "The Myth of Deadwood Dick." *Frontier Times* 43 (October–November 1969): 10–11, 48–50.

Gard points out in this straightforward, informative essay that Deadwood Dick appeared first as a fictional character in Edward L. Wheeler's thirty-three-volume series of dime novels in 1877–85. Once Wheeler's entirely imagined hero gathered widespread attention and acceptance, men came forward to claim they were the person on whom Wheeler based his protagonist. Gard briefly deals with six persons who claimed to be the original Deadwood Dick, including black cowboy Nat Love and longtime Black Hills resident Richard Clarke. The final paragraphs of Gard's helpful essay address Clarke's self-appointed status as Deadwood Dick and the controversies surrounding his spurious claim. Although Clarke's story was rife with errors, it captured the imaginations of others—and Clarke himself. In his remaining years and at his burial site he was lionized as the real Deadwood Dick. Dependable, useful essay.

399. Jones, Daryl. *The Dime Novel Western.* Bowling Green, Ohio: Popular Press, 1978.

This brief little book remains the best study of the dime novel Western. Jones provides a historical overview of the genre as well as close studies of the themes, settings, plots, and meanings that resurface in dozens of dime novels. Although the author devotes strong sections to backwoodsmen, plainsmen, outlaws, and cowboy heroes, these brief discussions command no separate chapter and are largely dovetailed into treatments of heroes. Still, Jones deals with the Edward L. Wheeler Deadwood Dick series and comments briefly on Calamity Jane as a close friend, lover, and wife of a hero disguised as an outlaw. Calamity participates in his attacks on corrupt people and places and saves his hide on more than one occasion. A source helpful for understanding the type of fiction that turned Martha Canary into the nationally recognized Calamity Jane.

400. La Telle, J. H. "Deadwood Dick—The Man Who Never Was." *Western Frontier* (November 1979): 31, 59.

The author briefly summarizes the making and marketing of Dick Clarke, a railroad section gang laborer, as the emblematic Deadwood Dick. As La Telle points out, no authentic Deadwood Dick ever existed, despite the widely known fictional character with that name in a lively dime novel series. So the Deadwood Chamber of Commerce decided to construct a Deadwood

Dick. From the late 1920s to the early 1940s, Clarke acted out his new, phony identity—to the enjoyment of visitors such as President Calvin Coolidge, ambitious tourism entrepreneurs, and starry-eyed little boys. The author does not reveal that several other men were christened Deadwood Dick, both before and after Clarke.

401. Ralph, Reckless. "Calamity Jane, The Queen of the Plains." Street and Smith's *New York Weekly*, 16, 23, 30 January; 6, 13, 20, 27 February; and 13 March 1882.

An eight-part serial, this poorly written and weakly organized dime novel is a story of revenge. Calamity, often in disguise, sets out to kill twenty-six vigilantes who have murdered her father figure, Mountain Jim. While revenging Jim's murder, Calamity also searches for her own father and mother. Eventually, with her sidekick Jesse James, Calamity gains ownership of a Deadwood gambling den. When she finds her father, he is worried about her antisocial behavior, but the storyteller says that though she gambles and kills people, Calamity is pure—that is, not guilty of sexual sins. Calamity forgives her father for abandoning her, and they return, together, to the grave of Calamity's mother in Colorado.

Like so many dime novels, this one is difficult to take seriously—as literature, and primarily as biography and history. The characters are exceedingly shallow and stereotyped, the plot overflows with unbelievable actions, and the historical details are wrong or distorted. Here, the emphasis is on Calamity the legendary Wild Woman of the Old West. Some Montanans thought the author of this series was Henry Horr of Montana, using the penname of Reckless Ralph, but no evidence has surfaced to support that contention.

402. Smith, Henry Nash. *Virgin Land: The American West as Symbol and Myth.* New York: Vintage Books, 1970. Originally published 1950.

This classic book, one of the most important volumes ever written about the American West, makes a case for ideas about the West—here termed myths and symbols—being as important as facts about the region. Often named as the pioneering volume in the "myth and symbol school" of the American Studies field, *Virgin Land* focuses on three specific myths: "Passage to India," "The Sons of Leatherstocking," and "The Garden of the World." Smith contends these powerful beliefs helped transform what readers, writers, planners, politicians, and historians came to think and "do" about the West.

Smith deals with Calamity Jane in his subsection on dime novels, a pioneering analytical treatment of the popular genre. In a chapter entitled "The Dime Novel Heroine," Smith points out that Calamity belongs with other Amazon-like heroines of the Edward L. Wheeler dime novels, such as Hurricane Nell, Wild Edna, and Phantom Moll. Often dressed in men's clothing, they ride, shoot, fight, and love like their male counterparts. Although subsequent critics have refined and sometimes challenged Smith's broad generalizations in this chapter, some of his descriptions of dime novel heroines, including Calamity Jane, still ring true. Smith broke new ground to show how the study of popular literature—often dismissed as worthless writing by previous academics—could open windows on new understandings of American culture. This work remains eminently useful for comprehending Calamity's roles as a dime novel heroine.

403. Tonkovich, Nicole. "Guardian Angels and Missing Mothers: Race and Domesticity in *Winona* and *Deadwood Dick on Deck*." *Western American Literature* 32 (November 1977): 240–64.

The author of this essay, diligently pushing her feminist themes, is a strong literary critic without much interest in the actual Calamity Jane and the inauthentic Deadwood Dick. The essay is useful for illustrating the writer's thesis that a dime novel such as *Deadwood Dick on Deck* breaks out of the stereotypical formats and characterizations of fainting females in domestic fiction and the wilting women of too many Westerns. More useful for students of literary criticism and theory than for historians and biographers.

404. Wheeler, Edward L. Deadwood Dick Series. New York: Beadle and Adams, 1877–85.

The thirty-three volumes in the Deadwood Dick series, part of Beadle's Half-Dime series, are also listed with further information in Albert Johannsen, *The House of Beadle and Adams and Its Dime and Nickel Novels: The Story of a Vanished Literature*, 3 vols. (Norman: University of Oklahoma Press, 1950). This source includes more extensive facts on each novel and also about the series author, Edward L. Wheeler. The following discussions describe plot summaries and Wheeler's handling of Calamity characters. A full-length study of the Deadwood Dick series would be a valuable project for an ambitious researcher willing to wade through thousands of pages of stereotyped characters, rambling plots, and diverse themes to capture the importance of a wildly popular series of dime novels at the end of the nineteenth century.

405. *Deadwood Dick, The Prince of the Road; or, The Black Rider of the Black Hills.* October 1877.

The first of the thirty-three volumes in Wheeler's Deadwood Dick series for Beadle and Adams, this typical dime novel introduces the two main characters of Deadwood Dick and Calamity Jane, sends them galloping through the Black Hills, and ends with most of the story line quickly, if not entirely satisfactorily, tied up in the final chapter. Deadwood Dick, actually a badly treated young man from the East named Ned Harris, appears in disguise as a much-feared highwayman. He has been victimized by bloated capitalistic rascals and is now on a trail of revenge.

Calamity jumps on scene as his companion. She is described in words entirely stolen or very closely paraphrased from Maguire's description in *The Black Hills and American Wonderland* (286), published just a few months before this dime novel. Dressed as a man in buckskins, she wears a "jaunty Spanish sombrero," has "hair of a raven color," and "comes of a Virginia City, Nevada, family of respectability and intelligence." Unfortunately, she "was *ruined*" and "set adrift on the world." But by dint of fortitude, toughness, and courage she has made her own way. "Her character has not suffered blemish since the day a foul wretch stole away her honor." And then come the slightly altered words of Lord Byron, via Maguire: she had a "slightly sunburned" face but "yet showing the traces of beauty that even excessive dissipation could not obliterate."

Riding with Deadwood Dick and other gallant fellows, Calamity fills onlookers and storytellers with awe and rumor. Set in the early boom days of Deadwood, the novel is a morality story featuring stick characters, fortuitous and chance circumstances, and incredible disguises. No matter, dime novel addicts loved the story, called for more, and bought copies by the hundreds of thousands.

This novel established the pattern for the Calamity Jane character in most of the volumes in the Deadwood Dick series: a youthful woman/man, of frenzied actions, on the road continuously and fearlessly, and for the most part bouncing through the Hills or other mining areas helping the hero right past wrongs. So smitten is Deadwood Dick with Calamity that he proposes marriage on the final page. But she refuses, telling him, "No . . . I have had all the men I care for. We can be friends, Dick; more we can never be." Still, the possibility of romance between Dick and Calamity was woven throughout most volumes in the series. Much more important for the imagined Calamity, the dime novels turned her, overnight, into a sensational fictional heroine and brought her name before hordes of enthusiastic readers.

406. *The Double Daggers; or, Deadwood Dick's Defiance. A Tale of Regulators and Road-Agents of the Black Hills.* December 1877.

Calamity bursts into this story on page 10, described in words taken from Maguire's book (286). Armed with two Colts, "clad in male attire . . . tanned buckskin, fringed," her form is "plump and graceful." And then Maguire's words, a la Lord Byron: "the face not really handsome; yet a rough and dissipated career had not altogether 'Swept away the lines where beauty lingers.'" Wheeler adopts the literary tricks of writers about the West from James Fenimore Cooper forward. Repeated chases and pursuits allow Calamity to gallop through the many gulches near Deadwood and to hide out in the caves and hidden camps nearby. Characterized as the "girl dare devil" and often speaking in rural vernacular, Calamity has abandoned her family in Nevada who earlier tossed her out of their home. Now she has become well-to-do, owning producing mines in the Hills and property in Deadwood. In addition, she is committed to protecting "the weak and oppressed." Dismissing men *and* women, she has "very few friends—for the simple reason I don't want many," she tells one listener.

In the closing scene, Deadwood Dick, who is one of Calamity's few accepted friends, marries another woman. Wheeler's narrator enters the narrative to say about Calamity: "I don't think . . . [she] will ever marry; her life will continue that of a dare-devil and reckless adventurer that she is, until the end." That prediction proved false.

407. *Buffalo Ben, The Prince of the Pistol; or, Deadwood Dick in Disguise.* February 1878.

Killings by the dozen, numerous chases and pursuits, attempted hangings, shootouts, disguises galore, and complex romances—all these and more in this, the third volume in the Deadwood Dick series. But almost no Calamity Jane. She does not appear until the closing chapters and plays only a very minor part. Deadwood Dick dons several incredible disguises, including one as a woman fortune-teller, is married to the beautiful Leone, and dashes in and out of the creaky plot. Generally, the work is badly organized, leaving several unanswered questions along with Calamity on the sidelines for nearly all the plot. A disappointing dime novel, with but a smidgen on Calamity.

408. *Wild Ivan, The Boy Claude Duval: or, The Brotherhood of Death.* March 1878.

Calamity Jane is entirely absent from this installment. She neither appears, nor is she even mentioned. Instead, Wheeler creates an unwieldy plot, with several subplots all featuring an attractive young woman. Deadwood Dick is married to an especially beautiful Leone, but in reprehensible jealousy she imprisons her husband. When freed, he sends Leone away, despite her penitent and remorseful pleadings. "Your jealousy led you into the commission of an act that no true, loving wife would have done," he tells her; "We were very happy together, until—until—until—." Dick also vows to leave off his road-agentry; he will no longer be "an outlaw, if his fellow-men will let him alone." But "if they strike me on account of the past, I will strike them back—*to the death!*" As they do, and he does, in later volumes of the series.

Entering the scene is Old Avalanche. A vernacular, Bible-quoting veteran scout, he resembles the older, wiser Natty Bumppo in the later Leatherstocking Tales. Officially known as Alva Lanch Hogg, Avalanche rides a scrawny, aging horse named Prudence Cordeliar and is accompanied by an assertive goat, Florence Night-in-a-gale who butts her way through several conflicts. The jumbled plot, combined with superhuman actions of Old Avalanche, his two beasts, and other men and women, and the total absence of Calamity and the slighting of Deadwood Dick, make this one of the less interesting and significant volumes in the series.

409. *The Phantom Miner; or, Deadwood Dick's Bonanza. A Tale of the Great Silverland of Idaho.* May 1878.

As in the previous dime novel in the Deadwood Dick series, Calamity is absent here. Her name is not even mentioned. But Deadwood Dick and his wife Leone, separated because of her earlier fractious jealousy and betrayal, are reunited. When she comes to the isolated Idaho hamlet of Eureka, she brings their infant son Deadwood Dick, Jr., born while they were separated. We also learn of the eastern parents of Dick, their giving him up for adoption, and his joining the Harris family. Author Wheeler tries to thicken his plot with several disguises, overlapping subplots, and the central role of Old Avalanche and his eccentric goat Florence Night-in-a-gale. But the story is muddled with impossible happenings, including a fake Phantom Miner, a ghostlike apparition that scares everyone. In the fast-closing end, Dick, Leone, and their baby son strike out for new adventures in the "great wide West."

410. *Omaha Oll, The Masked Terror; or, Deadwood Dick in Danger.* July 1878.

Calamity is absent from this dime novel, but Deadwood Dick, in one of his many disguises, appears as Omaha Oll, the Masked Terror. A tipping point seems to occur about one-third of the way through the work: a disastrous fire immolates Old Avalanche, Dick's ancient sidekick; Leone, his attractive wife; and Deadwood Dick, Jr., his infant son. But a resurrected Old Avalanche saves Dick from a shooting in the final scene and tells Dick that, though his son died in the fire, Leone is not dead. They escape and canter away, headed to the Black Hills to save Leone. The novel tumbles into a morass of incredible subplots, featuring more than a dozen back-and-forth, back-and-forth clashes between violent vigilante groups and equally violent men—and women. The southwestern Colorado setting, which Wheeler does not know (he speaks of it as prairie country and the main trail west), is superficially described as Mexican/Spanish, lawless, and containing a few wandering Navajos.

411. *Deadwood Dick's Eagles; or, The Pards of Flood Bar.* August 1878.

Although a constantly revolving bevy of men and women scamper through these pages, Calamity Jane is not among them. Set in the gulches, valleys, and mining bars of the Black Hills, this dime novel features, again, numerous gunfights and killings, threatening Indians, and several women captured with nary a threat to their virtue. Deadwood Dick, in several disguises, flits in and out for a few pages, and so does his very attractive wife, Leone Harris. A final scene features a sword fight between two women, in which Lenore kills the vicious desperado Edith Stone.

412. *Deadwood Dick on Deck; or, Calamity Jane, The Heroine of Whoop-Up.* December 1878.

Calamity is featured on the cover of this dime novel, one of only two of the entire series so illustrated. In the opening paragraphs she is introduced in familiar terms: morally besmirched in Virginia City, Nevada, she fled the rascal seducer and "tuck ter these rovin' life," as one old mountaineer recounts. She is not a "hard case" despite these rough beginnings. If she is to rebound and succeed, it is because she has to—"if a female ken't stand up an' fight for her rights, et's durned little aid she'll get." The narrator then enters the story, acting as if he has been to Deadwood and seen Calamity firsthand. None of the several paragraphs of description of Calamity has any basis in fact, save what was stolen from Maguire (286).

Calamity is at center stage and participates in much of the pell mell action that overflows in this fantastic fiction. Wheeler also says Calamity, once named Jennie Forrest, had been betrothed to Charley Davis in Denver. When Charley leaves for the East, "terrible things" overtake Calamity. What they were exactly is not revealed. During the early chapters, Calamity seems to fall for Deadwood Dick, but gives way to another woman, whom Dick marries. This novel focuses more on Calamity's actions than most of the other volumes in the series.

413. *Corduroy Charlie, The Boy Bravo; or, Deadwood Dick's Last Act.* January 1879.

Calamity does not appear in this dime novel set west of the Black Hills in the town of Quartz City. Here, Leone Harris, Deadwood Dick's wife, falls into drunkenness and unfaithfulness. She is shot down, along with her new lover, near the end of the novel. Mayhem and murder rule most of the plot, with Dick involved in much of the violent action. Wheeler's innocence of western geography betrays him when he places the large National Park near the Black Hills. Again, several subplots, numerous new characters, and far-fetched events undermine the literary quality of this dime novel.

414. *Deadwood Dick in Leadville; or, A Strange Stroke for Liberty. A Wild, Exciting Story of the Leadville Region.* June 1879.

Although Calamity appears on the cover of this dime novel, one of two to so feature her, she is absent for more than half of the novel. She is depicted as a strong, courageous woman, so fierce that the villain knuckles under to her. As Calamity tells another character, "I enjoy a free fight, when it is for the right." Calamity's definition of "right," however, includes violence. There are more vicious murders in this book than in other volume of the series.

Even though the setting is said to be Leadville, the descriptions of generic mountains, gulches, and valleys lack specifics. Wheeler attempts to disguise his innocence of western geography and landscapes by avoiding naming any specific site near Leadville. His lack of knowledge betrays him, however, when he places Nevada and Virginia City north of the Black Hills. Plot details are almost as unbelievable as the author's mistaken geography. For example, in the final pages Deadwood Dick allows himself to be hanged—so that he may be resurrected!

415. *Deadwood Dick's Device; or, The Sign of the Double Cross. A Wild, Strange Story of the Leadville Mines.* July 1879.

An incredible plot and a revealing portrait of Calamity Jane seesaw through this novel. Nearly every chapter includes shootings or poisonings, dozens (if not hundreds) in the course of the sensational plot. Deadwood Dick falls in love with a new pretty girl, Stella, but she is treacherously poisoned on the day of their marriage.

Calamity appears throughout the novel. Not many critics comment on this work, but Calamity serves as Deadwood Dick's sidekick, rescuer from death, and counselor. But here she experiences definite ups and downs. Dick accuses her of plotting to kill Stella, quickly apologizes, and then gives her leadership of his dozens of men. In a particularly illuminating passage, Wheeler has Deadwood Dick describe Calamity's "perception . . . as keen as the edge of a razor." He had asked her to marry him, but she refused. Would she change her mind now? She hovers near him, "a sort of guardian angel." "A wild, strange character she is—virtuous, and true as steel, beyond peradventure, yet so wild and strange as to seem a part of the wilderness through which she roams." In a few words, Wheeler caught the conflicting legends beginning to cluster around Calamity: a Wild Woman of the Old West but also an Angel of Mercy.

416. *Deadwood Dick as Detective. A Story of the Great Carbonate Region.*
26 August 1879.

Calamity is absent from the pages of this dime novel. Deadwood Dick does meet and marry, however, another beautiful young woman, Edith Yates, his third wife. In the small mining town of Rough Shod, in a gulch near Leadville, Dick, disguised as Phineas Porter, a detective, protects the innocent and assails the guilty. Dick defends himself and his vigilante actions by pointing out that he had been "outlawed from civilization"; he is no longer "a free man permitted to go among my fellow men as such." So he must remain active and a vigilante outside a crime-ridden society. This is a much-traveled theme in Wheeler's series. Concurrently, the author depicts the West as a new place where one can start over, free from past injustices. Unfortunately, baneful legacies of the past, like a virulent, contagious cancer, inflict themselves on the present. But once happily married to Edith, Dick sets out once again to another part of the West, hoping to free himself from a coercive and unjust society.

417. *Deadwood Dick's Double; or, The Ghost of Gordon's Gulch. A Tale of Wild-Cat City.* 13 January 1880.

Calamity Jane does not appear in this novel. Deadwood Dick is married to his new and third wife, Edith, living near Leadville. Wheeler reiterates Dick's character: he will abide no infringement on what he considers his rights and freedoms. He confronts, and is willing to kill, those who attempt to abridge or remove his liberties. Wheeler introduces a Calamity-like character in Slippery Sal, a dialect-speaking, ever-ready-to-fight frontier woman. Unfortunately, the author mitigates much of the work by introducing or repeating several fantastic elements: Deadwood Dick's mesmerizing abilities to freeze opponents, a ghostlike apparition haunting the forests, the resurrection of a settler killed and buried, and the unbelievable disguise of Deadwood Dick in the character of Slippery Sal. Dick, reiterating that he is a "free man" now that he has given up the road as an outlaw, nonetheless warns listeners, especially opponents, that he will strike back like an angry rattlesnake against any who malign his character or challenge his freedom.

418. *Blonde Bill; or, Deadwood Dick's Home Base. A Romance of the "Silent Tongues."* 16 March 1880.

Calamity and Deadwood Dick course through much of this novel. Via many disguises and vigilant, courageous actions, Dick outwits the Silent Tongues, a vicious group of avaricious rascals. He also makes clear that he wants to escape from road-agentry and become a miner, but the outlaws force him to take violent control, which he does with a vengeance.

Described as beautiful and vivacious, Calamity lusts after Dick, even though she refused his interest earlier. "A devil in man's attire once crushed every true womanly instinct out of my heart," Calamity testifies. Still, she bemoans her present situation: "No one cares for me; I am regarded as a creature as wild . . . a dare-devil, who would as lief take a human life as to smoke a cigar." But Dick trusts Calamity, asking her to lead some of his force. The author closes his pell-mell narrative, suggesting "in a dim future, it is not improbable that Dick and Calamity will enter into a long partnership for life."

419. *A Game of Gold; or, Deadwood Dick's Big Strike.* 1 June 1880.

Author Wheeler slides into incredulity in this installment. Disguised as Little Toothpick, Calamity comes to where Deadwood Dick is living in an isolated, mysterious mining town in Colorado. Wheeler would have readers believe that Calamity, dressed as a young man (which she is in many of the series volumes), is so thoroughly disguised in dress, appearance, mannerisms, and speech that Dick, the keenest of men, cannot recognize his longtime sidekick and girlfriend. As Little Toothpick, Calamity swiftly appears and as quickly disappears throughout the novel.

Calamity wants to test Dick's love for and loyalty to her. So, in disguise, Little Toothpick casts aspersions on Calamity's character and actions, hoping to discover whether Dick agrees. He does not, firing back, "Cast no slur upon her character . . . [S]he is all in all to me." When Little Toothpick continues her captious criticism, Dick again quickly responds that another young woman may be more beautiful than he "ever imagined a human being could be," but "Calamity Jane is pretty [, and she] is dear to me." Hearing and relishing Dick's endearing comments, Toothpick reveals her identity as Calamity. In the closing scene, Calamity and Dick set off "through the wild mess" of ruin, headed for "other wild and exciting scenes of the mighty West."

420. *Deadwood Dick of Deadwood; or, The Picked Party. A Romance of Skeleton Bend.* 20 July 1880.

Set in a mining boomtown in Billy-Goat Gulch, not too far from Leadville, the plot of this novel tests the love of Deadwood Dick and Calamity for one another. The "faithful" Calamity waits for Dick to establish and work a mining claim in Skeleton Bend. Calamity is described as a young woman of "merry composition . . . [with] little to merit the ominous name she bore except to those who incurred her wrath." But when she sees Dick embrace and kiss an attractive widow, Dick is afraid he has "looked upon her face for the last time." The widow does explain things, however, and Dick and Calamity are "united in matrimony" in the final paragraph. Calamity is gone for much of the novel, with limited descriptions of her character and actions.

421. *Deadwood Dick's Dream; or, The Rivals of the Road. A Mining Tale of Tombstone.* 19 April 1881.

This dime novel set in Tombstone (not in Arizona but in Colorado) opens with a dream of Deadwood Dick's that proves to be the unfolding plot. With Calamity Jane off scene, several other women appear alongside Dick. One of them, 'Shian (Cheyenne) Sal reminds him of Calamity, "his faithful girl-pardner." The central emphases in the novel are on Deadwood Dick's character, his fierce competitiveness, his relentless defense of his personal honor, and his willingness to take on his detractors. Wheeler seems committed to supporting Dick's preachments about honor, courage, and perseverance.

Again, the author, through use of disguises and mistaken identities, suggests that appearances are often at odds with reality.

422. *The Black Hills Jezebel; or, Deadwood Dick's Ward.* 31 May 1881. Later reprinted as *Deadwood Dick's Ward; or, The Black Hills Jezebel.* 30 March 1887.

Calamity never appears in this novel. Another heroine, Kentucky Kit, reports that Calamity told her that Deadwood Dick and she "were about as good as promised to get married, when they dissolved, by mutual consent, and went different ways." Deadwood Dick has been married perhaps a half-dozen times already, but "always lost his wife one way or another, shortly after." The frenetic actions and Wheeler's anti-Negro biases may have alienated discerning readers.

423. *Deadwood Dick's Doom; or, Calamity Jane's Last Adventure. A Tale of Death Notch.* June 1881.

Calamity is introduced halfway through this dime novel as a "notorious free-and-easy, reckless waif of the rocky Western country." Deadwood Dick has invited her down from northern mining districts to Death Notch, on the way from Pioche, Nevada, to Helena, Montana. He wants to settle down and experience peace and quiet. If Calamity will join him, "the hand you have so long sought shall be yours." Finding him dead and buried, she mourns at his grave. But Wheeler's hero and heroine rarely remain dead and buried; Dick comes forth, in disguise, and rescues Calamity in several threatening episodes.

Calamity becomes a tool here of Wheeler's thematic and structural predispositions. The revenge motif is played out in a series of nonstop actions, with characters often disguised. They are of the Wild West, which wants to throw off any ties to an evil and effete East. Violence abounds, but no sexual abuse. In the end Calamity is "used" for fictional purposes more than she is characterized.

In the final paragraph, Calamity and Deadwood Dick are married. They had joined in matrimony in *Deadwood Dick of Deadwood* (July 1880 [420]), but Wheeler does not explain why a second trip to the altar is necessary in this novel of June 1881.

424. *Captain Crack-Shot, The Girl Brigand; or, Gypsy Jack from Jimtown. A Story of Durango.* September 1881. Reprinted as *The Jimtown Sport; or, Gypsy Jack in Colorado.* February 1888.

Calamity is in Durango, Colorado, a booming gold-mining town, but she does not appear until halfway through the novel. Meanwhile, Gypsy Jack, a disguised Deadwood Dick, arrives, looking for "the dearest treasure of my latter life—my wife," who proves to be Calamity Jane. The villain Captain Crack-Shot, a nineteen-year-old female rascal, claims that Calamity has been an unfaithful wife and run off with her lieutenant. Gypsy Jack/Deadwood Dick contradicts these wild assertions, saying he has come for "only one woman, and that woman the one who has been true to me, through thick and thin." Calamity, Dick, and the latter's wonder dog Skip set out to defeat the bad guys. Skip comes to the rescue frequently and wins most of the battles. In another fantastic scene, Dick kills a giant bear and several vicious wolves. Along the way, Wheeler's anti-Mormonism and his negativity toward Indians are much in evidence. The hero and heroine win over all these human and animal competitors, with the aid of Skip. At the end they leave and set out for "a life [of] commingled peril and adventure."

425. *Sugar-Coated Sam; or, The Black Gowns of Grim Gulch. A Deadwood Dick Episode.* 18 October 1881. Reprinted as *The Miner Sport; or, Sugar-Coated Sam's Claim.* 4 March 1888.

Calamity Jane appears about halfway through this work, disguised as the miner Bumblebee Bob. Badly injured in one of several melees in the novel, she spends most of the remaining pages in bed, very sick, barely conscious, sometimes wildly off-track. In the closing pages, she escapes from the shack where she is being nursed and disappears. At the end of the novel, she is still missing. So, even though Calamity is on scene in the second half of the novel, her role is tangential, almost muted.

The novel exhibits three departures from most other installments of the series. It vies for being the most violent, with floods of mayhem, murders, the shooting of women, and even decapitation. It is also the most anti-Mormon of the Deadwood Dick dime novels, although Wheeler was also frequently negative about the Mormons in other novels. In addition, via the enigmatic character William Henry Shakespeare, the novel contains more poetry—no, verse—than other volumes in the series.

426. *Gold-Dust Dick. A Romance of Roughs and Toughs.* 3 January 1882. Reprinted as *Deadwood Dick Trapped; or, Roxey Ralph's Ruse.* 24 April 1899.

Well into this novel, Deadwood Dick asks a rough miner, "Where is Calamity Jane?" Earlier, Dick and Calamity, the married couple, had become separated. In answer to his plaintive but directive question, Dick is told Calamity may be dead. The villain of the story, Tra-la-lee Charlie, gambler and vicious murderer, has snatched Calamity away, beaten her, and now she has fallen among the "savage" Aztec Indians. When finally located among the Indians, she is afraid, tearful, and piteous to behold—not the usual courageous, forceful Calamity of this series. Yet she escapes and, with a more Calamity-like young woman Roxy Ralph, rides to the rescue of Dick. In the penultimate paragraph, Dick and Calamity depart "for a more remote and inaccessible part of the West, wherein to hide their identity."

Wheeler's plot lumbers along. For one, he tries to incorporate too many separate strands into his story. There are the pro– and anti–Deadwood Dick elements in Pistolville (located in an ever-present gulch in the "Sierras"), the events surrounding the Ponca and Aztec Indians (treated, as usual in Wheeler's dime novels, as murderous savages), and a romance or two. Generally, Wheeler is not successful in telling this story or in working in a believable Calamity Jane.

427. *Deadwood Dick's Divide; or, The Spirit of Swamp Lake.* 8 August 1882. Reprinted as *Deadwood Dick's Disguise; or, Wild Walt, the Sport.* 17 July 1889.

The on-and-off marriage journey of Deadwood Dick and Calamity Jane is at the center of this novel. Dick thinks Calamity has let him down, so he quickly abandons her. Hurt and angry at her husband's actions, Calamity pursues him to the isolated Swamp Lake and the adjacent settlement of Doomsday. A much-traveled local tale says Dick drowned in the lake with his huge "swag" of gold. Calamity proves the yarn untrue, and in a series of nonstop chases and murderous conflicts, Calamity and Dick resolve their alienations, but not before they have, sarcastically, attacked one another. Once Dick apologizes to Calamity—he had "believed her unfaithful"—she relents. In a lightning-quick conclusion, tying together plot fragments, Calamity and Dick are reunited and leave. Although nothing unusual happens in the fictional careers of Deadwood Dick and Calamity Jane here, they are on scene for most of the novel and their imagined lives are given rather extensive comment.

428. *Deadwood Dick's Death Trail; or, From Ocean to Ocean.* 12 September 1882. Reprinted as *Deadwood Dick's Mission; or, Cavie, the Kidnapped Boy.* 9 October 1889.

This dime novel illustrates well Wheeler's storytelling approaches. He mentions Calamity Jane's name a half dozen times, keeping her before readers, but she is not brought on stage. Deadwood Dick stands off a pretty young woman's rather innocent advances because of his love for Calamity. He looks forward to returning "up country, [where they live] on a little ranch of our own." And there is an added pull: he wants to return to "their peaceful valley . . . in the anticipation of a little Deadwood Dick, to brighten their after lives."

Several of Wheeler's excesses strain a reader's credulity. For one, Deadwood Dick proves a superhuman. On one occasion he dispatches a full dozen roughs in one slugging match; in another scene, while falling down and off balance, he is able to shoot well-hidden opponents. Dick also appears, almost at the call of the narrator, to save innocents several times from treacherous villains. In the course of the novel Dick disguises himself at least a half dozen times, and some of his closest acquaintances cannot recognize him even though he speaks to them at elbow's length. Even more ridiculous, the author would have us believe that a half dozen English royalty can, without directions or cues, meet in the outback of the wild West. Finally, the story betrays Wheeler's prejudices: Mexican "greasers," violent Westerners nearly always on the verge of lynching someone, and, as usual, male Mormons as polygamous tyrants. These excesses make it difficult to take these works seriously. Presumably dime novel readers did not.

429. *Deadwood Dick's Big Deal; or, The Gold Brick of Oregon.* 26 June 1883.

Although often overlooked in discussions of Calamity Jane and the dime novel in general, this work features Calamity and Deadwood Dick throughout its pages. They are separate though together. Both arrive disguised in out-of-the-way Right Bower, a mining hamlet situated in an unnamed part of the West. Throughout the novel, they are alienated from one another. Dick tells a good friend he witnessed Calamity's infidelities, her kissing and frequently visiting with another man in her cabin. (The "other man" proves to be Calamity's ne'er-do-well brother Ralph Chester.) Seeing these evidences of her unfaithfulness, and jumping to negative conclusions, Dick abandons Calamity and their son. He and Calamity are, he declares, "sworn enemies forever," their "mission on earth . . . to wreak vengeance on each other." Old pal Avalanche, maintaining friendships with both distraught husband and wife, tries to reconcile the two, but both are so set in their feuding and their quest to find and snatch away their son, Deadwood Dick, Jr., they have no feelings of remorse, sympathy, or sadness. Dick, valiant, manly, and dependable, can also be unyielding, quick to judge, and vituperative. Beautiful, energetic, and motherly, Calamity can also be unsympathetic, insensitive, and vindictive. Unable to reconcile, they leave the final scene separated. As Wheeler puts it in his closing phrases, "one thing seems certain—his [Dick's] and Calamity's paths in life lead wide apart." The novel exhibits Wheeler's excesses: too many disguises; multiple mistaken identities; Dick's superhuman insights and resurrections; and unfathomable contingencies and chance happenings; but, withal, this dime novel is one of the most interesting tales about Calamity Jane and Deadwood Dick.

430. *Deadwood Dick's Dozen; or, The Fakir of Phantom Flats.* 18 September 1883.

Calamity Jane is neither on stage nor even mentioned in this novel set in Phantom Flats, said to be in the gold hills of Arizona. Wheeler follows here a now-familiar plot in his series, bringing earlier feuds from the East and replaying them in the frontier West. Through swiftly shifting scenes, the author incorporates several subplots into his shaky narrative.

Deadwood Dick, that "daring Apollo of the West," is up to his usual trick of snatching away control from the viciously unjust and placing it in the hands of the needy, powerless, and upright. His goal, he tells an acquaintance, is "to work against . . . rascals." Dick admits that he is a man "the barbed arrows of the world have pricked, until I may be in a degree calloused; yet I am still a man, with a kindly regard and appreciation for the honest oppressed." With no mention of Calamity, Wheeler is allowed more space to expand on the character and actions of Deadwood Dick, which he does extensively in this novel.

431. *Deadwood Dick's Ducats; or Rainy Days in the Diggings.* 18 March 1884.

Calamity Jane is not here or mentioned, and neither is Deadwood Dick—for the most part absent except in disguise. Wheeler again, through innumerable coincidences, brings together several people, related in some way, in the mining town of Devil's Diggins in southern Arizona. Masked and disguised, father and son, sister and sister, boss and workers, and former business partners fail to recognize one another even at arm's length. The "galoots," Wheeler's favorite term for the mining town residents, are depicted as frequently drunk, often swayed erratically by emotions, and innocent of much intelligence.

A few unusual ingredients mark the novel. Roaring Ruth, a young, vivacious woman of Calamity-like character, owns an incredible burro, which drinks whiskey, can tell time, and discerns what cards are, face-down. The animal is more intriguing than most of the characters. A ghostlike apparition scares the rascals, and a ventriloquist (perhaps Deadwood Dick) startles the good guys. Wheeler's own naiveté about the West is demonstrated here in his depiction of southern Arizona as full of tree-lined mountains and experiencing heavy annual rains each fall.

432. *Deadwood Dick Sentenced; or, The Terrible Vendetta. A Nevada Tale.*
15 April 1884.

No mention of Calamity here. But Deadwood Dick is nearly continuously on scene, often in one of his many disguises. Early on, he becomes involved in a replay of the Hatfield-McCoy feud, a deadly vendetta that twists and turns the steps of Wheeler's dime novel hero in the vicinity of the mining town of Nowhere, Nevada. The clan war, emanating from the South, spills out into the Far West, embroiling Deadwood Dick with many mining town "galoots," pretty girls, and whiskey-driven criminals. Dick survives, as he always does, by his wiles, support from new followers, and Wheeler's overweening use of coincidences. Plus, Dick mesmerizes his opponents at opportune moments, especially to help him win one side of the murderous clan war. On the opposing side, devilish villains let wolves both devour the body of a little boy they have allowed to starve and eat away flesh of his not-yet-dead father. It is perhaps the most repugnant scene in the entire Deadwood Dick series.

Wheeler creates, again, the image of boomtown roughs easily driven like a band of dumb sheep by a skilled rabble-rouser. Nearly always, they are readily swayed, notoriously unstable emotionally, and drink-fueled. Deadwood Dick, that "lion-hearted ex-knight of the road," rises far above them in his courage, bravery, and skills.

433. *Deadwood Dick's Claim; or, The Fairy Face of Faro Flats.* July 1884.

Wheeler kept readers involved in the Deadwood Dick–Calamity relationship by frequently changing the details. Here they are clearly separated. Once lovers, they are now deadly foes. The "pards" were husband and wife, but "a foul lie," laments Dick, "separated us, and forever." Calamity, primarily "an angel in love," has become a "fiend, in hatred." She remains absent for most of the novel, and in the final scene Dick sadly buries the body he thinks to be that of Calamity in "a lonely forever." Again, with Calamity gone from much of the action, Deadwood Dick's deeds receive major attention here.

434. *Deadwood Dick in Dead City.* April 1885.

Although once dead in the grave, a resurrected Calamity reappears here about halfway through this installment. Deadwood Dick is told that "the woman you buried . . . was not 'Calamity Jane.'" They have been alienated from one another, but Calamity urges "let us not go down the hill hating one another [even] though we both have passed thro' many bitter experiences." Calamity finds a little boy to mother (an unusual emphasis in a Wheeler dime novel), and Dick and she bury their conflictive past and embrace. In the closing scene, Dick wonders if "the custody of the boy will serve to tempt Calamity to the charms of home life, and subdue her wild, roving spirit." It did not in the next handful of volumes in the series.

435. *Deadwood Dick's Diamonds; or, The Mystery of Joan Porter.* 2 June 1885.

Set in Carson City, Nevada, this dime novel features a reunited Deadwood Dick and Calamity. Dick has given up the road and become a detective; Calamity has taken up gambling. Disguises are so often employed, and so often unbelievably, that even Dick does not recognize his disguised wife—until she speaks. Wheeler betrays both his anti-Semitism and his often-overdone and contrived employment of blind chance and unforeseen circumstances. At the end, Calamity returns to a Wyoming valley ranch to be with her adopted son, Rex. The "two wild spirits of the wild West," Dick and Calamity, "will be separated for a time."

436. *Deadwood Dick in New York; or, "A Cute Case." A Romance of To-Day.* 18 August 1885.

Calamity is absent from this entire dime novel, save for one action of hers that occurred before the plot begins. All the action takes place in New Jersey and New York City. If the plot and setting are unusual for a Wheeler work, so too are the diction, syntax, and style. Did Wheeler write this dime novel, or was it the product of a ghostwriter?

437. *Deadwood Dick's Dust; or, The Chained Hand. A Strange Story of the Mines. Being the 35th and Ending Number of the Great "Deadwood Dick" Series.* 20 October 1885.

The subtitle is correct in indicating this was the last of the Deadwood Dick series, but it was the thirty-third, not the thirty-fifth, installment. The plot is so jumbled, filled with so many unanswered questions, and so unfinished in quality that one wonders if Wheeler grew ill and was unable to complete the work himself.

Calamity appears on page 2 as the "famous girl sport of the West." She is the "same Calamity as of yore—handsome, dashing, and looking not a day older than" in the Black Hills, several years before. Wheeler betrays his usual anti-Mormon biases here, with an un-Saintly man and other rascals eventually hanging Calamity. Dick also dies in a last-minute shootout.

Before his death and hearing of Calamity's violent demise, Dick asks that they be buried together. Calamity's gravestone reads "Frank with friends, fearless of foes." So the final pages of the Deadwood Dick series close with Calamity's shocking death, followed in short order by Dick's, and then their being buried together.

OTHER FICTION, LITERARY
WORKS, AND CRITICISM

Entries in this section are arranged alphabetically by author, with the J. T. Edson series listed in chronological order. Numbers in parentheses cross-reference other entries in this guide.

438. Brooks, Bill. *Deadwood*. New York: Pinnacle Books, 1997.

Although this novel follows closely the sex-and-violence formula of the Adult Western, Brooks proves to be a better than average writer. A superb gunman, Quint McCannon, arrives in Deadwood in the opening pages to solve the murders of several prostitutes. In approaching his dangerous task, McCannon proves to be on a par with Wild Bill Hickok as a shooter.

The initial description of Calamity prefigures the author's later depiction of her. "She's less attractive than a chamberpot" (p. 63), an oldster says of her. Then, he adds as a warning, hanging out with Calamity might give you the clap. Calamity is a drunk and a troublemaker, with "a narrow, homely face that was bereft of any femininity." She is, the author adds, "a mistake of nature" (p. 79). More negativity floods in: Calamity's "breath is sour as kraut" (p. 113), and she smells "the way no woman should smell, worse than a muleskinner" (p. 278). Yet she covets sexual intimacy, and suggests she and McCannon might have their own "sweet time" (p. 113).

The actual Calamity worked as a dancer, waitress, and entertainer in Deadwood, but in Brooks's novel she is a hopeless souse, turning tricks and wobbling up and down the streets. Then, unbelievably, Calamity does an about-face in the final pages, taking up with a drummer salesman and heading for Denver, where they will start over. In short, Brooks provides a very constricted, stereotypical view of the New Gray Calamity, pointing forward to a similar depiction of Calamity in the HBO series *Deadwood* (489).

439. Cain, Jackson. *Hellbreak Country*. New York: Warner Books, 1984.

Cain's novel belongs among the Adult Westerns depicting Calamity as little more than a sex-crazed young woman. Here, her electric lovemaking with Wild Bill and with the novel's lead character, Torn Slater, fills several pages. The author's distortions of history and additions of several implausible events weaken the work's artistic integrity. For example, Cain brings together several of the Old West's demigods, even though they never saw one another. The James and Younger gangs are depicted as pursuing Calamity and her acquaintances across the West toward General Custer's mishap in Montana. Cain's Calamity is with Custer in Arizona, even though she was never there. And the historical Hickok did not throw aside Agnes Lake and take up with Calamity and then bring on Belle Starr as his lovers. Obviously, the author knows little about the life of Calamity and is very willing to distort it for his fictional purposes.

440. Caple, Natalee. *In Calamity's Wake: A Novel*. New York: Bloomsbury, 2013.

Caple proves herself a skilled novelist but also a heavy-handed manipulator of historical and biographical facts in this smoothly written work of fiction. Employing some of the techniques of magic realists (combining facts and sleights of hand) and drawing on the approaches of other writers, the author produces an intriguing example of what she calls "metahistoriographic fiction" (p. 224). Undoubtedly, readers devoted to experimental fiction are likely to praise the work; historians wanting novelists to play square with their sources will have many questions.

Caple's plot follows the story of Miette, the daughter of Calamity Jane, who searches for her mother in the Badlands of the northern West. Syncopating chapters from Calamity, Miette, and several other characters, the author follows a journey motif in telling her story. Most of the narrative is told from Miette's perspective, taking her through parts of Canada, Montana, Indian communities, and, vicariously, through the lives and writings of other persons. Bits of poetry, revised quotations from original Calamity Jane sources, and many imagined conversations are combined in the meandering plot. Caple's writing is innovative, imaginative, and, at times, ethereal with magic realism.

Historians and biographers acquainted with Calamity Jane's life will have more trouble with the novel. The author frequently mixes up chronology, invents false information, and outrageously distorts facts. She has Wild Bill alive well beyond his death in 1876, has Calamity in Buffalo, New York, when President McKinley is assassinated, and misinforms readers about several other facts. And she borrows from the false Jean Hickok McCormick story, has Wild Bill and Calamity as lovers, says Calamity claimed she had a daughter by Wild Bill, and creates a father figure Calamity never had. She juxtaposes events taking place in Coeur d'Alene, Idaho, with those in Buffalo, New York, happenings seventeen years apart. Canadian and Catholic ingredients, far from the truth, are also added. Regrettably, Caple allows her experimental writing techniques to undermine the possible historicity of Calamity Jane's story. The historical inaccuracies are all the more surprising since the author clearly had at hand McLaird's definitive biography (290), which clearly disproves much of the "history" of this novel.

441. Cole, Judd [John Edward Ames, pseud.]. *Wild Bill: Santa Fe Death Trap.* New York: Leisure Books, 2000.

Writing as Judd Cole, John Edward Ames produces a novel far afield from the historical Wild Bill and Calamity Jane. He has them in New Mexico in the mid-1870s, Bill on vacation but forced into law enforcement and Calamity driving a herd of camels! Hot for Wild Bill, Calamity is introduced as "a hard-cussing hellcat" (p. 8). Later, in trying to elude the fast-closing Calamity, Hickok describes her as having a "face [that] terrified buzzards" and adds that "the smell coming off her could raise blood blisters on new leather" (p. 164). Save for her foul mouth, this fictional Calamity, in a rather weak novel, is not even a faint shadow of the historical figure. Ames/Cole employs Calamity as a sideline figure in his other Wild Bill novels, including *Wild Bill: Dead Man's Hand* (New York: Leisure Books, 1999). The author's scant knowledge of the historical Wild Bill and Calamity Jane is evident in his popular history, *The Real Deadwood* (231).

442. Dexter, Pete. *Deadwood.* New York: Random House, 1986.

This is one of the most influential novels about Calamity Jane. It is the work of a talented novelist who knows how to deal with characters, context, and plot. The novel was widely commented on, gained thousands of readers, and became a major source for the HBO *Deadwood* series (489). Unfortunately, the novel's limitations are almost as dominant as its strengths.

Dexter is a master of humor, pointing out the foibles of a coterie of Deadwood characters, including Calamity, Wild Bill, Charlie Utter, and Agnes Lake. He also wanted, perhaps, to counter the excessively romantic Calamity who had appeared in the Doris Day *Calamity Jane* movie (485). To achieve his goal, Dexter resorts to excessive parody and satire. Dexter's satirical portrait of Calamity rules his novel. Calamity smells like the ripe mules and horses she rides. Nor is she much cleaner than the filthy tents and lean-tos where she flops. Calamity is so rancid that a fresh crop of mold grows unnoticed on her neck. No man pays much attention to her, even though fornication and sexual violence are rife in Dexter's Deadwood. Unwashed, unloved, and underappreciated, Calamity seems less a woman that a two-legged screaming eagle bent on shooting off toes, bragging of her "husband" Wild Bill, and out-drinking all others, men and vile drunkards alike.

The parody gets away from Dexter. Once he has satirized Calamity and the other characters, he has little left to draw readers. The New Gray Calamity is portrayed as a drunken, filthy, promiscuous antiheroine. The excessive satire leaves a Calamity not wanting to help the less fortunate or fulfill her desire to be a wife and mother. David Milch, the producer of HBO's *Deadwood*, adopted most of this negative portrait of Calamity into his TV series.

443. Dixon, Dorothy. *Yellowstone Jewel*. Leather and Lace no. 9. New York: Zebra Books, 1983.

This is a house-produced Adult Western in another series of sex-and-violence novels. Wild Bill is Calamity's electric lover. Even though as a young woman Calamity loses her virtue to a Lieutenant Somers, it is Hickok who captures her. Their road to love begins in Abilene, where Calamity competes against and wins a contest with Agnes Lake for Wild Bill's attentions. Following somewhat the Jean Hickok McCormick false story (246), Dixon has Calamity and Hickok spending a long winter in the Rockies together, even though he is now a married man. The author takes an unusual approach to Calamity's story: rather than beginning with Calamity as an adult she traces her early years, moving from girl to young woman. In her fiction, Dixon clearly relies on the stories by Duncan Aikman (230) and White Eye Anderson (322), but juxtaposes that more dependable information with misstatement and false assertions. Dixon's Calamity is indeed an unromantic, gray figure driven by an excessive, often-expressed lust for Wild Bill.

444. Dufour, Hortense. *Le diable blanc: le roman de Calamity Jane* [The White Devil: The Story of Calamity Jane]. Paris, 1986.

This novel by a prolific writer (in French) is another indication of how popular the life of Calamity Jane is among the French. Dufour has Calamity tell her own story, and it is the story based on the fraudulent Jean Hickok McCormick claims (246). The first-person narrative buys into the Wild Bill–Calamity Jane romance and the daughter (Janey) born to Hickok and Calamity. The author emphasizes the depression Calamity went through when her marriage did not work out, and she was forced to give up Janey to the O'Neils. Dufour makes clear her reliance on the Hickok McCormick false story by asserting that she read the book *The Letters of Calamity Jane to Her Daughter* (246), said to have been written by Calamity but, as James D. McLaird has persuasively shown (376), written not by Calamity but probably by Hickok McCormick. Dufour based her novel on hit-and-run research and does not demonstrate much knowledge about Calamity's life.

445. J. T. Edson, Calamity Jane novels.

British author J. T. [John Thomas] Edson probably wrote nearly 150 novels—perhaps more. Among these numerous works were about a dozen Calamity Jane novels, and several other books in which Calamity played at least a supporting role. Edson did not know much about the historical Calamity, even though the good biographies by J. Leonard Jennewein (278) and Roberta Beed Sollid (326) were available to him. He did include a few bits of biography in his Calamity works, but most of what he said about her was entirely fabricated. His Calamity is a very attractive young woman, assertive, extraordinarily sexually active, and willing to embrace any new adventure, especially if it includes a handsome, virile, young demigod. Edson often partnered Calamity with another historical character, frequently a competitor such as Belle Starr or Ella "Cattle Kate" Watson. But male partners, for example Danny Fog and Mark Counter, were imagined heroes, many of whom make dual appearances in another Edson series, the Floating Outfit. (Wild Bill Hickok and Buffalo Bill Cody are mentioned but do not serve as central characters.) Several of Edson's Calamity Jane novels are set in Texas or on the central plains, two areas where she spent little time—or none at all. Edson was proud to assert that his novels were "action-escapism-adventure fiction." Or, as he told another writer, he was not writing historically accurate novels or polished literary works. Instead, he was churning out books for man-on-the-street readers (and perhaps women, too) who relished his Westerns.

446. Edson, J. T. *Trouble Trail*. London: Brown Watson, 1965, 1968.

The initial volume in Edson's Calamity Jane series, this novel illustrates the pattern and emphases he employed in most of his fiction about her. In later editions of this work, as well as in subsequent novels, Edson adds footnotes and appendixes to provide more information on Calamity. Most of those later descriptions, sometimes word for word, repeat what this opening volume states about Calamity.

Calamity appears on virtually every page. In the opening chapter Edson describes his heroine physically: She is "a girl in her late teens and . . . stood maybe five foot seven in height." She has a "shortish, curly mop of red hair; and the face framed by the hair was good looking without being ravingly beautiful." She is "tanned and sprinkled with attractive freckles." Her "face had happy blue eyes, and a slightly snub nose and a mouth which looked made for laughter and kissing, but which could cut loose with a hide-blistering flow of coarse invective when a situation called for it" (p. 6).

Next, Edson describes Calamity's dress, an element all Calamity novels emphasized. "The man's shirt and jeans she wore," the author begins, "looked like they had been bought a size too small and further shrunk during washing. Clinging firmly to her torso, the round full swell of her breasts straining against its material, the shirt's upper three buttons lay open and revealed there was little other than girl under the cloth" (pp. 6–7).

Along the way, Edson tells us that Calamity's mother and father went west. After her father's disappearance or death, her mother placed young Martha and her siblings in a St. Louis convent and also "disappeared into the West." At age sixteen, Martha escaped west and fell in among ranchers and lawmen who taught her the necessities of life: about guns, whips, cooking, fist-fighting, wagon-driving, and how to become a tough, courageous western woman. Within two or three years, she is a trail-driving veteran, known throughout much of the West as a young woman who loves her freedom, leadership, and men. And sex, too, although maybe that lust is not widely known. All these characteristics are magnified in this novel.

The plot also foreshadows what readers might expect in Edson's Calamity Jane series. A wagon train, military escort, and accompanying scouts make their way into the West. Once the major characters are introduced, especially four very different women in a series of catty and physical brawls, the train and the major characters move through one traumatic escapade after another. The overly dramatized adventures include a narrow escape from an Indian attack, a lively buffalo hunt, and a daring rescue of a military leader from the Indian camp. Edson frequently enters his narrative, sometimes himself and other times through his characters' reflections and actions. The novel's characters can change overnight, and the author repeatedly discusses eastern-western and class differences he thinks to be among his actors.

In sum, the series opens with Calamity as a rambunctious, opinionated, and very sexual protagonist. She relishes her intimate encounters with a handsome, stud-like scout (the encounters are off scene, of course) and encourages another virginal young woman to experience "it" as soon as possible, which she does. Calamity wields a vicious whip, welcomes knockout tussles with other women, and, leaving off her past, embraces a beckoning future. Readers were introduced to a heroine whom the author obviously relished and wanted his audiences to embrace too.

447. Edson, J. T. *Troubled Range*. New York: Dell Publishing, 1969. Originally published 1965.

This three-part Western opens with a longish section on Calamity Jane, Belle Starr, and the superhuman Texan Mark Counter. Mark appears in all three segments but Calamity only in the first part. Historical characters, outlaw Bill Doolin and Cattle Annie and Little Britches, are introduced in the third part, more as battlers and sex objects than as historical characters. Along the way, Edson adds a few footnotes, primarily to cite other books he has written.

Calamity is depicted as only eighteen, just two years after she escaped from the St. Louis convent where her mother had left her. Two years later she "already bore a name fast becoming famous" (p. 1). She is known to freighters, soldiers, and dance-hall girls. Handy with a whip, Edson's Calamity is pretty, sexy, alluring, and potty-mouthed. Although claiming to be "Wild Bill Hickok's gal" (p. 4), she soon beds down with Counter. A few hours later that rascally Texas lothario is intimate with Belle Starr. Not unexpectedly, Calamity and Belle engage in a titanic, six-page brawl, leaving them as two badly torn-up sexpots. Set in an undated and undescribed Montana, the first section of the novel is replete with Louis L'Amour–like details about guns, western paraphernalia, and activities.

448. Edson, J. T. *The Wildcats*. London: Brown Watson, 1965.

The first section of this two-part work, entitled "Better Than Calamity," features Calamity's several competitions with a lively, strong, and attractive Madam Bulldog. The latter, although named after a woman Calamity competed with in Livingston, Montana, is not treated historically here. She outdoes Calamity in swearing, gun-fighting, and a nearly ten-page she-brawl. Not until during the battle do we learn that Madam Bulldog is actually Calamity's mother, Charlotte Canary. Edson tries to convince his devoted readers that, after a few years of separation, neither recognizes the other until Calamity blurts out that her real name is Martha Jane Canary.

Edson's fictional trademarks are in evidence. The incessant action of his plot leaves little room for expanded characterization. The author also announces the meanings of happenings rather than allowing occurrences to dramatize meaning. Again, guns of all types are described, as are women's sexy dresses, or lack thereof. Calamity acts out her earlier familiar roles: a troublemaker with a grin, a sharpshooter, a brawler, a willing and enthusiastic bedmate, and a woman equally proficient with a whip and a rapier-like tongue. Edson provides little historical background for the characters or setting. Even though the second section introduces two well-known western characters, Poker Alice and Madame Moustache, they are reimagined as two very attractive and sexually alluring young women, which, at least in the case of Poker Alice, was a stretcher of gigantic proportions.

449. Edson, J. T. *The Cow Thieves*. London: Brown Watson, 1965.

Set in Texas where cattle thieves are at work, this Edson novel includes Calamity and her riding partner Danny Fog. Calamity travels endlessly, handles guns like a veteran, fights rustlers alongside Fog, and shares his bed. An energetic and courageous youthful woman of considerable sass, she fends off possible attacks from other lustful men.

Edson follows his previously manufactured story that Calamity has escaped from a convent, where her single mother, Charlotte, had placed her as a girl. Riding west from St. Louis, she enters Texas and soon gains a notable, widespread reputation; in fact, men and women know her name and her notoriety as an indefatigable and not-to-be-crossed young woman. All nonsense historically, of course. This imagined biography of Calamity parallels a similar fictional biography created of another historical figure, Ella "Cattle Kate" Watson. Again, Edson majors in exaggerations and entertainment, barely minoring in biography and history.

450. Edson, J. T. *The Bull Whip Breed.* London: Brown Watson, 1965.

Although Calamity is clearly the central character in this novel, the setting and plot are remarkably at odds with those in most Edson Westerns. Set in the unusual site of New Orleans, this work features Calamity as a girl in the city, tracking down a vicious murderer, the Strangler, who is killing off women of the street. In several scenes Calamity shows off her prowess with the bullwhip, hence the novel's title. Edson had warned unwary readers about his approach in an unpaginated author's note at the beginning: "This story does not pretend to be a factual account of the life of Martha Jane Canary, but is merely the kind of adventures Calamity Jane might have liked to have."

Adventures indeed. In one thirty-page section, in a pell-mell string of sensational scenes, Calamity serves as bait to catch the murderous Strangler, fights off four toughs bent on destroying her, and escapes from the clutches of the Strangler. Along the way, the author unpersuasively tries to compare a lively, masculine, healthy West with an immoral, crime-ridden, and unhealthy East (New Orleans!). Not one of the stronger installments of the Calamity Jane series.

451. Edson, J. T. *The Big Hunt.* London: Brown Watson, 1967.

The absence of a clear, well-organized plotline undermines this volume in the Edson Calamity Jane series. The author is unable to integrate the major characters and their separate stories in a coherent narrative.

This fictional Calamity both parallels and differs from her image in the other volumes of the series. A vivacious, wisecracking, and courageous redhead, Calamity adroitly wields her whip and delivers several telling blows in her fisticuffs and wrestling matches. Differences occur too. Calamity is one of the boys in an undated story set during buffalo-hunting days. No romance story here, even though one of her usual sidekicks, Mark Counter, appears and then is quickly gone. Nor is there a vicious, she-cat brawl in these pages, as there are in so many other Edson Westerns.

452. Edson, J. T. *Guns in the Night.* London: Corgi Books, 1968.

Edson spins an unusual plot here, set in Indian Territory in the late 1870s. He portrays several murderous conflicts among settlers, white-schooled Indians, reservation Indians, and the magical trinity of the Floating Outfit regulars, Mark Counter, Dusty Fog, and Ysabel Kid. Marrying is a concomitant, usual theme. Some of these men, as well as several of the fellow riders in Edson's fiction, have the morals of promiscuous rabbits, but not here. The Kid and Dusty will soon marry willing wives-to-be but, tragically, Mark loses his sweetheart, Belle Starr, in a violent attack.

Edson's Calamity, although relegated to a supporting role, nonetheless reveals new information about herself. She practices birth control by following instructions she has learned from an Indian herbalist, and though she and Belle Starr have both been intimate with Mark, Calamity has never thought of marrying him. Still, in a closing scene she speaks of possibly joining a freighter who wants her for a partner—and maybe as a wife. She is thinking about that.

Some of Edson's techniques and ideas seep out here. He is not trustworthy in his details, jumbling together false facts and imagined stories in treating the life of Belle Starr. He also betrays his pro-Southern sentiments and anti-Reconstruction prejudices. Nor are his treatments of Indians and their opponents balanced. Still, readers likely found his treatments of Mark, the Kid, and Dusty—and Calamity as well—inviting and intriguing.

453. Edson, J. T. *The Bad Bunch*. London: Corgi Books, 1968.

Calamity makes a cameo appearance at the end of this novel. Set just after the close of the Civil War in the Southwest, the work features a coterie of renegade women known as the Bad Bunch. Two recognized historical figures, Belle Starr and Belle Boyd (the latter known as the Confederate or Rebel Spy) appear throughout the novel, Calamity only at the end. Starr and Boyd fit the correct chronology but are depicted as much different from their actual personas. Calamity (still Martha Canary) would have been only nine or ten in 1865–66. She briefly lives up to her lust for fist-fighting and snap shooting. Not a major work on Calamity.

454. Edson, J. T. *Calamity Spells Trouble*. London: Corgi Books, 1968.

The title of this novel summarizes its contents. Wherever Calamity rides, trouble ensues. In this work set in the early 1870s along a stagecoach route in northern Utah Territory, Calamity seems to attract robbers, shootouts, fistfights, and woman-on-woman brawls. And most assuredly she willingly and frequently couples with two men. Although only eighteen, Calamity skillfully drives a stagecoach, wields handguns and a wicked whip like a veteran, and wisely counsels a handful of persons about their dilemmas.

Edson betrays here his bewildering fascination with guns—naming, describing, and loving them throughout the novel. In addition, he dishes out

several lengthy paragraphs describing western practices and devious steril-
ization of operating knives, practices of gunsmithing, life at stage stations,
the construction of stagecoaches, and the variety of gun holsters. Perhaps
the author was convinced that descriptions such as these would lend an aura
of realism to what is a skip-and-run, adventure Western.

455. Edson, J. T. *The Fortune Hunters*. London: Corgi Books, 1969.

Calamity jumps on stage for about thirty pages in the middle of this work.
She is depicted in familiar terms: sexy, dressed in the tightest of clothes,
hungry for superman Mark Counter, and an individualistic, do-it-my-way
young woman. When Calamity claims she will be a good girl, the author
enters the narrative to tell the reader "Calamity was never to be trusted when
she sounded as innocent as a church-pew full of choirboys" (p. 66). A minor
but characteristic role for Calamity.

The novel's plot is the unbelievable story of an eccentric, millionaire
Texas rancher who plans his own false death to control his inheritance.
Along the way, Edson betrays his anti-liberal and pro-Confederate leanings,
and death is "delivered wholesale" (p. 182).

456. Edson, J. T. *The Small Texan*. London: Corgi Books, 1969.

Calamity enters the narrative in the second part of this three-part novel. The
book features Dusty Fog, Ysabel Kid, and Mark Counter, with one or two
other members of the Floating Outfit crew. Calamity joins them as a minor
figure in this series of stories set in Kansas cow and farming towns.

Calamity is painted in familiar terms. She is a fly-off-the-handle young
woman with an overly assertive attitude, a flapping mouth, and indiscreet
actions. Her Texan sidekicks continually warn her not to act precipitously
and get them into trouble. Most of the time she harkens to counsel. Toward
the end of her supporting role, Calamity even wears a dress and serves as a
phony wife.

Edson advances some of his favorite conclusions and displays his
historical shortcomings. In the words of one character, Westerners need to
make their own decisions and avoid the wrongheaded conclusions of "liber-
alradical soft shells" [*sic*] from the East. And the Union Yankees were lucky
to defeat the valiant Southerners like Dusty Fog. Some, especially Edson
himself, tout his historical accuracies, but here he is wide of the mark in
speaking of a man being appointed governor of the state of Kansas. Gener-

ally, Edson fails to understand differences between western territories and states in the post–Civil War years.

457. Edson, J. T. *Cold Deck, Hot Lead*. London: Corgi Books, 1969.

The archetypical Wild West Calamity appears in this Edson novel. She is lively, profane, and deadly with a whip and guns. She is also shapely from head to toe, attractive but not beautiful—and already a living legend: "Happy-go-lucky, living each day fully, Calamity Jane had won the admiration and friendship of many people" (p. 37). And she wins a brutal fight with another pugilistic woman in which their clothes are torn off, their breasts left bare.

Unusual characteristics are in evidence, too. Calamity has become a healer, having learned the healing arts from an ancient Pawnee woman. She is also more explicit about the choices to be made. Speaking of marriage and settling down, Calamity retorts she would "'hate like hell for *that* to happen'" (p. 82). In fact, no coupling takes place, even though lecherous men try to move in on her. This Calamity hunts, lives off the land, and cherishes her individualistic freedom.

458. Edson, J. T. *White Stallion, Red Mare*. London: Corgi Books, 1970.

This novel in the Calamity Jane series contains unusual ingredients for an Edson work. Set in post–Civil War days in Kansas trail-end, farm, and stage-stop towns, this volume has Calamity traveling with Ysabel Kid, one of the main characters in Edson's voluminous Floating Outfit series but rarely part of the Calamity Jane novels. Part Comanche, the Kid becomes Calamity's stealthy, knife-wielding partner and lover.

Edson also incorporates information here about Robert Howard Canary and Charlotte Martha Canary, Calamity's parents. A wanderer, a gambler, and something of a ne'er-do-well, father Robert wins a small Kansas ranch in a card game and bequeaths it to his daughter Martha/Calamity Jane. (In an earlier novel Martha's father had already died.) She clashes with a woman hard case planning on capturing the ranch to plunder its timber. Besides the imagined information about Robert and Charlotte, the plot includes the usual dozen killings and even follows two simultaneous subplots that allow for Calamity's womanly clashes as well as the deadly male gunfights. In one dramatic scene, Calamity is tied to a log and nearly run through a buzz saw before she is saved at the very last moment from brutal death. The author even drags in an environmental mini sermon attacking Calamity's female competitor for timber clear-cutting and fouling nearby streams.

459. Edson, J. T. *The Remittance Kid*. London: Corgi Books, 1978.

Edson writes that the happenings in this novel, a prequel to *The Whip and the War Lance* (461), "precede" those in that work. But this work, lacking even a mention of Calamity Jane, is an odd one to place in the Calamity Jane series. Set in Chicago in the 1870s, it deals with an Irish revolutionary group fomenting rebellion. Belle Boyd, the famed Rebel Spy, and the Remittance Kid, an Englishman, are in undercover police work; they are the novel's two positive protagonists. Edson emphasizes class differences among his characters and mentions the "homosexual tendencies" of one man, the "liberal" politics of governments, and the socialism of several villainous characters.

460. Edson, J. T. *J. T.'s Hundredth*. London: Corgi Books, 1979.

In this fifteen-part anthology of stories to celebrate the publication of his hundredth volume, Edson includes one story about Calamity Jane. In addition to "Part Seven, Calamity Jane in Deadwood, August 2nd, 1876" (pp. 226–48) the author attaches an appendix with his imagined biography of Calamity (pp. 435–37). In introductions to the anthology and to Part Seven, Edson reveals that he began to write about Calamity because he thought that moviemakers were failing to utilize "her character traits to their fullest potential" (p. 226). So he set out to portray her as "a kind of pre-Women's Lib liberated woman" (p. 227). She would compete—and succeed—in a man's world.

Edson marries history to falsehood in this brief story. He mostly follows history in writing about Jack McCall and his shooting of Wild Bill Hickok but is counterfactual in this treatment, his only extended coverage of the Wild Bill Hickok–Calamity Jane relationship. He grafts onto these semi-factual ingredients a wholly unsubstantiated, largely imagined story of a conspiracy to bring down the famed gunfighter. Edson ends the story, falsely, with Calamity tackling McCall in a butcher shop and threatening—but finally withholding—his demise with a cleaver. In closing with this misrepresentation, Edson followed misinformation that Calamity included in her flawed autobiography (241).

461. Edson, J. T. *The Whip and the War Lance*. London: Corgi Books, 1979.

Edson imbues this novel, one of the final installments in the Calamity Jane series, with an international flavor. Canadian and American advocates of a *méti* (mixed-blood) rebellion and a separate state for the *méti* in Canada engender the opposition of the Remittance Kid, Belle Boyd, and Calamity Jane. In a series of nonstop confrontations from Kansas to Montana, Calamity and her sidekicks gradually defeat the *méti* contingent. As something of a sequel to *The Remittance Kid* (459), this work includes several characters from that earlier novel, in fact resurrecting some killed in the previous book.

Calamity is depicted in now-familiar terms. A provocateur of the first order, she assertively attacks opponents, verbally, with her fists, and with her deadly whip. Some of these actions, admittedly, are needed for her undercover work with the Kid and Belle to defeat the *métis*. Calamity even couples with one of the leading villains.

Edson also grafts onto his Western plot the *méti* legend of a maiden warrior, the Jan-Dark, whom Calamity battles and defeats in the novel's closing scene. Edson mishandles the facts of Montana history, and his dictatorial authorial hand often resorts to deus ex machina interventions to control a wayward plot. Still, readers undoubtedly were drawn to the author's three leading characters—Calamity, the Kid, and Belle Boyd. They are lively, appealing figures.

462. Edson, J. T. *Calamity, Mark and Belle*. London: Corgi Books, 1980. Reprinted as *Texas Trio*. New York: Charter Books, 1989.

From midcareer onward, Edson often reused his earlier writings, sometimes expanding on them, frequently rearranging earlier stories. Such is the case with this later novel. In its first iteration in 1965, the nub of the novel appeared as "Part I, The Bounty of Belle Starr's Scalp," in the novel *Troubled Range* (447). In 1979 and again in 1990, Edson reprinted *Troubled Range*; these reprintings contained minor revisions, including added footnotes of explanation. Part I of the first edition of the novel, fifteen years later, was greatly expanded into *Calamity, Mark and Belle* (1980). Included in the expanded version were fact-filled appendixes on Calamity and one of her amours, Mark Counter. Nearly all of the "facts" about Calamity in her appendix were imagined, wide of any historical truth.

Readers of earlier volumes in the Calamity Jane series will easily recognize her. Edson characterizes Calamity in well-worn terms: she is young, assertive, rambunctious, attractive but not beautiful, smoothly contoured, sexy, promiscuous, gregarious, foulmouthed, and a nonstop wanderer. She travels with two of her well-known companions, Belle Starr and Mark Counter, and couples with Mark. That Texas cad steams up the blankets with

Belle a few pages later. As one might expect, Calamity and Belle engage in a titanic, exhausting brawl.

Edson wants readers to believe that within two years after escaping from the convent where her mother had placed her, Calamity is known throughout the interior West. Bullwhackers, saloon owners and dance-hall girls, ranchers and cowboys, virtually everyone, has heard about Calamity. Her name turns heads and catches breaths. Even though she has been appearing for fifteen years in Edson's Westerns, Calamity has not aged. Forever young, she captures the attentions and imaginations of the other characters—and readers—she meets.

463. Edson, J. T. *J. T's Ladies*. London: Corgi Books, 1980.

In this collection of six stories is "Part Six[:] Martha 'Calamity Jane' Canary in Mrs. Wild Bill" (pp. 170–212). Edson also provides a brief appendix sketching out how he has treated Calamity in his dozen and more novels about her. In his "action-escapism-adventure fiction" (Edson's words), he decided to avoid the masculine domination of that genre by starring some "ladies." Although Calamity Jane was the only heroine to have her own series, Belle Starr, Belle Boyd, and several other women also ride through Edson's novels.

Calamity is something of sideline character in the Mrs. Wild Bill story. Scheduled to box another villainous woman, Calamity is captured and spirited away. Agnes Lake Thatcher (Hickok), standing in for Calamity, surprisingly wins the brutal match, in which the two competitors blast away at one another bare breasted. Those fisticuffs take up much of the story.

Unfortunately, Edson has the history entirely wrong. Agnes Hickok and Calamity Jane never met, the Hickoks did not buy a house/hotel in Cheyenne, and Agnes never participated in boxing matches. Thus, Edson produces an action-packed story with flashes of the familiar Calamity; but she is off scene for much of this story weakened by inaccurate historical details.

464. Edson, J. T. *The Hide and Horn Saloon*. New York: Corgi Books, 1983.

Although Edson numbered this novel as one in the Calamity Jane series, she does not appear in it. Something of a prequel to *Cut One, They All Bleed* (465), the novel is set in the small Texas town of Tennyson, and the plot deals primarily with Madam Bulldog (Charlotte Canary, Calamity's errant mother) and her beginnings as owner of the Hide and Horn Saloon. Madam Bulldog, who does not want to be called Mrs. Canary, is a grown-up Calamity: assertive, courageous, dangerous, sexy, and in charge. The usual gunfights and fistfights (including those between women), details of guns and card games, and descriptions of the seductive contours of women and the burly physiques of heroes and villains—all are here. But Calamity is not.

465. Edson, J. T. *Cut One, They All Bleed.* London: Corgi Books, 1983.

Although Edson listed this Western in his Calamity Jane series, she plays a sideline role. She does not appear until halfway through the novel and is not the central figure thereafter. Otherwise, her role is mostly unsurprising: fistfight with Madam Bulldog (off scene), who proves to be her mother, and gunfights with the Cousins gang and town rascals. Others, especially Trudeau Front de Bouef and his salacious mother, Jessica, serve as the villains, and Calamity's sometime partner Mark Counter as a fill-in good guy. Edson stresses his usual ingredients: sex, gun battles, violent fistfights, and antiliberal ideology. He also draws heavily on his earlier *The Wildcats* (448) for his coverage of Calamity, Mark, and Madam Bulldog here. More unusual is the author's use of two middle-aged (but beautiful and sexy) women in roles usually reserved for women half their age. One of the three appendixes summarizes the Calamity Jane novels and Calamity's actions in those works. A less-than-satisfactory installment in the Calamity Jane series.

466. Edson, J. T. *Wanted! Belle Starr.* London: Corgi Books, 1983.

Although several sources list this work as part of the Calamity Jane series, it contains nothing on her. Instead, Belle Starr, another of Edson's bevy of sexy, attractive, and assertive heroines, prances through the novel. Several of Edson's other favorite characters, including Belle's male sidekicks from Texas, make an appearance. And as always, there is a vicious fight between two frontier women.

467. Evans, Tabor. *Longarm in Deadwood.* New York: Jove Books, 1982.

Part of the voluminous, house-written Longarm series, this novel overflows with violence and crude sex. The major protagonist, one Custis Long, spends more time seducing willing women than he does upholding the law. He is a crusty, fast-gun artist driven to fulfill his own lusts. Unfortunately, Calamity is reduced to a drunken nymphomaniac, a hot-blooded, lascivious woman. The novel greatly exaggerates the tangential connection between Calamity and Wild Bill and undercuts even that story with numerous mistakes, including even calling Hickok "Jim." Nor should readers be taken in by the misleading suggestion that the opponents of Hickok were the real dispensers of justice and the controllers of the "hard cases." Another example of the Adult Westerns so popular from the 1970s onward.

468. Fontes, Ron, and Justine Korman. *Calamity Jane at Fort Sanders*. New York: Disney Press, 1992.

This brief novel, no. 8 in Disney's American Frontier series, is meant primarily for youthful readers. The authors resort to nonstop, sensational action and purple prose to entice their pre-adolescent readers. One sentence, like many others, exhibits the authors' predilection for breathless description: Calamity is labeled "the wildest woman west of the Mississippi" (p. 3).

Worse for readers wanting fiction solidly based in historical fact are the incorrect descriptions and events. The rearranged facts about Calamity's girlhood and a totally invented narrative dampen down the value of this lively historical fiction. The authors work in unhistorical contacts with groups of Indians and soldiers that Calamity never had. Conversations and unspoken ruminations also allow unrecorded revelations about Calamity's deceased parents and her sister Lana/Lena and brother Elijah.

For the most part, the authors allow their imaginations free rein. In that twilight zone between fact and fiction, when the authors veer toward fiction the historical Calamity Jane gets lost. The second half of the novel features Calamity's rescue of Captain Egan, although not quite as she claimed it in her suspect autobiography (241). The Indians are positively treated, and Calamity is a vivacious, lively, and nontraditional young woman. Indeed, the authors tout Calamity as an early feminist, suggesting that she could be president. Conversely, considering the intended readership, Calamity's alcoholism, promiscuity, and nonstop swearing are absent.

469. Hueston, Ethel. *Calamity Jane of Deadwood Gulch*. Indianapolis, Ind.: Bobbs-Merrill, 1937.

Telling Calamity's story has not been an easy task for novelists. Aside from the Deadwood Dick dime novel series, one or two other dime novels, (401, 471) and Mrs. Spencer's novel (481), no other writer of fiction dealt with Calamity before this work. It can be said to be the first novel of appreciable literary quality to deal with Calamity. The novel is clearly a work of historical fiction, the Calamity sections more historical and the other parts imagined fiction. Its strengths and limitations are equally balanced.

Hueston utilizes a good deal of Calamity's biography. She writes of Calamity's going north with General Crook and her time in the Deadwood area. She speaks of Calamity's dealings with Wild Bill Hickok and Colorado Charlie Utter. And the author persuasively deals with Calamity's complex character. When she is "on the warpath," writes Hueston, "Crazy Horse is a Christian dude alongside Calamity Jane" (p. 25). But she also wants to help, telling another character, "There ain't nothin' above love . . . Nothin'" (p. 165).

The author falls into trouble when she tries to graft the story of Phoebe Ann Norcutt, the hyper-religious daughter of missionaries to Indians, onto a Calamity Jane novel. Too many unbelievable and fortuitous happenings travel alongside Phoebe. Her romantic attachment to an Indian killer is one of those dubious happenings.

But Hueston, more than most male writers and like Mrs. Spencer earlier, raises the possibility that Calamity could and did have women friends. Phoebe and Calamity, though disagreeing on much, find avenues of friendship. While "birds of opposite feathers get themselves in noisy nests sometimes," Hueston writes, she also notes that "birds of a contrary plumage seem [sometimes] to . . . [make] a night of it" (pp. 124, 121), suggesting that two such different people as Calamity and Phoebe can be friends. What Hueston did better than any previous author was to suggest that woman-to-woman stories ought to find their way onto the Western stage alongside masculine and romance stories.

470. Ihle, Sharon. *Wildcat*. New York: Harper Paperbacks, 1993.

Ihle's historical romance mixes several disparate ingredients. It combines romance, history, fiction, and sex, with a bit of violence thrown in as spice. Of note, the author follows a plotline no other Calamity Jane novel has utilized. Ann Marie Cannary [*sic*], portrayed as Calamity's young sister, travels to Deadwood to find Martha, to be again with family. In telling this fictional story, Ihle insists that she has "tried to present as many historical facts as possible" (p. 374). But she too often abuses history. She rearranges historical facts to fit her novelistic needs—for example, falsely having Wild Bill Hickok arrive in Deadwood before the Custer disaster. She asserts, too, that Wild Bill and Calamity "were at least friends, and probably for a brief period lovers" (p. 375). The best evidence reveals they were no more than acquaintances, not romantically or sexually involved.

The author attempts to provide a greatly expanded Calamity but begins with her drunkenness, bullwhacking, and promiscuity. The expansions come in Ihle's attempts to show Calamity as a loving sister, guilt-ridden for not helping her Canary siblings and desiring to help Ann Marie (Stormy) in her up-and-down romance with Lucky Luke McCanles. The romance between Ihle's two imagined characters—Stormy and Lucky Luke—is not smoothly handled, often substituting created fiction for known history. This novel belongs among the Adult Westerns in its explicit treatment of sex, but is much less violent than most recent Calamity novels.

471. Ingraham, Prentiss. *Buffalo Bill and Calamity Jane; or, A Real Lady from the Black Hills.* New Buffalo Bill Weekly no. 177. New York: Street and Smith, 1916.

This short story, novella in fact, is part dime novel, part nonsense. Writer Prentiss Ingraham, said to be the author of more than five hundred novels (one hundred or so on Buffalo Bill alone), follows an unusual, perhaps unique, route in treating Calamity Jane here. He portrays a smallish man disguised as Calamity in the first half of the story. She is pictured as about thirty-five, of masculine build (surprise!), and assertive and combative. Ingraham, who died a dozen years before this story was published, wasted little time with historical research. Set in New Mexico, the brief piece includes the historical characters of Buffalo Bill, Wild Bill Hickok (mostly absent), and the disguised Calamity. But the story places them where they never were together, doing things they did not do. Superficial and contrived.

472. Jameson, Mike. *Tales from Deadwood.* New York: Berkley Books, 2005.

Prolific author Jameson structures his novel on two subplots. One deals with historical figures Wild Bill Hickok, Colorado Charlie and Steve Utter, the Anderson brothers, and Calamity Jane on their way to Deadwood in early summer 1876. The other follows the imagined character of Dan Ryan, trying to make his way as a miner and sometime townsman in the Deadwood area. Jameson draws on well-known historical sources for his bits of history, but his story is more invented than historical reconstruction.

Jameson's Calamity Jane is a pain in all parts of the anatomy, a drunk who is driven by sexual hunger. Accompanying the Hickok-Utter train traveling from Fort Laramie to the Black Hills, Calamity pesters Wild Bill for drinks from his keg, tries to butt into his affairs, and offers her bed to the newly married pistoleer on more than one occasion. Hickok tries to keep her away from him and out of trouble, but is often unsuccessful in his efforts. Jameson, although dealing with a period overlooked by most novelists— Calamity's life in 1875–76 before she arrived in Deadwood—provides a very negative portrait of her. She is profane, drunken, lustful, and precipitous in her actions; redeeming character qualities are rarely in evidence.

473. Logan, Jake. *Dead Man's Hand.* New York: Playboy Press Paperbacks, 1979.

Another one of the Adult Westerns featuring explicit sex and extraordinary violence, this volume encapsulated the ambivalent New Gray Calamity that emerged after the 1960s. It is part of a voluminous series of novels written by a stable or two of anonymous writers whose works were published under the house name of Jake Logan. This novel, actually from the pen of Donald McCaig, features the super stud John Slocum, who beds many, many willing women through the more than four hundred volumes that appeared in the Jake Logan series from the mid-1970s until about 2014. The Calamity pictured here is little more than the sexual toy of supermen, including Slocum and Wild Bill Hickok, on the same night, in the same bed. Calamity makes clear her gender desires: "Women bore the hell out of me . . . never liked 'em," "but men don't. Not strong men" (pp. 155, 156), The height of violence comes in a twenty-page vicious fight between Slocum and Hickok near the end of the novel. Logan/McCaig distorts Calamity by scrambling the chronology of her life and adding many events not true to her character. History lite—or none at all.

474. Lynde, Sidne, and Stan Lynde. *Calamity Jane: "Queen of the Plains."* Billings, Mont.: Montanacrafts and Rimrock, 1975.

An illustrated narrative poem, this brief account generalizes about Calamity's character without providing much specific information. The authors seem most interested in Calamity's storytelling talents, as one refrain reveals:

> The stories Calam could tell
> Would raise your hair on end.
> She didn't care if they were true or not,
> And neither should you, my friend. (p. 2)

Several of the authors' historical details are incorrect or suspect. They have Calamity born in 1852, include the false story about Captain Egan naming her "Calamity Jane," and assert that she chased and cornered Jack McCall after he assassinated Wild Bill. The poetry is informal, folksy verse.

475. McMurtry, Larry. *Buffalo Girls.* New York: Simon and Schuster, 1990.

McMurtry's work is probably the most touted novel about Calamity Jane and her friends. It gained a wide readership and was made into a movie, *Buffalo*

Girls (1995), starring Anjelica Huston as Calamity and Melanie Griffith as her intimate friend and bordello matron Dora Du Fran (484).

McMurtry's Calamity fits comfortably into the New Gray Calamity (neither saintly nor evil) popular in the years following the 1960s. Like the heroine in Pete Dexter's novel *Deadwood* (442), McMurtry's heroine is a gritty, amoral woman, with nothing of the romantic, adventuresome woman in the Doris Day tradition. Indeed, the Calamity of *Buffalo Girls* fails in nearly everything. Unable to adjust to a closed frontier, she boozes and cries her way through much of the novel. She falls off the stagecoach in Buffalo Bill Cody's Wild West arena show, she cannot use a gun (and thus is unable to compete with Annie Oakley), and fails to *do* anything but live off others. Following the off-track story of Jean Hickok McCormick (246), McMurtry presents a woman increasingly out of step with her surroundings, hoping to be a good mother but a failure at that as well.

In addition, McMurtry provides valuable commentary on the molding power of a closing frontier in his Calamity Jane. When Calamity writes to her imagined daughter, she says, "I *am* the Wild West, Janey, no show about it, I was one of the people that kept it wild, why should I want to make a spectacle of myself before a bunch of toots and dudes" (p. 14); but, contrary to her own assertion, she does join Buffalo Bill's Wild West to perform. And her mountain man friend Bartle Bone adds to the conflict Calamity feels between her memory of a roaring frontier and her participation in a phony show. As Bone says, "What Wild West . . . If Billy Cody can make a poster about it there ain't no Wild West" (p. 18). Calamity stubbornly resists that conclusion, however, trying to live on her dying memories. McMurtry also adds another important ingredient by suggesting the narrow, constrictive roles that were forced on women in the Old West. Despite an excessive grayness in his Calamity, McMurtry suffuses his novel with cultural meanings about a closing frontier and the roles of women on that frontier.

476. Markley, Bill. *Deadwood Dead Men*. Nashville, Tenn.: Goldminds, 2013.

In his first novel, Bill Markley combines a mystery story featuring Captain Jack Jones, a Chicago newspaper reporter, with the actions of several historical persons in Deadwood in August 1876. Calamity Jane, bartender Harry Young, newspaper editor A. W. Merrick, entrepreneur Seth Bullock, and others play minor supporting roles. Marley's Calamity—foulmouthed, assertive, and helpful—participates in several "rumored" historical events, including her reactions to Preacher Smith's preaching and murder, a tobacco-spitting incident in a theater, and her professed love for Wild Bill. Most historians do not support this novelist's contention that a ring of rascals, ruling Deadwood in 1876, hired Jack McCall to assassinate Hickok, although most agree with his comments about Deadwood being a place without law and order. More demanding editing and further revision would have elided needless repetitions, clichés, and deadening conversations. But Markley is strong on history, and his major characters are attractive and interesting.

477. Mitchum, Hank [Dwight B. Newton, pseud.]. *Stagecoach Station 11: Deadwood*. New York: Bantam Books, 1984.

Even though this novel fits comfortably into much of the Adult Western genre appearing after the 1960s, it does exhibit several differences. First of all, the real author (Hank Mitchum is a house name) is Dwight B. Newton, a veteran writer, author of dozens of well-researched historical Westerns. Here he warns readers he will deal with several other historical figures in addition to Calamity and Wild Bill. Actor/theater owner Jack Langrishe, entrepreneurs Charlie and Steve Utter, and villain Jack McCall are some of the rather historically accurate figures portrayed in this novel.

  More a ballet of blood than a drama of erotic promiscuity, this work demonstrates that even within the narrow confines of the Adult Western, there were/are margins for competent characterization and social commentary. For instance, when Wild Bill queries Calamity's understanding of "ladies," she retorts: "Oh, hell! . . . I guess I know a lady when I see one. I been chased out of towns by some of the best!" (p. 59). But when another young woman does not cast Calamity on the scrap heap of criticism and wants to be her friend, Calamity quickly reciprocates and promises friendship. Even though Calamity is driven to drink, she is not the nymphomaniac portrayed in many of the Adult Westerns. And Mitchum/Newton is, by and large (save for his overemphasis on Wild Bill Hickok), more trustworthy in his uses of history and biography than most authors of Adult Westerns. He even suggests that Calamity does not idolize Wild Bill because she is more interested in furthering her own mythic status.

478. Morris and Goscinny. *Calamity Jane*. A Lucky Luke Adventure. Canterbury, Kent, UK: Cinebook, 2007. Original title: *Lucky Luke—Calamity Jane*, by Goscinny and Morris. Paris: Dargaud Editeur, 1971.

Here we have one installment of the Lucky Luke series, which features a bumbling but heroic cowboy in the far reaches of the American West. A forty-six-page graphic novel/comic book, this work of fiction plays around the edges of history. Calamity's earthy, grubby, profane, and assertive qualities are emphasized—along with her detestation of ladylike prescriptions. However, a few other emphases, including a declaration of love for Wild Bill, are off track. The novel's intention is not serious history but parody, satire, and humor.

479. Roberts, J. R. [Robert Randisi, pseud.] *The Gunsmith 146: Return to Deadwood.* New York: Jove Books, 1994.

The publication of this volume proved that Adult Westerners were still being published at the end of the twentieth century. And the contents and approach of this sex-and-violence novel placed it at the center in the Adult Western tradition. Prolific author Randisi, writing under the house name of J. R. Roberts, adopts the familiar plot with Gunsmith Clint Adams starring as a fast-shooting stud bent on clearing up a murder mystery, out-shooting opponents, and satisfying lustful women.

Calamity had written to Adams asking him to come to Deadwood to help her. She had been accused of murder and needed his aid in capturing the real murderer. Calamity is depicted as a drunk and a lush, and maybe still in love with the murdered Wild Bill Hickok. Once Gunman Adams comes on scene, Calamity is reduced to a secondary figure as he mows down opponents and moves from bed to bed. The Gunman also helps Calamity recover money stolen from funds set aside for her daughter's education. Even though the author hints that Calamity represents a long-gone Deadwood belonging to a wilder West, his plot suggests otherwise in his picturing the town as a dangerous, still-violent, and sex-driven place. Stereotypes abound, and literary artistry and historical accuracy are mostly absent.

480. Robinson, Gillian. *The Slow Reign of Calamity Jane.* Kingston, Ontario: Quarry Press, 1994.

This is a curious volume. The Canadian poet Robinson has written a series of poems loosely based on some of Calamity's life but relying primarily on her own imagination. Robinson's imaginings allow her to create conversations among Martha/Calamity, her mother, and Calamity's nonexistent daughter Janey. The author's feminist desires drive her into a far country of made-up dreams, including Calamity's love affair with Wild Bill, a longtime relationship with cowboy Teddy Blue right up to her death, and letters and a diary she never wrote.

To attempt to plumb Calamity's consciousness, to understand her feminine dreams and desires, is a commendable and worthwhile endeavor. But to play recklessly with known facts and to invent events whole cloth is to greatly distort the historical character one is trying to follow and understand. Robinson's volume will benefit most those bent toward the imaginary and be of least help to those wanting to grasp the hard facts of Calamity's controversial life.

481. Spencer, Mrs. William Loring. *Calamity Jane: A Story of the Black Hills.* 1887; Reprint, Mitchell, S.Dak.: Dakota Wesleyan University Press, 1978.

This first full-length novel about Calamity Jane by a woman (Mrs. George E. Spencer, or Mrs. William Loring Spencer, her given name) is more valuable for its sociocultural contexts than its literary content. It was the only full-length novel published about Calamity before the 1930s. Several parallels link Spencer's work with dime novels: she makes extensive uses of disguises, and the effete, crook-infested East is compared to an open, rough frontier West. Calamity Jane illustrates the latter.

But it is in Spencer's handling of an unlikely friendship between Calamity and Meg Stevens DePew, a new, virtuous wife just arrived with her snooty lawyer husband from the East, that the author breaks new ground. Calamity is depicted as an enigmatic wild rider, gambler, and controversial young woman in the Black Hills. Meg does not know what to think of her but dislikes the class biases of other women in Deadwood who treat Calamity as a social skunk come in from the outback. Although Meg is a rather poorly drawn character, her willingness to befriend Calamity rings true. Gradually, they form a strong, loving woman-to-woman relationship, despite her husband's strong opposition.

Spencer also provides an intriguing image of Calamity as an oxymoronic woman/man. She dresses and acts like a man but has strong womanly desires. In one illuminating image, the author deftly catches these conflicting impulses: Calamity's "pretty foot and ankle" attract attention as she springs "into her saddle." Combining the early Fox interview (361), a few of Calamity's scattered comments, and this provocative novel, one can suggest, tentatively, that some part of Calamity aspired to be a typical pioneer woman, hoping to find her way as a wife, mother, and homemaker.

FILMS AND CINEMATIC CRITICISM

482. Films

Films are listed alphabetically by title, and movie reviews alphabetically by author. Numbers in parentheses cross-reference other entries in this guide.

483. *Badlands of Dakota.* 1941. Universal. Frances Farmer as Jane, Richard Dix as Wild Bill Hickok, Robert Stack as Jim Holliday, Broderick Crawford as Bob Holliday, Ann Rutherford as Anne Grayson.

Set in Deadwood, this Western film features two brothers, Bob and Jim Holliday, who vie for the same attractive young woman. Bob, a tough guy and saloon owner, turns out to be an outlaw, making matters very difficult for his younger brother, Jim, now the marshal of Deadwood. Phony and actual Indians as well as killer Jack McCall provide several threats and actual violence. Wild Bill Hickok is assassinated in the closing half of the film, and General George Custer tries to protect Deadwood from the real Indian intimidations. In a distortion of historical chronology, the film depicts Custer helping to save Deadwood before riding off to his demise at the Little Bighorn.

Jane (she is not called Calamity Jane), played appealingly by Frances Farmer, is portrayed as the tomboy acquaintance (maybe girlfriend) of Bob Holliday. At first Jane sides with Bob in his conflicts with Jim and others. Then she becomes a truth-teller and violence-avoider by informing on Bob's extralegal acts and shooting him as he plans to cut down Jim. Bob dies in her arms. Some critics touted Farmer's role as the outstanding performance of her career, which, sadly, quickly stopped when she descended into mental instability and institutionalization, though she eventually recovered. Some thought Jane and Wild Bill should have gotten more film time, but they are not portrayed as sweethearts here. Others thought Farmer stole the show.

Ostensibly a historical work, the plot and characterizations belie correct chronology and distort actual events.

484. *Buffalo Girls.* 1995. CBS-TV. Anjelica Huston as Calamity Jane, Melanie Griffin as Dora Du Fran, Gabriel Byrne as Teddy Blue, Peter Coyote as Buffalo Bill Cody.

Based on Larry McMurtry's novel of the same name (475), this two-part TV series likewise followed the Jean Hickok McCormick story but alongside it presented a feminist story of the woman's Old West. Anjelica Huston was superb in portraying an ambivalent Calamity being pushed aside with the closing of the frontier.

Like most of the cinematic Calamities from the 1980s onward, Huston's Calamity wants a man's love and companionship but without sacrificing her self-respect and desire for independence. When Buffalo Bill tells her he wants to make her "famous," she responds, "I *am* famous." Later, when Cody describes her as "an original," she quickly retorts "my reputation is all I got, and it's not for sale." She also tells Bill, "I'm gonna let you make me immortal."

Many of Huston's sparkling one-liners illustrate the conflicting desires that drive her. In speaking of the Old West having left her behind, she confesses "I got nowhere left to go," and she is going nowhere. Or, as she tells one of her old-time mountain man friends, "We've seen some glory days, you and me." "Wifing and whoring" are the only two options for a woman, Calamity asserts; and since neither had worked out for her, she has dressed as a man. Men seemed to misunderstand her; maybe because too many of the "damn fools never seen teats before," she barks after being thrown out of Custer's army. Her good friend and soulmate, Dora Du Fran (a bordello madam), says, "No man has ever loved" Calamity, perhaps because she does not know how to dress and act, perhaps because she sometimes smells like she has been in a "hugging contest with a skunk." All these challenges tell Calamity that she cannot trust men, but women she can. "To all us Buffalo Girls, we got to stick together," she tells Annie Oakley after hearing of that woman's similar hard knocks background.

No one should approach this series for an accurate portrayal of such historical figures as Calamity, Buffalo Bill Cody, Wild Bill, Dora Du Fran, or Teddy Blue (the well-known trail-drive cowboy). It is largely an imaginative re-creation, almost all fictional, of the life and times of Calamity Jane. But it is also an appealing attempt to dramatize the converging legends surrounding Calamity, especially those of Wild West Woman and aspiring Pioneer Woman.

485. *Calamity Jane*. 1953. Warner Brothers. Doris Day as Calamity Jane, Howard Keel as Wild Bill Hickok.

No film captured the romantic image of Calamity Jane that was so popular in the half century after her death as the movie *Calamity Jane*, starring Doris Day. A lively musical, the movie has little pretentions to historicity, but it does play hard on some of the same themes that also powered Cecil B. DeMille's earlier and very popular *The Plainsman* (493).

Day's Calamity comes dashing on stage as an enthusiastic tomboy not much interested in men or femininity. Her transition toward femaleness is the platform on which the movie builds. Wild Bill Hickok, in whom Calamity is initially not much interested, teases her about not dressing or acting like a woman. At first she cares not, but once another woman steals a beau who does interest her, Calamity begins to change. Now, Hickok becomes, increasingly, a target of Calamity's ardor. As Sammy Fain's prizewinning lyrics put it, her "heart is now an open door . . . her love is secret no more." In the final scenes Calamity and Wild Bill marry and ride off on the Deadwood Stage to their honeymoon.

Calamity Jane sanitizes its heroine. No drunkenness, profanity, or promiscuity for this Calamity. Her most powerful drink is "sarsaparilla," and the worst swearing is denouncing rascally miners as "two-bit gamblers," "mangy groundhogs," and "slab-sided coyotes." There is not a hint of the historical Calamity's pliable sexuality. Instead, we are treated to a romantic, pretty, and perky heroine (which Doris Day easily fulfilled) who dances, stomps, and sings herself to matrimony. All historical veracity is shoved aside in the dash toward cinematic entertainment. The film remains to this day the embodiment of the romantic portrait of Calamity Jane that many choose to embrace.

486. *Calamity Jane*. 1984. CBS-TV. Jane Alexander as Calamity Jane, Frederic Forrest as Wild Bill Hickok, Ken Kercheval as Buffalo Bill Cody.

Jane Alexander's portrayal of Calamity Jane in this made-for-TV movie demonstrates how far filmmakers had moved away from the romantic heroine in Doris Day's *Calamity Jane* of 1953 (485). It also illustrates the New Gray Calamity that had come on scene in the post-1960s. Regrettably, it also epitomizes the continuing tight hold of the Jean Hickok McCormick fraudulent story on invented Calamities, particularly in films and novels.

The plot followed McCormick's off-track yarn. Calamity and Wild Bill Hickok fall in love, produce a child (Janey), and then break up. Unable to care for Janey, Calamity gives her up for adoption to the O'Neil family, who take her off to England. Calamity's heart breaks with that act and the continuing separation of mother and daughter. Calamity yearns for a continuing relationship with Wild Bill.

Jane Alexander, despite being burdened with a story line that was historically inaccurate, was up to the demanding task of portraying a Calamity torn between conflicting desires. Calamity covets Wild Bill's love, she desires motherhood, and she wants a home—like other pioneer women. She also pursues her freedom, protects her self-esteem, and touts her ability to make her own way. She tells Wild Bill that she can "be a good wife" to him, but when he declares he cannot be marshal and have a wife, she retorts "I can take care of myself, Bill."

The movie is far from historically accurate in its details about Calamity and Hickok. Still, we get a good deal of interesting possible insights about Calamity in her conversations/pretend letters with daughter Janey. On one occasion Calamity tells her daughter (although Janey does not know it is her mother speaking), "What I know about wifing you could stuff in a saddlebag." Even more shocking to Janey is the revelation, "Well, I guess it's the same for us ladies here or there. You either get paid for washing a man's drawers or for pulling them down." Most of all, this movie clearly demonstrated what a talented actress could do in portraying a complex, angst-ridden Calamity.

487. *Calamity Jane: légende de l'Ouest* (2014). Gregory Monro, director and producer. Arte France and Temps Noir, Paris.

This eighty-two-minute documentary by a French filmmaker provides a generally dependable overview of Calamity's life. It is the only major documentary of Calamity's full life. The English version, titled *Calamity Jane: Wild West Legend*, emphasizes Martha/Calamity's early life, with less on the 1880s and beyond. No stress is placed on Clinton Burke and Robert Dorsett, her last two "husbands." Nor does the film include much about interpretations of Calamity after her death in 1903. The documentary does a good job of placing Calamity in contexts of a changing West and contests between the East and the West. The three major talking heads are James D. McLaird, Linda Jucovy, and Richard W. Etulain. A helpful source that illustrates the intriguing and persisting popularity of Calamity Jane in France.

488. *Calamity Jane and Sam Bass.* 1949. Universal. Yvonne De Carlo as Calamity Jane, Howard Duff as Sam Bass, Dorothy Hart as Katherine Egan, Lloyd Bridges as Joel Collins.

With a complicated plot and many action scenes, this film is not always easy to follow. Bass comes to Texas and is soon involved in a series of events revolving around horse racing. Bass, through dubious means, acquires the famous "Denton Mare," the star racehorse of northern Texas. Once that four-footed animal arrives, the two-legged heroines are unhorsed.

De Carlo plays a lively and sexy Calamity. When Bass helps her with Thunderbolt, her overactive horse, Calamity is smitten with Bass. She is jealous of his attentions to Kathy Egan. Later, Jane joins a group that is turning outlaw. After Bass seems to abandon Kathy (he thinks she loves another man), he and Jane embrace. A series of events forces Bass outside the law, and he is shot by pursuers. Although making clear his love for Kathy, he dies in the arms of Jane. De Carlo, replicating several of her other roles, plays an attractive, alluring Calamity; but the horses, shootouts, and other action scenes push her to the margins. Almost nothing about the historical Calamity Jane appears in this film.

489. *Deadwood.* 2004–2006. HBO. Robin Weigert as Calamity Jane, Ian McShane as Al Swearengen, Timothy Olyphant as Seth Bullock, Molly Parker as Alma Garret, Paula Malcomson as Trixie, Keith Carradine as Wild Bill Hickok.

This thirty-six-segment TV series and Doris Day's *Calamity Jane* (485) in 1953 may be the most popular films ever made about Calamity Jane. At the opposite extremes—Day the romantic Calamity and Robin Weigert the gritty realist—the two movies revealed the sharp shift in depictions of Calamity over a half century. Both works captured huge audiences.

The HBO *Deadwood* almost did not come into being. David Milch, the series' talented, assertive producer-writer, was contemplating a series on ancient Rome, but was talked into doing something on the Old West that dramatized themes similar to those he planned for Nero's Rome. In thinking about the sweep of American history, Milch decided he would focus on community building: how though divergent in class, ethnic and racial backgrounds, and geographical origin, the United States had forged a nation. How had that happened? What forces, what types of people, what kinds of power relationships were at work in the centralizing story?

In interviews and comments on the three-year series, Milch pointed to two avenues he would follow in formulating the series and getting at its central emphases. First, he would draw on historical sources and, combining them with imagined characters and scenes, he would produce programs that were not "a slave to history" but nonetheless would be "historically accurate." Second, he would look carefully at the *process* of community building, how in the absence of *law*, residents of Deadwood might move toward citizen consensus, no matter how many stuttering steps were needed to arrive at those tentative agreements. Anyone who has seen the series knows that saloon owners, such as Al Swearengen (actually Swearingen) and Cy Toliver, are brutal power lords who harass, even rape, some of their dance-hall girls and kill off their opponents. Opposite them were Seth Bullock, Wild Bill Hickok, and others who try with their fists and guns to bring law and order, sometimes through violent means. Some groups, like the Chinese and the call girls, are almost separate societies, but they must nonetheless kowtow to the power brokers.

How was one to place Calamity Jane in the maelstrom of this nascent, semicivilized settlement? Consider the dilemmas facing a film director trying to tell an enticing story about Calamity early in the twenty-first century. The historical facts—Calamity's being an alcoholic, a possible prostitute, and a decidedly unfeminine woman—were ruthlessly confining. Earlier, more romantic filmmakers such as those producing *The Plainsman* (493) and *Calamity Jane* (485), avoided unpalatable realities, depicted Calamity in much less gritty terms, and brought onboard the pretend love affair between Calamity and Wild Bill, a romance that seemed to capture audiences through the decades. The more realistic films of the late twentieth century, such as *Calamity Jane* (486) and *Wild Bill* (498) would not allow a new film to backtrack to romantic nonsense. A new portrayal of Calamity had to fit with contemporary society.

Director-writer Milch decided to create a realistic but very narrowly conceived Calamity Jane. Played superbly by Robin Weigert, Calamity is a drunken mess. She wanders the streets so soused that she cannot, at first, carry out her desired aid in the pest house and for some of the settlement's children. Weigert's Calamity, both like and unlike her historical counterpart, is something of an *isolato*, separated from others in the early installments because of her alcoholism and antisocial behavior. Gradually, however, she finds friendship with Joanie Stubbs, one of the empathetic dance-hall girls. Some read this as a lesbian relationship.

Unhappily, strong though Weigert's depiction of Calamity is, it is constricted and truncated. We get nothing of her work as a dancer, waitress, or hostess. Weigert's Calamity gives no indication that she worked for Swearingen and other saloon owners; she is too drunk and separate in the *Deadwood* series to be a part of the forming community. Separation is a problem, too, for the saloon owners; they cannot hear and understand the sermon of the Preacher from St. Paul that we are all parts of the same body, not to be divided and separate from one another.

Deadwood attracted and retained a huge, enthusiastic audience. The acting was strong, the scenes well laid out, and the themes easily to follow. But it was historically inaccurate. In fact, even though Milch asserted that the series was on-track historically, he and his actors did not seem to know well the lives they were portraying and, in the case of Weigert on Calamity, not much interested in learning those biographical details. Those intrigued with Calamity Jane should remember *Deadwood* for its powerful artistic presentations, not for its close connections to history.

490. *In the Days of '75 and '76.* 1915. Black Hills Feature Film Company. Freeda Hartzell Romine as Calamity Jane, A. L. Johnson as Wild Bill Hickok.

The first film with a starring role for Calamity Jane, this movie was filmed in northwestern Nebraska near Chadron. Featuring Freeda Hartzell Romine, a local young woman, as Calamity, the hour-long film (seven reels) includes more unhistorical ingredients than solid facts. It also adumbrates other Calamity movies produced up through the 1950s.

The film opens in Butte, Montana, where Calamity lives with her widowed mother and her in-the-way younger brother, and where she first meets Wild Bill. Halfway through the movie they marry, and Calamity/Romine helps Hickok with his scouting and mining. The story carries through to Hickok's assassination, and Calamity stays around to gain justice against Jack McCall, the villainous murderer. Calamity is nearly virginal, dressing in white before and after her marriage. She is domestic, loyal, and traditional, with nary a hint of swearing, drinking, or possible prostitution. Although sometimes seeming like one of the guys—as the only woman in several scenes—she is guilty of no antisocial or immoral behavior. For the most part, the descriptions of Calamity here are not defensible historically.

Several of the themes in this first film were repeated in movies about Calamity over the next five or six decades. Her story would be inextricably interwoven with Wild Bill's; there would be a romance between the two, perhaps leading to marriage. Generally, Calamity is depicted here as an unusual pioneer woman (hanging out with men, wearing buckskins, serving as a bullwhacker, and handling a whip and guns), but she is not portrayed as drunken, profane, or selling sex. This rather cleaned-up version of Calamity would carry through Doris Day's landmark *Calamity Jane* in 1953 (485).

491. *The Legend of Calamity Jane*. 1997–98. Warner Brothers Kids Network TV series. Barbara Scaff as the voice of Calamity Jane, Frank Welker as Joe Presto, Clancy Brown as Wild Bill Hickok, and Mark Rolston as Bill Doolin.

This TV production, an animated adventure series, featured a strong, assertive Calamity Jane as a justice-bringer and enforcer in the Old West. The series had an international flavor, having been produced by the French company Contre Allée, France 3, and Canal + and distributed by the British firm Itel and Warner Brothers in the United States. Thirteen episodes were filmed and broadcast outside the United States, but it was pulled from the U.S. market after only three episodes aired.

Barbara Scaff was the voice of the adventuresome, active, and opinionated Calamity Jane. She and her sidekicks Joe Presto and Wild Bill Hickok are the good guys, helping Indians who have been mistreated and aiding others who have been bullied. Calamity wields a deadly whip, belts evildoers in fisticuffs, and outmuscles other rascals. In fact, she reminds one of the heroine in British novelist J. T. Edson's Calamity Jane novels (445–66).

Although Warner Brothers and other promoters touted the series as based on the life of Calamity Jane, it rarely was. In several episodes, Calamity is shown supporting the Comanche and other Indians, taking on opponents in the Civil War, pursuing outlaw Bill Doolin, and participating in several nonwestern events. All these were invented history; Calamity was neither in these places nor a participant in these events. Warner Brothers never explained why it quickly withdrew the series, but some speculated it was too violent and included too much gunplay for its intended pre-adult audience.

492. *The Paleface*. 1948. Paramount Pictures. Jane Russell as Calamity Jane, Bob Hope as "Painless" Peter Potter.

Anyone searching for a serious cinematic treatment of Calamity Jane should not stop here. The film should not be taken seriously. It is primarily farce

and burlesque. Bob Hope as "Painless" Peter Potter, a bogus dentist, inad-
vertently becomes involved in an attempt to stop smugglers selling guns and
dynamite to Indians. Hope/Potter bumbles his way through several episodes
of unbelievable, charade-like events. Hope is ludicrous—and implausible.

The buxom Jane Russell as Calamity Jane also fails. Although shown to
be a superb shot and able handler of the reins, Russell's Calamity is far too
glamorous. She wears long, sexy dresses in the opening scenes of the film
and tight buckskins in the closing scenes. Her clothing accentuates Russell's
more-than-ample figure but detracts from anything close to the historic
Calamity.

The film parodies several ingredients central to old-fashioned Westerns.
Heroes are antiheroes, the Indians are satirized, the shootouts are mostly
false, the romance is phony, and the run-up to a high-noon gunfight ludicrous in every segment. The catchy, Academy Award–winning tune "Buttons
and Bows" is the most memorable part of the film. Generally, the comedy
piling up to parody eliminates any serious historical value for the film and its
underwhelming depiction of Calamity Jane.

493. *The Plainsman*. 1936. Paramount Pictures. Jean Arthur as Calamity Jane,
Gary Cooper as Wild Bill Hickok, James Ellison as Buffalo Bill Cody, Helen
Burgess as Louisa Cody.

Cecil B. DeMille's Western starring Gary Cooper as Wild Bill Hickok, Jean
Arthur as Calamity Jane, and James Ellison as Buffalo Bill, although not the
blockbuster DeMille's biblical epics were, nonetheless was the first film with
a major, very popular role for Calamity Jane. It was an extravaganza of the
first order, depicting the winning of the West on a grand scale. Moving well
beyond historical reality, DeMille brought together Wild Bill, Calamity, Buffalo Bill, and General George Custer in a series of dramatic events that never
occurred. DeMille seemed unworried about the historical accuracy of his
film; he wanted to tell *his* story rather than to re-create history.

Arthur was called upon to portray a very complex Calamity. She was
to be nearly wild in her actions as a stage driver and whip wielder, but sufficiently feminine to attract a Hickok/Cooper said to be uninterested in
women. One revealing incident dramatizes this bifurcated image of Calamity. Sent to aid soldiers pinned down by Indians, Calamity slips out of the
appealing dress she has worn to attract Hickok, revealing the buckskins she
wears underneath, in which she rides to help. Here, in one scene, Calamity/
Arthur reveals her oxymoronic character: a wild feminine woman. In the

film Calamity does not drink, swear, or act immorally, but she is forward, independent, and outspoken.

When it became known that DeMille planned a Hickok–Calamity Jane romance in *The Plainsman*, members of the Hickok family threatened to sue to thwart the cinematic depiction of a romance that they argued had never happened. At first DeMille and his staff were not sure how to depict Calamity; they did not want her to be a whore, or even too lusty in her actions. Instead, they chose to tell a romantic, nonsexual story that included an active, energetic, and sometimes rule-breaking woman who wanted to marry and set up a stable home. That hybrid heroine embodied several of the tensions at work in the historical Calamity.

494. *The Plainsman.* 1966 (remake). Universal. Abby Dalton as Calamity Jane, Don Murray as Wild Bill Hickok, Guy Stockwell as Buffalo Bill Cody.

The remake thirty years later of the DeMille classic *The Plainsman*, which starred Jean Arthur and Gary Cooper, contains elements of the original. Wild Bill and Buffalo Bill are trying to keep Indians from overrunning pioneers and chasing them out of a newly settled area. Calamity is their sidekick in the attempt to hold off the Cheyenne. As in the original, Calamity is much in love with the reluctant Hickok. Cody and his new wife, Louisa, model the love and marriage Calamity longs for with Hickok.

The 1936 *Plainsman* had director DeMille's flair and big budget, as well as the cinematic strengths of Arthur and Cooper. The remake had none of these, with director David Lowell Rich forced to use actors under contract to Universal. Abby Dalton as Calamity, with a phony southern accent, seems hopelessly secondhand next to the Hickok and Cody characters. As usual, history and biography are pushed aside for Hollywood entertainment, with the now-familiar Calamity–Wild Bill romance story taking center stage. The acting and plot of the film are so limited that the remake deserves to remain in the shadow of the original *Plainsman.*

495. *The Raiders.* 1963. Universal. Judi Meredith as Calamity Jane, Robert Culp as Wild Bill Hickok, Jim McMullan as Buffalo Bill Cody, and Brian Keith as John G. McElroy.

Calamity joins Wild Bill and Buffalo Bill, hoping to help pacify warring elements in the post–Civil War plains and Texas. A Texas cattleman and former Confederate military leader, John G. McElroy, tries to shove aside one railroad in order to build another spur line that would facilitate shipping his beeves to market from Texas to Kansas. The railroad refuses. When emotions got out of hand and a fight seems eminent, Hickok, Cody, and Calamity show up.

The petite Meredith seems an unusual choice to play Calamity, but the five-foot, two-inch heroine, a former figure skater, is up to the task physically. She had appeared previously on the *George Burns and Gracie Allen Show* and as a guest star in several Hollywood Westerns. In trying to play a calloused freighter for the railroad, however, Meredith seems out of her element. Perhaps the incredible plotline—bringing the three western demigods on scene in a place and time where and when they had not met—doomed the film from the start. At any rate, viewers understandably forgot the movie and Meredith as Calamity.

496. *The Texan Meets Calamity Jane.* 1950. Columbia Pictures. Evelyn Ankers as Calamity Jane, Lee "Lasses" White as Colorado Charley, and James Ellison as Gordon Hastings.

The plot of this mediocre Western opens with Deadwood hosting its annual celebration in honor of the late Wild Bill Hickok. Calamity Jane sponsors the gathering because Wild Bill was the only man she ever loved.

In Deadwood, Calamity owns a saloon, which Frank Mullen gave her for saving his life. But Mullen's niece Cecelia is now contesting Calamity's ownership, arguing that her Uncle Frank had bequeathed the saloon to her. The plot includes several conflicts among Calamity and those supporting and opposing her.

Although Ankers's Calamity is a strong woman, she does not jump out from the screen. An English beauty who had played in several horror films in the 1940s, Ankers seemed unable to capture the rougher, less feminine appearance and actions of Calamity Jane. Her attachment to the memory of Wild Bill is clear, as well as the tenacity of her convictions, but not much beyond that. A possible romance with "The Texan" (Ellison), a lawyer who aids Calamity in keeping her saloon, never sizzles and eventually fizzles. Perhaps the attractive, curvaceous Ankers was miscast for this role. In the next decade, she chose marriage and motherhood over movies.

497. *This Is the West That Was.* 1974. NBC-TV. Kim Darby as Calamity Jane, Ben Murphy as Wild Bill Hickok, Jane Alexander as Sarah Shaw, Matt Clark as Buffalo Bill Cody.

This made-for-TV Western featured the Old West heroes and heroine Buffalo Bill, Wild Bill, and Calamity Jane, first in the famed McCanles shootout with Wild Bill and later in Deadwood. It is primarily a movie of satire and parody. The Old West giants are depicted as ordinary, flawed humans rather than towering heroes and heroines. Simultaneously, the film asks viewers to think about the ordinary origins of extraordinary names and reputations.

Kim Darby has trouble carrying the load expected of the complex Calamity she portrays. For one, she is too small and girlish to project the buxom, masculine qualities expected of her. Still, she at least voices the ambiguity she is supposed to represent. In one telling scene, Cody asks Calamity about "couth," a concept foreign to her. Rather than defining the idea, Calamity tells Cody that there are three things she can do: she can (1) be a barmaid (and maybe a prostitute) like other girls in Blind Pete's saloon; (2) marry, but she hasn't found the man she wants; or (3) labor like a hardworking man. When Cody tells her he's speaking about her dress, actions, and failure to take baths, she retorts that she does take baths and asks Cody if "couth" will cause Wild Bill to take a second look at her.

The film portrays Calamity as naming both "Wild Bill" and "Buffalo Bill," implying how important she is in "this West that was." She is also shown nursing Wild Bill back to health. More intriguing, she is depicted as being brighter than either Hickok or Cody. As she says, "I always could figure out things." Most of all, Calamity is presented as something of an innocent urchin. She is neither a brawling broad nor the more romantic Jean Arthur of *The Plainsman* (493), and certainly not the Doris Day of *Calamity Jane* (485). A genial satire with probing questions about Calamity and the Old West.

498. *Wild Bill*. 1995. United Artists. Ellen Barkin as Calamity Jane, Jeff Bridges as Wild Bill Hickok, Diane Lane as Susannah Moore, Keith Carradine as Buffalo Bill Cody.

Continuing the transition away from the romantic Doris Day image of Calamity Jane, this film and HBO's *Deadwood* (489) in 2004–2006 represent the extreme to date in pushing toward a gray, gritty, and realistic interpretation of Calamity. Even though the movie perpetuates the off-base Jean Hickok McCormick story (246) and is wrong in nearly all its specifics about the Calamity–Wild Bill relationship, it nonetheless provides numerous suggestive comments about gender roles, femininity, and sexuality for late-twentieth-century audiences.

The film opens with Wild Bill's casket headed for the grave. That emotion-saturated event drives Calamity to review and rethink her relationship with Hickok. Then we get dozens of scenes with the two, from Kansas to Deadwood, almost none of which is historical. The important parts of the movie for Calamity hunters are her thoughts about her undying love for the great pistoleer. She never ceased to lust for him, but often had to push herself on the reluctant gunman. She wonders if he loved her, but she satisfied herself with the one-night stands she enjoyed. Most often she had to start the encounters because he would not. On one of the several intimate occasions, they made love on the pool table in a tavern, only to have their intense lovemaking interrupted by swinish intruders.

Dressed in buckskins, wearing a mannish hat and her hair in a braid, Barkin tries to engage Hickok in conversations about love, sex, and relationships. When he remains silent on these, to him, sticky topics, she sounds out the Kid about them. When Hickok hears her speaking about men taking advantage of women, he explodes in anger. She accepts her outsider female role (there are no typical wives here), but she wants others to treat her like a woman and is upset when she thinks they do not. She is something of a sociocultural housekeeper, cleaning up the saloon, looking after Bill and other men and women, and preparing food. In short, this is the Old West seen through the eyes of a woman who sometimes has male tendencies but wants to be loved—even cherished—as a woman. The film clearly reflects cultural-intellectual currents swirling around just before and well into the twenty-first century.

499. *Wild Bill Hickok*. 1923. Paramount Pictures. Ethel Grey Terry as Calamity Jane, William S. Hart as Wild Bill Hickok, Kathleen O'Connor as Elaine Hamilton.

No copy of this film is known to exist, but its content can be discerned from the script on file in the William S. Hart Papers in the Natural History Museum of Los Angeles. Hart, a leading Western actor and a stone-faced man with mountains of self-appreciation, would not have allowed a female lead to steal the limelight from him, even though he might fall in love with her. The famed actor claimed the film was historically accurate, based on a story he had written. It was not, even though such historical figures as Abraham Lincoln, General George Custer, Bat Masterson, and Calamity appeared on stage.

Calamity (Ethel Grey Terry) is in love with Wild Bill (Hart), but his eyes are on another woman in Kansas, until he learns she is already married. Realizing that, he leaves Dodge City and travels to Deadwood. With her heartthrob gone, Calamity turns to smoking, drinking, and mannish buckskins. Later, the two are together again in the Black Hills—up to the killing of Wild Bill. Jack McCall, having earlier unsuccessfully wooed Calamity, gnashes his teeth at her just before he is hanged. Hart claimed to know a good deal about Hickok and Calamity, but his film owed more to his point of view than to facts.

This film of 1923, along with *In the Days of '75 and '76* (490), revealed much of the pattern for the earliest movies about Calamity Jane. Perhaps because Hickok and Calamity were buried next to one another in Deadwood, or perhaps because bringing together two western demigods on screen would guarantee large audiences, moviemakers in the first half of the twentieth century could not let go of the Calamity–Wild Bill story. Usually it led to romance, and most often Hickok was the more prominent figure in these movies. Another decade or two would pass before a Calamity figure could be *the* central one in a movie.

500. *Young Bill Hickok.* 1940. Republic. Sally Payne as Calamity Jane, Roy Rogers as Wild Bill Hickok, George Hayes as Gabby Hayes.

This film contains most of the familiar ingredients of traditional Westerns released in the 1930s and 1940s: black and white hats (villains and heroes), romance, chase and pursuit (several), and a happy ending. And with Gabby Hayes as a major character, humor.

Set in the closing months of the Civil War, the movie takes place in Hayes City, which is trying to ship California gold east to help the North win the war. Confederate sympathizers attempt to steal the gold, leading to shootouts and dramatic rides. Bill Hickok (Roy Rogers) is a stage station operator who through his heroic actions makes a name for himself as Wild Bill Hickok. (Calamity Jane first uses "Wild Bill" as his nickname.)

Payne's Calamity is in the Doris Day mold, a role still a dozen years in the future in *Calamity Jane* (1953 [485]). Perky, pretty, girlish, and dressed in formfitting buckskins, Calamity is interested in Wild Bill, but he has his eyes on another. Calamity and Gabby instill bits of humor in an otherwise traditional, sometimes cliché-ridden plot. Nothing about Calamity here suggests promiscuity, alcohol, or motherhood. Two or three times Calamity asserts she "is not a lady." Polite society, "I never get in it," Calamity states. Romance and adventure sideline, then obliterate, authentic biography in this treatment of Calamity.

501. Film Criticism

502. Beck, Henry Cabot. "'The Devil Always Gets the Best Lines': And He Does in *Deadwood*'s Second Season." *True West* 52 (March 2005): 22–28.

Writer Beck stresses how much the controversial HBO series *Deadwood* breaks from the John Wayne, *Gunsmoke*, and Lone Ranger Western film traditions. This essay opens with a description of the *Deadwood* Hollywood setting, followed by discussions of the major characters in the series, the costuming, and the moral or amoral tone of the episodes. The author does not critique producer David Milch's questionable treatment of Deadwood's history. (Milch claimed to be following known historical fact; most of the time he was not.) Robin Weigert, who played a complex, dark-hued Calamity, is quoted revealingly about her role: "The funny thing about playing Jane is, I found myself feeling very protective toward her. She seems very vulnerable to me" (p. 24). Useful descriptive but nonanalytical comments on the TV series.

503. "Boom or Bust." *Hollywood Reporter*, 8 May 1997, S-7–S-8.

This section on animation includes a brief reference to the new show *The Legend of Calamity Jane* (491). The writer suggests that the show, imported from France and the United Kingdom, may appeal to youthful audiences, especially because it revolves "not just around a girl but around a girl with a whip!" "Calamity Jane," the writer adds, "might be just the wake-up call sassy youngsters are looking for" (p. S-8). In hindsight, the show did not make much of a splash.

504. Eisloeffel, Paul J., and Andrea I. Paul. "Hollywood on the Plains." *NEBRASKAland* 68 (May 1990): 42–47. Reprint, *Journal of the West* 33 (April 1994): 13–19.

This brief piece provides much useful background information on *In the Days of '75 and '76* (1915 [490]), a silent film featuring Wild Bill Hickok and Calamity Jane. Interestingly, the film was shot by a Chadron, Nebraska, company well away from Hollywood in Nebraska and the Black Hills of South Dakota. Most of the essay deals with the Nebraska film company and its challenges in shooting schedules and locating local talent for the movie. The authors understand the errors in the film's plot. They note the excessively romantic treatment of the two leading protagonists in a relationship they correctly assert never occurred. Plus, the salty characteristics of Calamity are omitted, and none of Wild Bill's vices admitted. Eisloeffel and Paul are on target in concluding "this film portrays the pair in a fictitiously wholesome light, contrary to historical evidence" (p. 45). The same could be said for most films about Calamity up to the 1960s.

505. Graulich, Melody, and Nicolas W. Witschi, eds. *Dirty Words in Deadwood: Literature and the Postwestern.* Lincoln: University of Nebraska Press, 2013. See, esp., "Calamity Jane and Female Masculinity in *Deadwood,*" by Linda Mizejewski , pp. 184–207.

For the past generation or so, several leading specialists in western American literature have been debating the "authenticity" of writing about the West. These scholars often criticize historians for being much too tied to the facts of western experiences and too little open to creative "stories" about the past and present West. Perhaps. Most historians do want their histories, novels, and movies faithful to history, if it is known.

The eleven essays in this provocative anthology subscribe to an "authenticity" more like the "romances" of Nathaniel Hawthorne than the more realistic, fact-filled "novels" of William Dean Howells. Melody Graulich, longtime editor of *Western American Literature* and one of the leaders of the new "authenticity" movement, wants HBO's *Deadwood* to be "read intertextually." She urges commentators to understand how much the HBO series references works of American literature. Graulich's long introduction and most of the other essays, primarily by literary and film critics, praise the artistic, storytelling qualities of director David Milch. Indeed, this anthology is a paean of praise for Milch, with the essay writers finding nothing for which he should be questioned.

The one essay that deals extensively with Calamity Jane—the others do so only glancingly—is by Linda Mizejewski. This piece follows Graulich in its discussions of gender, sexuality, and lesbian topics. Even though the author cites James McLaird's definitive biography (290), she does not reference Calamity's stated desire for a husband and motherhood, or her negative responses to several women. Rather this author salutes *Deadwood* for being willing to treat a "butch, cross-dressing figure [who] may have been attracted to women" (p. 186). The author seems unwilling to point out that the photographs in McLaird show Calamity dressed much more often as a pioneer woman than as a buckskin-clad figure (of about twenty-five extant photographs she is dressed in buckskins in only six or seven). Nor does Mizejewski reference the works making a case for Calamity's femininity. In the end, she does not admit to readers that the hinted-at lesbian relationship between Joanie and Calamity (whom the author wrongly refers to as Jane rather than Martha Canary) owes more to the fertile imagination of David Milch than to the historical accuracy he wrongly claimed.

In the end, historians should continue to ask several large questions of *Deadwood* and other movies and novels. Is this what happened in Deadwood or elsewhere? Is this an accurate picture of Calamity Jane? Is this film or novel a slanted creation owing more to a moviemaker or novelist than to history? Historians, especially those with a literary-cultural bent, can point out the historical shortcomings of *Deadwood* and other similar creative efforts even as they praise the important sociocultural questions director David Milch raised in his popular series.

506. Special issue on the HBO series *Deadwood. Great Plains Quarterly* 27 (Fall 2007): 235–95.

This special issue of four essays includes few comments on Calamity Jane. The authors, all specialists in literary or film criticism and early in their careers in 2007, are much more interested in theoretical than historical-cultural commentaries. Historians, historical approaches to the film series, and Calamity Jane do not fare well here. None of the writers is much interested in the contextual backgrounds of the historical Deadwood or Calamity Jane.

In the third essay, "'Whores and Other Feminists': Recovering *Deadwood*'s Unlikely Feminisms" (pp. 267–82), Anne Helen Petersen deals with several women in the series but, inexplicably, for the most part excludes Calamity. Petersen knows films and feminism, but is short on western history and historiography, overlooking the best studies in western women's history, for example. She provides a narrowly focused plot summary of feminism in *Deadwood* while missing some of the subject's complexity (e.g., Calamity Jane and the sexuality of Alma), both of which diverge from director David Milch's and the author's comments and conclusions.

In the first essay, "*Deadwood* and the English Language" (pp. 239–51) Brad Benz runs aground in following Milch's assertion that he knows the speech of the Old West and has used it in his series. The author references other Westerns to generalize about western language but then, wrongly, argues that Milch's script is the way Westerners spoke. He is off track when he tries to show that swearing in HBO's *Deadwood* reflects the actual swearing in historical Deadwood. We do not know how residents of Deadwood spoke in the 1870s—even after more than a century of steady research.

In "No Law: *Deadwood* and the State" (pp. 253–65), Mark L. Berre-
tini deals revealingly and helpfully with David Milch's contention that the
TV series would portray a place (Deadwood in the 1870s) without law and
hoping to find order. The author suggests, convincingly, that individualists
like saloon keeper Al Swearengen (the spelling used in the series) and Seth
Bullock attempted to fight off the incorporating, homogenizing tendencies
of mining magnate George Hearst.

Following some of the same ideas, the final essay by Kyle Wiggins and
David Holmberg, "'Gold Is Every Man's Opportunity': Castration Anxiety
and the Economic Venture in *Deadwood*" (pp. 283–95), argues that two
conflicting themes about autonomy dominate *Deadwood*. Swearengen and
most inhabitants of the frontier boomtown favor an individualistic, isola-
tionist, and freedom-desiring autonomy; they compete with George Hearst's
"economic self-determination," an organizational, structured, and coher-
ing autonomy. Unfortunately, the authors' discussion, too often laden with
theoretical jargon and opaque syntax, is often difficult to follow, especially
when they descend into discussions of "castration and phallic violence" in
the series.

One wishes these authors and other commentators on HBO's *Deadwood* were more willing to evaluate carefully the comments of director
Milch; that is, praise his attempts at depicting a place without law trying to
find order, but dismiss his comments about the historical accuracy of the
series. Milch reveals that he knew very little about the history of this place
and the leaders of the area, and he was too willing to distort history and
personal life stories to fit his dogmatic, and sometimes arrogant, assertions
about truth, humanity, and society.

507. Hitt, Jim. "Belle and Calamity: Real to Reel." *True West* 33 (October 1986):
28–33.

Hitt rightly contends that Hollywood reshaped the real Belle Starr and
Calamity in most early movies about the two women. The author provides
capsule biographies of the two gritty females, then demonstrates how movies
distorted their lives by turning them into attractive, romantic heroines.

The biographical section on Calamity is very brief, but it features the
writer's opinions about Calamity's lack of femininity and her fascination with
masculine clothes and actions. *The Plainsman* (1936 [493]), *Calamity Jane
and Sam Bass* (1949 [488]), and *Calamity Jane* (1953 [485]) are exemplars of
the inaccuracies and excessive romanticism that early movies peddled. As

the author puts it, in these films Hollywood portrayed Calamity and Belle individually as "a warm, sensitive woman who only needs the love of a good man to set her free" (p. 33). The author might have come to different conclusions had he viewed the movies made about Calamity since the 1990s (after he wrote his piece), in which Calamity is often portrayed with grittiness, little romance, and considerable aberrant behavior.

508. Hutton, Paul A. "Westerns: Deadwood Redux." *True West* 52 (March 2005): 59–63.

This brief, photo-enriched essay by Paul Hutton provides an abbreviated overview of the treatment of Deadwood in cinematic and TV Westerns. Not surprisingly, the author uses text references and photos to spotlight several Calamity films. They include *Wild Bill Hickok* (1923 [499]), *The Plainsman* (1936 [493]), *Badlands of Dakota* (1941 [483]), *The Paleface* (1948 [492]), *Calamity Jane* (1953 [485]), *Wild Bill* (1995 [498]), HBO's *Deadwood* (2004 [489]), and a few others. Hutton also deals briefly with the importance of dime novels and other fiction in treating and shaping images of Deadwood, Wild Bill, and Calamity.

509. Key, M. David, and Angela Thomas, comps. *Hollywood and the American West: A Selective Bibliography.* Occasional Papers 22. Albuquerque: Center for the American West, University of New Mexico, 2001.

This handy bibliographical guide lists the important books and essays on Hollywood, the Western genre, actors and actresses, and individual films. The compilers have included numerous entries about audiences as well as about moviemakers. More than eight hundred unannotated items are listed.

510. Lackman, Ron. *Women of the Western Frontier in Fact, Fiction, and Film.* Jefferson, N.C.: McFarland, 1997.

This reference volume, covering new subjects, gathers useful information on the treatment of frontier women in "fact, fiction and film." The book is part narrative, part reference guide. Separate chapters deal with the lives of (1) gunfighters' wives and lovers and women outlaws; (2) female entertainers; (3) prostitutes, madams, and gambling ladies; and (4) "remarkable respectable women." Appendixes list and annotate silent and sound films and TV Westerns. A closing chapter treats a dozen well-known western frontier sites.

The opening chapter deals with Belle Starr and Calamity Jane, calling them "The West's Two Most Famous Women." The section on Calamity (pp. 21–36) includes biographical and cinematic discussions, as well as several photographs. The part on Calamity movies and TV appearances is brief but useful.

Regrettably, the biographical section on Calamity (pp. 21–32) is so rife with errors as to be nearly unusable. On the first page alone (p. 21), there are more than a dozen factual errors. The author gets the Canary family history wrong and has the story of Calamity's penultimate "husband" Clinton Burke in disarray. Burke was a minister's son from Missouri, not the scion of a "socially prominent San Francisco family" (p. 30). When the author insists that Duncan Aikman's (misspelled here as Aiken and Ailen) *Calamity Jane and the Lady Wildcats* (1927 [230]) is "one of the best of the Calamity Jane biographies" (p. 31), we know we are headed for trouble. Unfortunately, these kinds of careless and off-track errors mar every paragraph of the biographical discussion of Calamity.

511. Lavery, David, ed. *Reading Deadwood: A Western to Swear By*. London and New York: I. B. Taurus and Palgrave Macmillan, 2006. See, esp., "Myth Maketh the Woman: Calamity Jane, Frontier Mythology, and Creating American (Media) Historical Imaginings," by Janet McCabe, pp. 59–77; and "Whores, Ladies, and Calamity Jane: Gender Roles and the Women of HBO's *Deadwood*," by Kathleen E. R. Smith, pp. 79–90.

This collection of fourteen essays treating the major characters and themes of HBO's *Deadwood* series includes two essays on Calamity Jane and other women in the series. The first essay, by Janet McCabe, is a close reading of the "meanings" of Calamity in *Deadwood*. Although overflowing with esoteric and academic language and inadequate in its handling of the historical Calamity, the essay presents a provocative thesis: in the HBO series Calamity serves as a storytelling agent or device "to mediate on the uneasy relation between historical events, myth, and cultural fantasy, and screen memories and media re-presentation" (p. 77).

The second essay, by Kathleen E. R. Smith, is much more accessible. Utilizing the concept of the Cult of True Womanhood, Smith shows how the women in the HBO series do or do not fit in the categories of refined ladies, helpmates, and bad women. The author's discussions, including a brief one on Calamity, are illuminating and convincing. Smith shows, however, surprisingly little acquaintance with the best historical writing about women of the West published from the 1980s forward.

512. Lynch, Jacqueline T. *Classic Films and the American Conscience: Essays from "Another Old Movie Blog."* Kindle edition, 2012.

This compendium of dozens of the author's blogs includes a blog series on Calamity Jane movies. Lynch's discussions include commentary on *The Plainsman* (1936 [493]), *The Paleface* (1948 [492]), *Calamity Jane and Sam Bass* (1949 [488]), *The Texan Meets Calamity Jane* (1950 [496]), and *Calamity Jane* (1953 [485]), as well as several other Calamity movies. The author has made good use of McLaird's definitive biography of Calamity (290), sticking to verifiable facts and casting out misinformation, including the false Calamity–Wild Bill romance and the fraudulent Jean Hickok McCormick story. Lynch's readings include a good deal of plot summary and sound commentary. Useful movie readings.

513. Whiteside, William R. "Calamity Jane in Film and TV." 4 July 1999, 16 August 2000. In Etulain's collection.

This unpublished compilation lists twenty-eight movies and TV programs containing Calamity Jane characters. The entries include dates, actresses portraying Calamity Jane, studios, sources of information, and a few scattered comments.

Photographs

Following one photographic essay, photographs of Martha Canary are listed in as close to chronological order as can be determined.

514. McLaird, James D. "Calamity Jane Exposed." *True West* 52 (September 2005): 33–38.

This valuable photographic essay with minimal text and useful captions contains a dozen Calamity Jane photos and two others not of Calamity. Author McLaird provides strong photographic evidence here to counter the stereotypical pictorial portraits of Calamity as solely a cross-dressing woman in buckskins. Instead, McLaird shows that most of the time she was attired in long dresses typical of late-nineteenth-century pioneer women. These photos, among others, also appeared in McLaird's first-rate biography of Calamity (290).

515. **Photographs of Calamity Jane**

516. This is the earliest extant photograph of Martha Canary, then just becoming known as Calamity Jane in the summer of 1875, probably in July. She was traveling to the Black Hills with the Newton-Jenney Expedition. The photographer was A. Guerin, and the shot was taken at French Creek. Calamity would have been about nineteen years old. Courtesy J. Leonard Jennewein Collection, McGovern Library, Dakota Wesleyan University.

517. Said to have been taken in 1876–77, this photograph came from an unknown photographer. Sometimes it was printed with a caption identifying Calamity as General George Crook's scout. Some sources state the photograph was discovered under an old building in Deadwood. A second version of the photo has Calamity seated, with the same Stevens Buggy gun near her side. Courtesy J. Leonard Jennewein Collection, McGovern Library, Dakota Wesleyan University.

518. This illustration of Calamity appeared in Thomas Newson's Drama of Life
in the Black Hills (1878). It was probably based on a photograph now lost.
Etulain collection.

519. The noted photographer L. A. Huffman took this often-reprinted photograph, probably in 1882 rather than the 1880 date frequently given it. Calamity did not arrive in Miles City, Montana, where Huffman was located, until about 1882. It is the first extant picture of Calamity dressed as a woman rather than in buckskins. She appears a bit disconcerted at posing but certainly projects a much more feminine appearance than the earlier shots of her in male dress. Courtesy L. A. Huffman Collection, Montana Historical Society (MHS 981-573).

520. This infrequently printed photograph of a "plain Jane" Calamity was probably taken in the early 1880s. Photographer and site are unknown. Courtesy Robert G. McCubbin photo collection.

521. An attractive shot of Calamity, one of several where she dressed as a pioneer woman, this photograph may have been taken in Wyoming, perhaps in Rawlins. It is dated in the 1880s, probably in the middle of the decade. Courtesy Denver Public Library (F-38793).

522. Historians suggest that this photograph of Calamity was probably taken in Wyoming, perhaps Evanston, in the late 1880s. The outfit is the fanciest of her buckskins, which may have been a regalia she used for special occasions, parades, or western fairs. The photographer is unknown. Courtesy J. Leonard Jennewein Collection, McGovern Library, Dakota Wesleyan University.

523. Calamity, in a long black dress and hat, stands among soldiers guarding a train in Billings, Montana, in 1894. She is the fifth person from the right. Why she joined the gathering is unknown. Courtesy Montana Historical Society, MHS NRR box (strike image).

524. In 1895, before Calamity went on her trip with the Kohl and Middleton
tour group, she had photographer H. R. Locke take several shots of her in
various poses. Besides this seated one, others had her standing, and still
others had her looking in different directions. Calamity sold this photograph
and copies of her autobiography on her trip to the East and in the West after
she returned. Courtesy Montana Historical Society (MHS 941-417).

525. Not satisfied with her previous photographs, Calamity had photographer
C. E. Flinn of Livingston, Montana, shoot a new series sometime between
1896 and 1898. Flinn took photos of her facing front (this one) as well as facing right and left. Calamity sold these photos throughout the northern West
but especially to tourists in the Yellowstone Park area. Calamity's clothing
is essentially the same as in the previous picture. Artist Frederic Remington
obtained Calamity's suit of clothes, which the Buffalo Bill Center of the West
later purchased and now has in its holdings. Courtesy Montana Historical
Society (MHS 941-418).

526. In the late 1890s Calamity was in and out of central Montana. This photograph was likely taken in Utica, near Lewistown, in 1897 or 1898. There are one or two other photographs of this scene, in slightly different positions. Courtesy J. Leonard Jennewein Collection, McGovern Library, Dakota Wesleyan University.

527. Teddy Blue, famed trail-drive cowboy, claimed he first met Calamity in the Black Hills in the late 1870s. They met later, in 1897–98, in Utica or Gilt Edge, Montana, switched hats, and had drinks together. This is the first of two Blue-Calamity photographs. Courtesy Montana Historical Society (MHS 941-409).

528. The second of the Blue-Calamity photographs. Courtesy J. Leonard Jennewein Collection, McGovern Library, Dakota Wesleyan University.

"CALAMITY-JANE"

529. In the late 1890s, Calamity obtained a permit to sell her autobiography and photographs in the Yellowstone Park region. Here she is seen offering items to tourists who are part of one of the Burton Holmes travel tours. Burton Holmes, Travelogues. Vol. 12. New York: McClure, 1918, p. 38. Courtesy James D. McLaird Collection.

530. Mrs. E. G. Worden is credited for this on-the-street photograph, probably taken in Lewistown, Montana, about 1899. The long, dark dress and a hat were often Calamity's everyday public attire. Courtesy J. Leonard Jennewein Collection, McGovern Library, Dakota Wesleyan University.

531. This photograph, probably taken in Montana in the late 1890s, provides
another strong bit of evidence that more often than not Calamity dressed
like other frontier women. Buckskin attire was an anomaly, except for public
presentations. The photograph appeared for the first time in W. G. Patterson,
"Calamity Jane," Wide World Magazine (August 1903). Etulain collection.

532. This photograph and the next appeared in the writings of Lewis Freeman, a journalist who met Calamity in Livingston, Montana, in the spring of 1901. The first depicts Calamity smoking a cigar while preparing breakfast. From Lewis Freeman, Down the Yellowstone, 1922. Courtesy J. Leonard Jennewein Collection, McGovern Library, Dakota Wesleyan University.

533. The second photograph, also from Lewis Freeman, pictures Calamity seated among the beer barrels where the author found her in the back of a hotel in Livingston, Montana. From Lewis Freeman, "Calamity Jane and Yankee Jim" Sunset Magazine, July 1922. Courtesy James D. McLaird Collection.

534. When things did not work out for Calamity on her 1901 trip with writer
     Josephine Brake to Buffalo, New York, and the Pan-American Exposition,
     she bolted and joined Frederic Cummins's Indian Congress. Here she is
     among the tents of the Indian Congress. Courtesy Library of Congress (LC
     USZ 62-473390).

535. Calamity appears well dressed in this photograph taken in Pierre, South
Dakota, after her return from the trip to the Pan-American Exposition in
1901. She is dressed in becoming clothes likely given to her when she was
in Buffalo, New York. R. L. Kelley is the credited photographer. Courtesy
Montana Historical Society, Jack Ellis Haynes Collection, Box 14.

536. Photographer John B. Mayo talked Calamity into posing in front of Wild Bill's grave in the Mount Moriah Cemetery in Deadwood. But she impugned him into standing with her for one shot by his assistant before she stood alone in a second pose. The photos were taken in early to midsummer 1903, about one month before her death in early August. Courtesy South Dakota State Historical Society.

537. Once the previous photograph was taken by John Mayo's assistant, she agreed to pose by herself in front of Wild Bill's grave. Her fragile health is much in evidence. Courtesy Montana Historical Society (MHS 941-415).

Calamity Jane

538. Photographer Charles Haas took this picture of Calamity on the street of
Whitewood, a small town near Deadwood, in the summer of 1903. Taken
just a few weeks before her death, the photograph clearly revealed Calamity's
disintegrating health. Courtesy J. Leonard Jennewein Collection, McGovern
Library, Dakota Wesleyan University.

539. On 4 August 1903, just three days after Calamity's death, she was photographed in a mortuary in Deadwood. Standing beside the casket are Henry
and Charles Robinson. Earlier, Calamity had helped other members of the
Robinson family through illness. Courtesy Western History Collection,
Denver Public Library (F-23387).

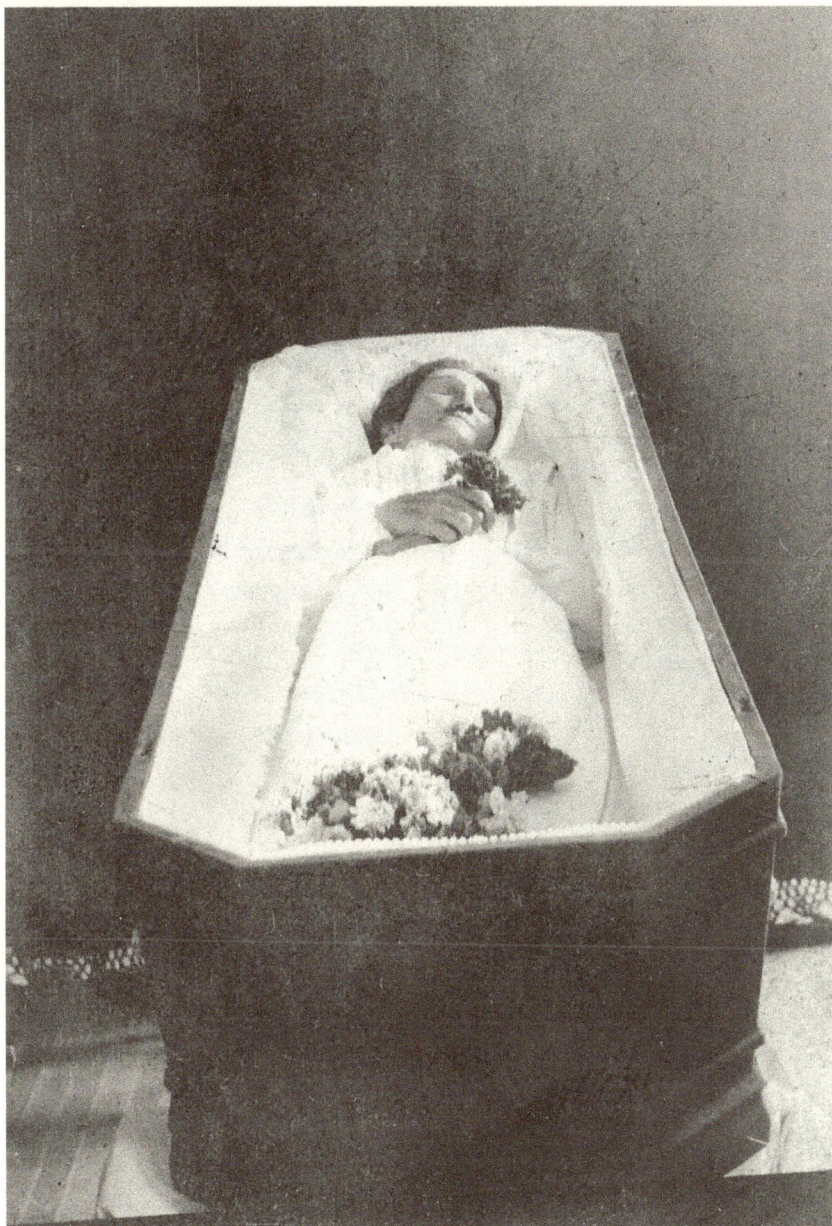

540. While Calamity lay in her casket, tourists and curiosity seekers began to clip bits of her hair. The funeral directors were forced to place a guard next to her casket and a wire screen over her head to protect her hair. Courtesy Montana Historical Society (MHS 941-420).

541. After funeral services in Deadwood's Methodist church, a graveyard service
in Mount Moriah Cemetery drew a huge crowd. Some sources say it was the
largest funeral in Deadwood's history to that date. Courtesy Western History
Collection, Denver Public Library (F-12210).

CALAMITY JANE
Unfinished Business

ALTHOUGH CALAMITY JANE may be the most written-about woman of the Old West, several unanswered questions remain about her life and the legends that coalesced around her. Missing documents, blank periods of her life, and shadowy information on legend-making remain challenges for biographers and historians wishing to write about Calamity Jane.

Several types of documents concerning Martha/Calamity's Canary family need to be uncovered. We know little, for example, about Grandfather James and Grandmother Sarah Canary and their large family in Virginia, Ohio, and Iowa before they scattered across the eastern and western sections of the United States. True, the U.S. censuses of Ohio in 1820, 1830, 1840, and 1850 provide bare-bones information about the Canarys in terms of name, age, occupation, literacy, wealth, and other categories; but information on their schooling, religious faith or lack thereof, changing residences, and other family details are for the most part missing.

Similar lacunae face researchers trying to tease out information about others close to Calamity. A limited number of verifiable facts have turned up about her sister Lena Pauline Canary Borner and her brother Elijah (Lige). Brief essays based on newspaper reports and a few legal documents are the only publications we have on Calamity's siblings. Calamity's half dozen or so "husbands" remain equally unresearched. Information on George Cosgrove, Frank[?] King, William Steers, Clinton Burke, and Robert Dorsett is, by and large, limited to journalists' or observers' comments on the men while they lived with Calamity. Almost nothing on Cosgrove, King, and Steers, and only scattered facts about Burke and Dorsett, have been located.

On Martha/Calamity herself we have less than a dozen or so strong documents about her life before 1876. More diligent research may turn up additional information about the Canary family in Princeton, Missouri, and Montana, the Mormon families that may have adopted Martha and her siblings in Utah, and Martha's connection to places and people in Wyoming before she traveled to Deadwood in the mid-1870s. The U.S. census of 1860 and the preterritorial Wyoming census of 1869 add valuable facts, but we need to place Martha more specifically in the years after her parents' deaths in 1866 and 1867. Where she was, and when, in the years from 1867 to 1875 still needs to be clarified.

Calamity's life from 1876 to 1890 is depicted in numerous newspaper stories of varied value. We learn a great deal about her unorthodox behavior, and charges that she was a drunk and a possible prostitute, but too little about her perambulations and actions. More energetic digging in newspapers; censuses of 1870, 1880, and 1890; and birth, death, and marriage records could turn up new facts.

The final years of Calamity's hectic life, from 1890 to 1903, display similar ups and downs of information. Calamity's dime museum tour with Kohl and Middleton in 1896 still lacks thorough documentation, and the details of her trip to Buffalo, New York, to participate in the Pan-American Exposition in 1901 remain shadowy. During these travels, Calamity often landed in jail for her drinking or bad behavior, but most of those jail records, if extant, have not yet been uncovered. Scattered journalistic accounts trace her ramblings in Montana, Wyoming, and South Dakota, but these stories are at best diffuse and undocumented, with no verification outside of newspaper articles. The recent discovery of Calamity in the U.S. census of 1900, living with "husband" Dorsett, suggests that other valuable documents may still be located with arduous research. In addition, Calamity's death certificate in Deadwood, extant in the 1950s, has been missing for many years; it needs to be relocated.

Documents concerning the lives of Calamity's family and acquaintances after her death also remain very elusive. We know of Elijah's imprisonments before and following her death and information on his death, but little besides. Probably all of Calamity's "husbands" outlived her, but where are their comments and reminiscences about her? We have Social Security and death records for several of these men but little else. Regrettably, we know almost nothing of daughter Jessie Elizabeth's life following her birth in 1887. Journalists glancingly mention her before 1903, and we have recently discovered her marriages in Montana in 1904 and 1908. But of her later life we know only the strange letters she wrote in the 1920s through 1950s to libraries and archives, searching for information about her grandmother or aunt, as she called Calamity, even though in 1908 she had acknowledged that Martha Canary was her mother.

The legend-making processes so important for understanding how Martha Canary became and remained Calamity Jane from the 1870s to the present day remain a fertile area for researchers. The unpublished papers of Deadwood authors Horatio N. Maguire and Thomas M. Newson, dime novelist Edward L. Wheeler, and novelist (Mrs.) William Loring Spencer may yet tell us more about how their pioneering works helped launch the legendary Calamity. No one has thoroughly examined the papers of biographers Duncan Aikman and movie-emakers William S. Hart and Cecil DeMille to study their characterizations of Calamity. The unpublished manuscripts of historians-biographers Nolie Mumey, J. Leonard Jennewein, Roberta Beed Sollid, and Glenn Clairmonte have yet to be thoroughly exploited; they may turn up other information about the Calamity legend-making evolution.

Over the years, prospective biographers who did not complete life stories of Calamity have left rich research deposits of archival gatherings about her. The papers of Clarence Paine at Augustana College in Sioux Falls, South Dakota, and Lloyd McFarling in the South Dakota State Historical Society in Pierre, are prime examples of these invaluable collections. In addition, the materials of J. Leonard Jennewein at Dakota Wesleyan University in Mitchell, South Dakota; those at the American Heritage Center in Laramie, Wyoming; and those of biographers Stella Foote, James McLaird, and Richard Etulain, when they become available, will be fruitful sources of information. The same is true for the papers of novelist Ethel Hueston, English writer J. T. Edson, and, perhaps, well-known author Larry McMurtry.

Truth to tell, many research projects, large and small, beckon writers interested in the life and legends of Calamity Jane. Some authors may be content to fill in gaps still apparent in her biography. Others may want to produce more expansive studies of Calamity's images in biographies, novels, still illustrations, and movies. Still others may wish to furnish feminist readings of Calamity, showing how she tried to navigate the constricted roles available to women in her time or what shifting gender roles she has occupied in interpretations of her. Whatever route one wishes to travel, the life and legends of Calamity Jane remain rich, redolent subjects for further investigation.

Index

Bold type indicates page numbers in the two opening essays and final essay; regular, nonbold type indicates item numbers in the remainder of the text.

RICHARD W. ETULAIN grew up on a sheep ranch in eastern Washington and graduated with high honors in 1960 from Northwest Nazarene College (now University) in Nampa, Idaho. He earned a master's in American literature (1962) and a Ph.D. in American history and literature (1966) at the University of Oregon. He taught at NNC (1966–68), Idaho State University (1970–79), and the University of New Mexico (1979–2001).

He has authored or edited more than fifty books. The best known of these volumes are *Conversations with Wallace Stegner on Western History and Literature* (1983, 1996); *The American West: A Twentieth-Century History* (1989, 2007); *Re-imagining the Modern American West: A Century of Fiction, History, and Art* (1996); and *Beyond the Missouri: The Story of the American West* (2007). His most recent works are *Lincoln Looks West: From the Mississippi to the Pacific* (2010); *Seeking First the Kingdom: Northwest Nazarene College; a Centennial History* (2012); *Lincoln and Oregon County Politics in the Civil War Era* (2013); and *The Life and Legends of Calamity Jane* (2014).

Etulain is currently at work on studies of Abraham Lincoln and the American West.

www.ingramcontent.com/pod-product-compliance
Lightning Source LLC
Chambersburg PA
CBHW020334100426
42812CB00029B/3126/J